# PLAY YARDS, PLAY THINGS

**Creative Homeowner Press**®

COPYRIGHT © 1993 CREATIVE HOMEOWNER PRESS®
A DIVISION OF FEDERAL MARKETING CORP.
UPPER SADDLE RIVER, NJ

This book may not be reproduced, either in part or in its entirety, in any form, by any means, without written permission from the publisher, with the exception of brief excerpts for purposes of radio, television, or published review. Although all possible measures have been taken to ensure the accuracy of the material presented, neither the author nor CREATIVE HOMEOWNER PRESS is liable in case of misinterpretation of directions, misapplication or typographical error. All rights, including the right of translation, are reserved.

Manufactured in the United States of America

Current printing (last digit)
10 9 8 7 6 5 4 3 2 1

Produced by Scharff Limited
Technical Reviewer: Drew Corinchock

LC: 92-74899
ISBN: 1-880029-14-6

CREATIVE HOMEOWNER PRESS®
A DIVISION OF FEDERAL
MARKETING CORP.
24 PARK WAY
UPPER SADDLE RIVER, NJ 07458

# TABLE OF CONTENTS

Introduction .................................................................... 4
Working Safely ............................................................. 17
Tools ............................................................................ 18
Fasteners .................................................................... 21
Woods ......................................................................... 27
Sanding and Finishing ................................................ 28
Planning Your Play Yard ............................................. 29

## Projects for Exercise
    Jungle Gym ............................................................ 34
    Teeter-Totter .......................................................... 43
    Balance Beam ....................................................... 45
    Carousel ................................................................ 47
    Adjustable Chinning Bar ........................................ 51

## Projects for Riding Toys
    Red Wagon ............................................................ 52
    Rocking Horse ....................................................... 56
    Toddler Sled .......................................................... 59
    Three-Wheel Seat Scooter ................................... 61
    Full-Sized Sled ...................................................... 63

## Projects for Playhouses
    Frontier General Store .......................................... 65
    Framed Playhouse ................................................ 68
    Log Cabin .............................................................. 73
    Elevated Playhouse .............................................. 78
    Play Castle ............................................................ 84

## Projects for Quiet Time
    Kiddie Picnic Table ................................................ 95
    Sandbox ................................................................ 98
    Drawing Easel ..................................................... 101
    Game Table and Stools ...................................... 104
    Adirondack Chair ................................................ 108

## Projects for Gardening
    Six-Sided Garden Plot ........................................ 111
    Wheelbarrow ....................................................... 113
    Window Box and Planter Stand .......................... 116

## Projects for Toys & Games
    Stick Pony ........................................................... 121
    Bad-Guy Bean Bag Game ................................... 122
    Basketball Backboard ......................................... 124

Glossary .................................................................... 126
Conversion Charts .................................................... 128

# INTRODUCTION

There is perhaps no more wonderfully natural sight in the world than children at play. As adults, we admire and envy the carefree enthusiasm of youngsters as they run, jump, climb, and swing their way through daily life. But a play yard is much more than just "fun and games." Its importance goes far beyond merely giving children a place to while away an afternoon. In a very real sense, a play yard is an outdoor classroom.

Play is the first stage in a life-long process of learning that every person experiences. The well-designed play yard and the equipment it contains gives children the opportunity to discover themselves, their environment, and other people. Play, in all its forms, thus becomes a vital part of a child's physical, mental and social growth.

The most obvious benefit of a play yard is physical exercise. Coordination and motor skills, strength, agility, balance, and endurance are all acquired and improved through exercise. Children love testing their physical limitations, to see how high, far, and fast they can go. A good play yard, first and foremost, provides ample opportunity for strenuous physical activity.

The play yard also fosters mental growth. Children learn communication skills and engage in problem solving. They learn to distinguish and make choices. Concepts such as shape, number, force, and frequency are developed. The best play yards stimulate a child's imagination; they challenge the mind as well as the body.

Children also acquire important socialization skills through play. They learn how to relate to each other through cooperation, sharing, and group decision making. These shared activities help a child turn away from the self-centeredness of infancy toward a greater reliance on friendships.

As beneficial as a play yard is to the child, it has its own special rewards for the creator as well. Whether you are constructing for your own children or grandchildren, nephews and nieces, or even the neighborhood kids, the feeling of satisfaction you get from building play things for youngsters is unmatched. There is an undeniable sense of pride in watching children enjoying themselves with something you built. You are truly creating a "labor of love" that will long be appreciated.

With this in mind, all of the projects in *Play Yards, Play Things* have been designed for durability and longevity. They were chosen for their sturdiness, attractiveness and safety. With a measure of craftsmanship and careful attention to detail, you will produce things that will be passed on from generation to generation.

The projects have been grouped according to the area of child development they are most suited to. The "Exercise," "Riding Toys," and "Toys & Games" projects are concerned mainly with the physical aspects; the "Quiet Time" and "Gardening" projects emphasize mental growth; and the "Playhouses" section stresses social skill above all else.

Projects are classified as either basic or advanced, depending on the woodworking techniques required to make them. If your woodworking experience is limited, start with several of the basic projects before moving on to the advanced. A complete Materials, Parts, and Cutting List is provided for each project. In essence, this list combines the standard bill of materials (or shopping list) with a parts list. The result is an all-in-one chart that has the added advantage of designating which parts are cut from which sizes of lumber.

Because safety is so important, each project lists specific safety equipment that must be worn during construction; this includes safety goggles, a dust mask, and a pair of quality cloth or leather work gloves. Familiarize yourself with the safety equipment, as well as the entire step-by-step instruction, before beginning a project. This will ensure that the work progresses as smoothly—and successfully—as possible.

# Projects for Exercise

### JUNGLE GYM

A well designed jungle gym is the crown jewel of any play yard. The basic structure is made up of two towers, which are connected by a trussed walkway. We've added swings, rings, slides, ladders, platforms and a seesaw, but the possible combinations are endless. You can include whatever suits you.

### TEETER-TOTTER

Few experiences are as exhilarating for a youngster as a ride on a teeter-totter. Your child will love having one right in his own backyard. This teeter-totter is built with pressure-treated pine to withstand the elements, so you can be sure it will be a source of enjoyment for years to come.

## BALANCE BEAM

This Z-shaped balance beam provides a fun challenge for children. Not only does it help improve balance and coordination, it also provides friendly competition. Children can play games that test who can stay on the beam longest without falling off. As an added challenge, the height of each leg is different.

## ADJUSTABLE CHINNING BAR

When it comes to providing arm and shoulder strengthening exercises for children, this chinning bar can't be beat. The bar adjusts easily, so it can "grow" to fit the size of your growing child.

## CAROUSEL

Children love to spin and turn so this compact carousel is bound to receive a hardy workout in any play yard. It is designed for young children with a combined maximum weight limit of 150 pounds.

# Projects for Riding Toys

### ROCKING HORSE

The rocking horse continues to be a classic favorite year after year. Feel free to customize your child's horse by using special paint effects. Its sturdy construction makes it suitable for indoor and outdoor use. If you plan to use it outside, be sure to finish it in such a way that it will be protected from inclement weather.

### RED WAGON

Even with all the innovative new toys on the market today, the red wagon continues to have great appeal. In order to haul everything from dolls to cats and dogs to rocks, it must be solidly built. If you like, you can add an enclosing rack.

### TODDLER SLED

This is a fun one for those snowy days in winter. Built especially for toddlers, this good-looking sled can easily seat two small children. The high sides and back provide safety and comfort.

### THREE-WHEEL SEAT SCOOTER

This attractive scooter is a happy site for children who haven't yet graduated to a tricycle. The simple design can be decorated with different colors and patterns. It is sure to be handed down from one generation to the next.

### FULL-SIZED SLED

This sled is for bigger kids. It can carry one teenager or several smaller riders who want to share a trip down the hill. Sturdier than the toddler's sled, this one is built to take more wear-and-tear.

# PROJECTS FOR PLAYHOUSES

### FRAMED PLAYHOUSE

This charming playhouse is framed using 2x3 lumber. Just like a real house, this one is complete with windows and shutters, doors and an attached front deck.

### FRONTIER GENERAL STORE

This playhouse is great inspiration for your child's imagination. Change the sign and the General Store becomes a hotel, a saloon, the country jail, or any other remnant of the old wild West.

## PLAY CASTLE

What kings, queens and knights wouldn't love this castle which is complete with dungeon and drawbridge. A ladder leads to the look-out towers and walkway, while a slide provides for a quick escape to the back of the lower level. Details such as barred windows, towers and flags bring this fantasy to life.

## ELEVATED PLAYHOUSE

Your children will love the elevated playhouse which combines the excitement of a tree house with the variety of a jungle gym. This structure includes a slide, an overhead set of bars, a swing set, monkey bars and ladders.

## LOG CABIN

With this precious log cabin your child can pretend that your yard is the American frontier and that he or she is one of those who first settled the wild West. A shingled roof, open window and doorway give it an authentic look.

# Projects for Quiet Time

### KIDDIE PICNIC TABLE

This table is a scaled down replica of the old American favorite. Not only is it perfect for sit-down outdoor activities, it also serves as a great space reliever at family picnics where children can dine at their very own table.

## DRAWING EASEL

Young artists love this easel which provides both a blackboard and a drawing pad holder. Since it is hinged at the top, it can be folded up and stored away when not in use. For safety sake it is equipped with a stop latch and safety chain.

## SANDBOX

Playing in the sandbox is a favorite pastime for most children. This one is especially attractive, made of redwood with seating all around. When the kids have outgrown it, the sandbox easily transforms into a double-decker planter.

## GAME TABLE AND STOOLS

The game table and stools have been scaled for a child's use. The game-board insert can be flipped over for instant conversion for backgammon or checkers. Four chip pockets act as holders for board games, card games or even crayons for the little ones who will use the table for arts and crafts.

## ADIRONDACK CHAIR

With its steeply angled back and long, curved seat (both slatted) this chair will quickly become a favorite of your children for reading, playing and those rare "quiet" moments. While this project is scaled to child size, it is nevertheless very durable and designed to withstand the expected abuse.

# Projects for GARDENING

### WHEELBARROW

Constructed to withstand hard knocks, the wheelbarrow is more than just an accessory useful to the budding gardener. It also can be used to carry loads of toys or other objects.

### SIX-SIDED GARDEN PLOT

This hexagonal shaped garden is the perfect size for a curious farmer or botanist. Your child will learn to enjoy nature and the thrill of growing vegetables and blooms.

### WINDOW BOX PLANTER AND STAND

This window box doesn't necessarily have to be hung out of the window. It offers an optional holder which can be screwed into any mounting area or you may choose to build the stand which accommodates up to six planters.

# PROJECTS FOR TOYS & GAMES

### STICK PONIES

Perhaps one of the oldest toys invented, stick ponies are also the simplest toys to make. For fancy riding, you can decorate the pony to suit your own imagination and the desires of the rider.

### BAD GUY BEAN BAG GAME

Children sharpen their throwing and aiming abilities with this game that never loses its appeal. It is especially fun for youngsters because a good throw makes the bad guy swallow the beans. Make plenty of bean bags for ammunition.

### BASKETBALL BACKBOARD

Since shooting hoops appeals to both the young and the young-at-heart, you're sure to get a lot of mileage out of this project. The backboard is adjustable, so it can grow as your children do. Hang the backboard on a post or simply mount it on the garage or another outdoor structure.

## play yards, play things
# WORKING SAFELY

When working with wood, especially when power tools are involved, safety must come first. Keep the following points in mind at all times to help prevent serious injury.

- Take the time to read the tool manufacturer's instructions before attempting to use a tool. Be aware of the limitations of your tools, and never try to force them to do things they were not designed to do.
- Never use a power tool on a workpiece that is not firmly supported or clamped. Likewise, never support a workpiece with your leg or any other part of your body if you intend to cut with a portable saw.
- Keep your hands away from the cutting end of blades, cutters, and bits. Use push sticks and hold-downs instead of touching the workpiece.
- Do not wear loose clothing, jewelry, and open cuffs that can be caught in a power tool. Make sure long hair is tied back or covered with a cap.
- Always work in an uncluttered, well-lit environment.
- Make sure all tools are sharpened before use. Never work with dull tools.
- Always unplug the power cord before changing a blade or bit.
- Wear safety goggles when hammering or doing any other job that generates flying debris.
- Always read and follow the label directions on containers of paint, stain, solvent, and other chemical products. When working with these products, do so only in well-ventilated areas.
- Wear a dust mask when sanding pressure-treated wood or when working around chemical vapors or concrete dust.
- Avoid skin contact with chemical sealers or concrete.
- Do not use power tools in damp or wet locations, or operate power tools when it is raining.
- Keep your work area clean and organized. Accidents happen when workers trip over scraps of lumber or tools left scattered about.
- Keep children and visitors away from the work site. The children will obviously be anxious to have the project completed. Never allow children around power tools or sharp hand tools. Older children can help with certain tasks, but only after power tools and other dangerous equipment are removed from the site.
- Enlist the help of another adult when needed. Many of the advanced projects involve lifting, cutting, and fastening of heavy timbers or lumber. Do not attempt any job you are not physically strong enough to accomplish safely. Keep your footing and balance at all times, especially when working off the ground.
- Lift heavy objects correctly. Keep your back straight and lift with your legs.

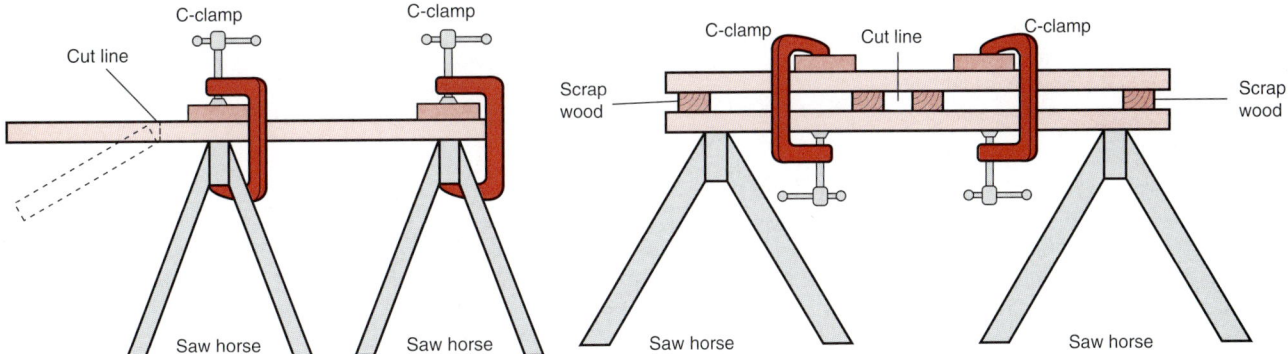

Use these safe methods when cutting with portable saws.

17

*play yards, play things*

# TOOLS

The importance of working with good quality, well-maintained tools cannot be stressed enough. Nothing ruins a woodworking job faster than an inferior tool. Following are the basic hand and power tools needed to build the projects in this book.

## *MEASURING*

The success of any woodworking project depends, first and foremost, on accurately taking measurements and transferring them from the plans to the wood. Do all measurements twice to ensure accuracy. If you do not get the same result each time, recheck your work. It is much easier to re-mark a measurement than to start all over when you realize a piece was cut too short. Mark all measurements with a sharp edge or pencil.

Whenever possible, use a pre-cut length or width of material as a guide, or hold the piece to be cut in place against parts that are completed, then mark and cut it to fit. While many of the following projects call for cutting all components to size beforehand to save time, you may prefer the cut-to-fit method because it helps reduce wasted material.

The steel tape measure, or flexible rule, comes in varying widths; the wider the tape, the better. Since this tool is only available in lengths up to 16 feet, however, the longer wind-up tape measure is recommended for siting larger projects, such as the "Jungle Gym."

Several tools are used to lay out angles for cutting. The framing square is an "L"-shaped piece of steel. Lay it across a board with one leg tipped down so that it butts against one edge, then mark the board for crosscutting. The try square, or T-square, consists of a moveable metal blade and a wooden handle. Use it for quickly checking the accuracy of 45° and 90° angles, and for checking the ends of boards to see that they have been cut square. The combination square is also used for checking angles, as well as for checking level.

The T-bevel has a parallel sided steel blade that can be adjusted to form any angle with the stock. To set the bevel to the desired angle, hold the stock against the base of a protractor, set the blade to the angle, and tighten the locking lever. The combination set is used for the same purpose, but it has a built-in protractor head. Simply clamp the combination set to a steel rule and mark off or measure any angle through 180°.

A level is essential to check for true vertical and horizontal. The longer the level, the more accurate the reading, so a 2-foot long spirit level is recommended for most of the projects in this book. The 9-inch torpedo level is useful for smaller projects and for checking underside levels. For siting larger projects, a line level is best; it is fitted with a hook at either end for hanging it on a taut line.

## *CUTTING*

The two basic handsaws used to cut standard lumber are the crosscut, for cutting across the grain of the wood, and the ripsaw, for cutting with the grain. A log saw is ideal for cutting timbers, such as those used in the "Log Cabin" project. A back saw or dovetail saw is good to have on hand for cutting smaller pieces of wood and molding. The fine-toothed coping saw can be used to make curved cuts, especially those with a small radius. When hand sawing, make sure that the wood is securely supported, and always start a cut on the waste side of the cutting line.

A miter box is invaluable for hand cutting 45° miters and accurate squared ends. The work is laid in the box and the saw blade fits in the slots cut in the sides. Make the first cuts with backward strokes, lowering the blade to horizontal as the cut progresses.

Cuts such as rabbets, long bevels, and off angles (for example, 32°) are made quickest and easiest with power saws. The best choices in this category are the table saw and the radial arm saw. If you are fortunate enough to have access to either of these incredibly versatile tools, you will be able to make all the basic woodworking cuts, plus cut dadoes, make moldings, and sand workpieces.

Several portable power saws are available to the home woodworker. While they cost only a fraction of the price of a table saw or radial arm saw, these tools get the job done nicely. The portable circular saw is used for making straight and angle cuts in long boards and plywood panels. The saber saw cuts curves; when fitted with a very fine blade, it can handle intricate cuts. If you will be doing projects that involve a lot of curve cutting, the bench type scroll saw is a good investment. This saw makes light work of intricate curves on small jobs.

Sawing guides are available to aid in making long cuts in dimensional lumber and similar workpieces. The basic aluminum saw guide breaks down into two 4-foot sections and has self-contained clamps. When the guide is clamped in place on the workpiece, its low or flanged edge may be used for marking, scoring, and cutting with a

# tools

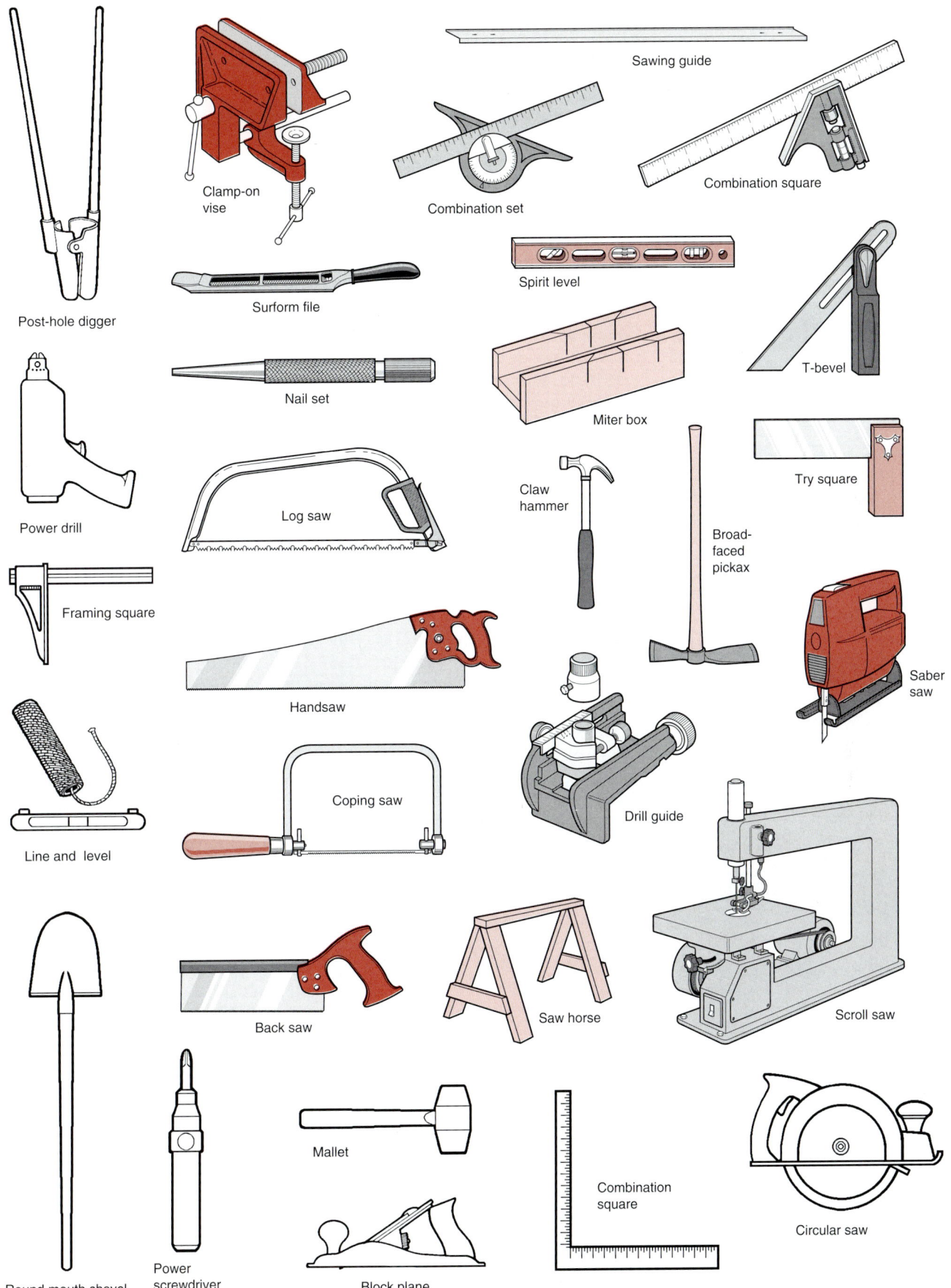

*tools*

utility knife. The flat edge or high side serves as a guide fence for portable saws and routers.

## DRIVING AND DRILLING

Hammers are available in countless styles and sizes, but the best choice for most of these projects is a 16-ounce claw hammer. A steel shaft gives the best driving power, and a rubber sleeve provides a comfortable, shock-absorbing grip. For driving larger nails or spikes, as in the "Log Cabin" project, a 28-ounce hammer with a longer handle is recommended.

In many cases, such as with the "Riding Toys" in this book, the aim is to remove all traces of the finishing nails used in construction. This is accomplished by countersinking the nail head and then filling the hole with wood putty. A nail set does the job of countersinking nails; just tap the nail about 1/8 inch below the surface of the wood.

A soft-faced mallet will be helpful in press-fitting dowels, such as the handhold mounts in the "Teeter-Totter" project. Using a conventional hammer in such instances could easily damage the wood.

With so many projects requiring holes to be drilled and dowel joints to be made, you cannot be without a dependable power drill. Besides its obvious uses, a drill can be easily converted into a circular, drum, or disc sander, and can be used with a wire brush to remove rust and finishes. Portable drills come in two types: electric and cordless rechargeable. To drill a hole perpendicular to the surface of the workpiece, use a drill guide; this accessory will center the hole while controlling both the depth and angle of drill entry.

A must with any drill is an accompanying set of driver bits, both standard and Phillips, of various sizes. Along with a power screwdriver, these will greatly speed up the task of assembling a project. For those jobs that call for countersinking wood screws, have a selection of countersink drill bits on hand. In most cases, 3/8-, 1/2-, and 5/8-inch bits will be sufficient.

## MISCELLANEOUS

Many of the projects in this book, notably those in the "Exercise" and "Playhouses" sections, involve excavating. Either a square mouth shovel or a broad-faced pickax is needed to break up the ground and rip up sod. The round mouth shovel is the best choice for digging. When narrow holes must be dug for posts, such as in the "Teeter-Totter" project, it is a good idea to rent a post-hole digger. This tool does the best job, and it is easier than trying to dig postholes with a pick and shovel.

The saw horse has long been used by carpenters as a sturdy work support. Today's lightweight, folding metal saw horses are perfect for the home woodworker. They require a one-time-only assembly and are topped off with a 2 x 4 rail, which can be used as a nailer. Use two horses side by side to hold long pieces of lumber for cutting to length. In such cases, be sure the waste piece extends past the horses and is sawn off past the horses.

Since it takes both hands to do most woodworking jobs, you should have a bench vise for clamping the work. Most good workbenches are fitted with a bench vise. If you do not have a workbench, buy a clamp-on vise that attaches to the edge of any sturdy table. Some vises have swiveling heads that allow you to change the angle of the work by adjusting the angle of the clamp. Be sure to use small wood blocks between the clamping areas on the vise and the table top to prevent damage to the table.

After cutting out a part, some additional work may be needed, including forming, shaping, and smoothing of the piece. A block plane is an adjustable, low-angle plane that is ideal for sanding a small radius on edges and corners that may be dangerous or uncomfortable when handled. It can also be used for trimming.

Surform tools, the modern variation of the rasp and file, perform three basic tasks. First, when stroked along the edge of the workpiece at a 45° angle, they remove the maximum amount of waste; lesser angles remove less stock. Second, they smooth the edge when stroked parallel to it. Lastly, they polish the edge when stroked at an angle slightly opposite the original angle.

## play yards, play things

# Fasteners

The two major types of fasteners used to build the projects in this book are nails and wood screws. Glue is also used, but to a much lesser degree. A good working knowledge of each of these fastening methods is essential to making durable, long-lasting wood creations.

## NAILS

While screws may be stronger and glue may be neater, nails are still the quickest and easiest fastener to work with. When selecting the type of nail to use, keep this in mind: choosing the right nail and driving it properly makes the difference between the completed job holding together or falling apart.

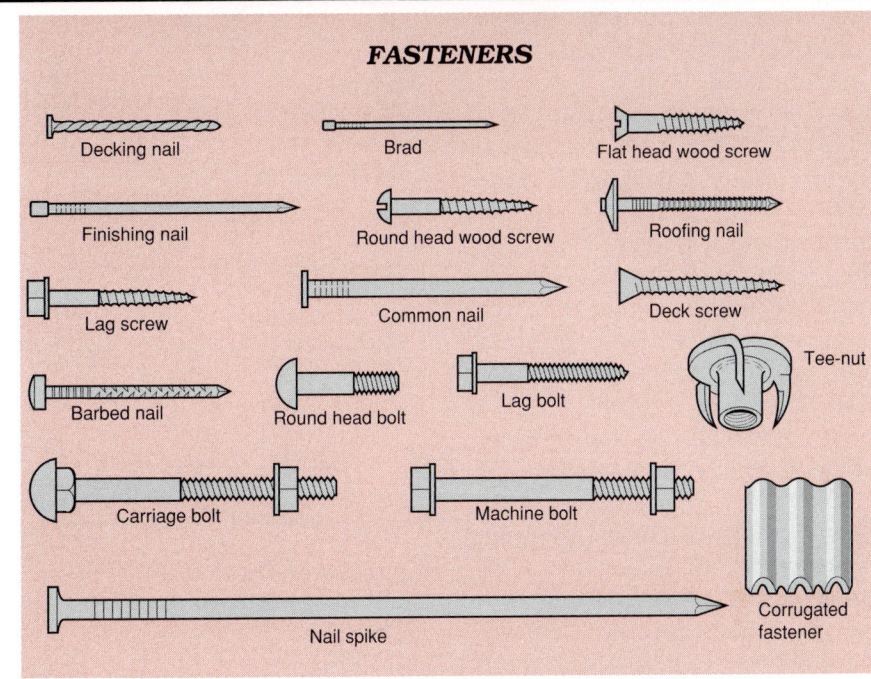

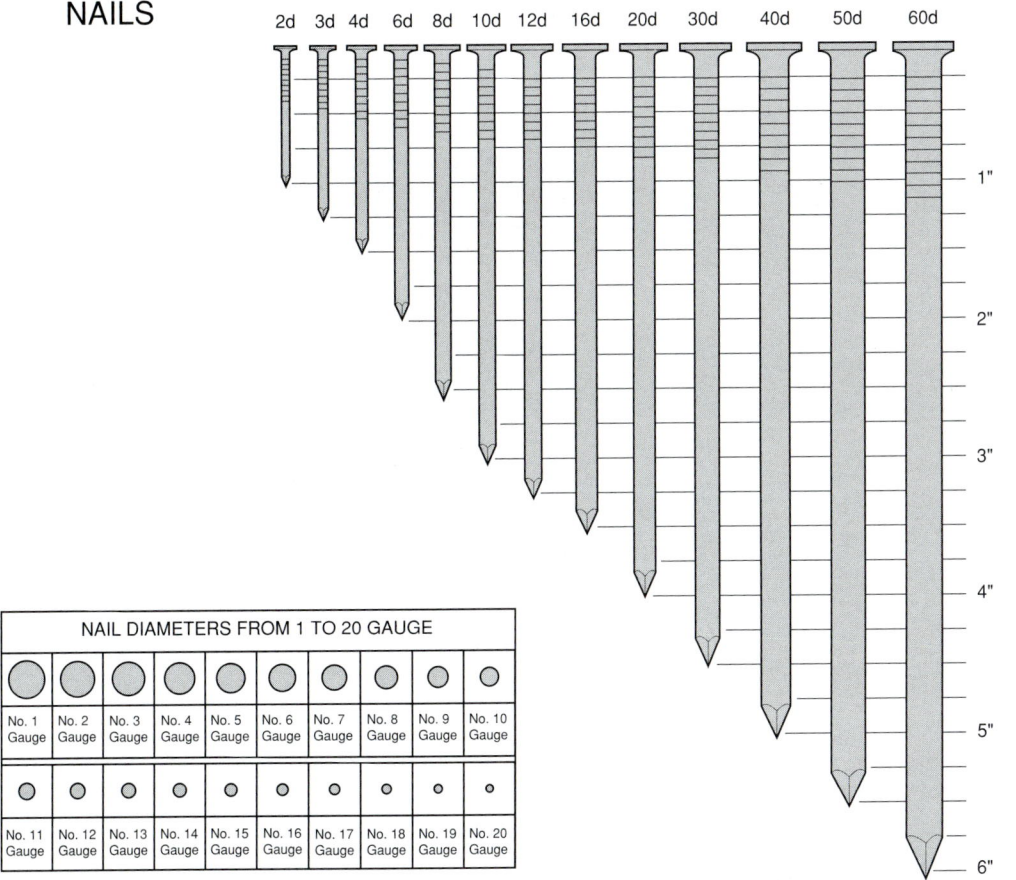

As the gauge number of a nail goes up, the penny size and diameter go down.

21

# fasteners

Nails made of steel are the most common, but they are susceptible to rust and should not be used on exterior projects. Instead, choose hot-dipped galvanized steel nails. Copper, brass, bronze, and stainless steel nails are also rustproof.

The length of a nail is indicated by its "penny" size, which goes back to the time when nails sold for a penny a pound. The letter designation for the word "penny" is the "d." Sizes range from 2d, which is 1-inch long, all the way up to 60d, which is 6 inches long. As a nail becomes longer, it also becomes thicker; the gauge number, or diameter, increases.

For these projects, two types of nails are used: common and finishing. Common nails have a flat head and a grooved shank that allows for good gripping. Common nails are ideal for fastening framing lumber, such as the 2 x 4s used in the "Frontier General Store" project. Finishing nails are thinner and have a much smaller head. They are most often set below the surface of the wood, leaving a small hole that is easily filled with putty. As their name implies, finishing nails are used for finished carpentry, such as in the "Riding Toys" and "Quiet Time" projects found in this book. A finishing nail that is 1 1/2 inches or smaller in length is called a brad.

Some nails are made with a spiral or screw-type shank to resist loosening or popping out over time. Because they are often used to nail deck boards in place, these nails are commonly called decking nails.

Other nail designs have special barbed ends that resist pull-out forces. Barbed nails should be used to install metal joist hangers, post anchors, truss plates, rafter ties, and other joining hardware subject to stress and force.

If you choose to shingle any of the playhouse roofs, be sure to use specially designated roofing nails of the proper size. For example, for 5/8-inch sheathing, 3/4-inch long roofing nails are the best choice because they will not penetrate the inside of the roof and become a safety hazard. There is a simple rule to follow when selecting nail lengths for both framing and finish work. When face-nailing hardwoods, the nail penetration into the bottom piece should be one-half the length of the nail. When face-nailing softwoods, the penetration into the bottom piece should be two-thirds the length of the nail. When edge-nailing, two-thirds of the nail must be in the thicker piece; this is true whether working with hardwood or softwood.

When working with plywood, the nail size depends on the thickness of the plywood. For 3/4 inch, use 8d. For 5/8 inch, use 8d or 6d. For 1/2 inch, use 6d or 4d. For 3/8 inch, use 4d or 3d. For 1/4 inch, use 3d nails or 1-inch brads. A 6-inch spacing between nails is adequate for most work.

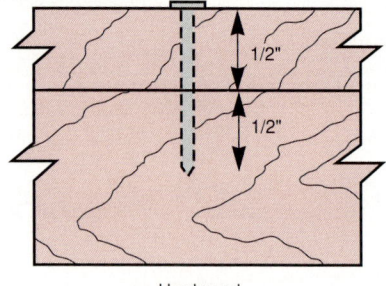

Hardwood

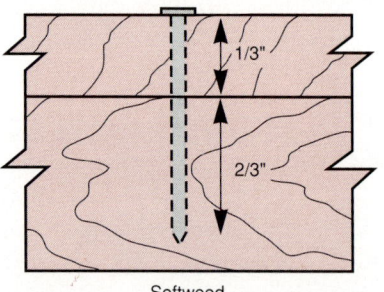

Softwood

Nail penetration should be at least one-half the length of the nail for hardwoods, and two-thirds for softwoods.

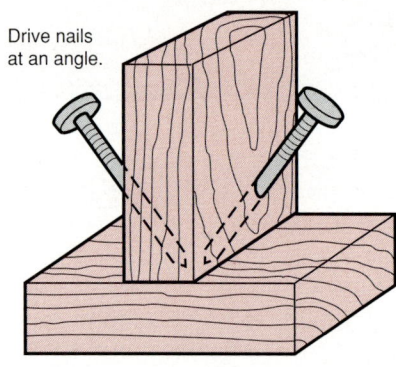

Toe-nailing is an effective method of increasing the holding power of nails.

When it is impractical to face-nail (such as when nailing studs to the floor in the "Framed Playhouse"), toe-nailing should be used. This consists of driving nails in at an angle from either side of the stud or beam. When toe-nailing, use a nail long enough to pierce one member being joined and into the other so that about half the length of the nail enters the second member. A 10d nail is the best choice for toe-nailing 2 x 4s.

Nails should always be placed carefully so as to provide the greatest holding power. Nails driven with the grain do not hold as well as nails driven across the grain. A nail driven with or along the grain can be easily pulled out. Also, any shearing stress placed on a nail driven with the grain may split the wood.

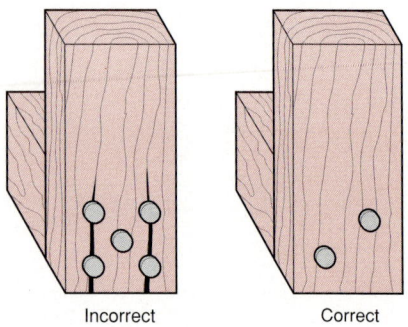

Proper positioning of nails is very important. The five haphazardly driven nails on the left have less effective holding power than the two strategically driven nails on the right.

# fasteners

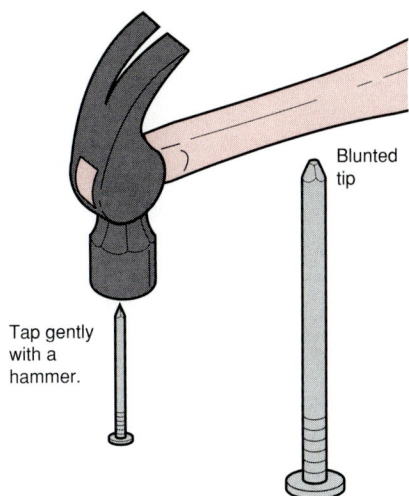

Blunt the ends of sharp nails with a hammer to avoid splitting the lumber.

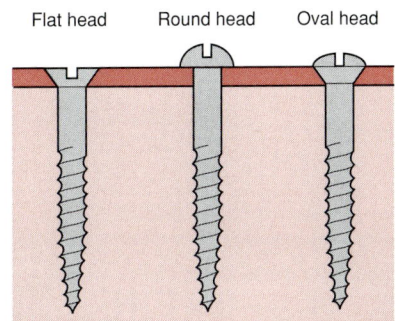

Flat head wood screws are used when you want the head below the surface of the wood; round head and oval head wood screws protrude above the surface.

gently with a hammer, or by filing it lightly. Particularly when driven in near the edge, blunt-pointed nails also have increased holding power.

## WOOD SCREWS

All wood screws consist of three parts: the head, which is slotted so that the screw can be driven with a screwdriver; an unthreaded body or shank immediately below the head; and a threaded portion which tapers to a point at the tip. Screws are most often classified according to the shape of their head, either flat, round, or oval. Screw heads can be straight-slotted or recessed. The most popular screw with a recessed opening is the Phillips, because it allows the maximum turning force to be applied.

Steel screws are generally the strongest, but unless they are specially plated to resist rust, brass screws are better for use outdoors. Chrome- or nickel-plated screws are also ideal for exterior use.

The size of the wood screw is indicated by the length and body diameter (the unthreaded part) of the screw. Lengths vary from 1/4 inch to 6 inches. Screws up to 1 inch in length increase by eighths, screws from 1 to 3 inches increase by quarters, and screws from 3 to 6 inches increase by half inches. For measurement purposes, the length of a flat head wood screw is the overall length, while the length of a round head wood screw is measured from the point to the underside of the head. An oval head wood screw is measured from the point to the edge of the head.

Placing nails too close to the end grain or too near the edges of the wood will also produce splitting. When driving more than one nail, always stagger the nails so that none are in the same grain line. A few nails of the proper type and size, properly placed and driven, will hold better than a great many nails driven close together.

Dense woods should be nailed with blunt-pointed nails to prevent splitting the wood. You can blunt the point of any nail by tapping it

Body diameter is designated by gauge or shank number, running from 0 (smallest) to 24 (largest). The gauge number can vary for a given length of screw.

## WOOD SCREWS

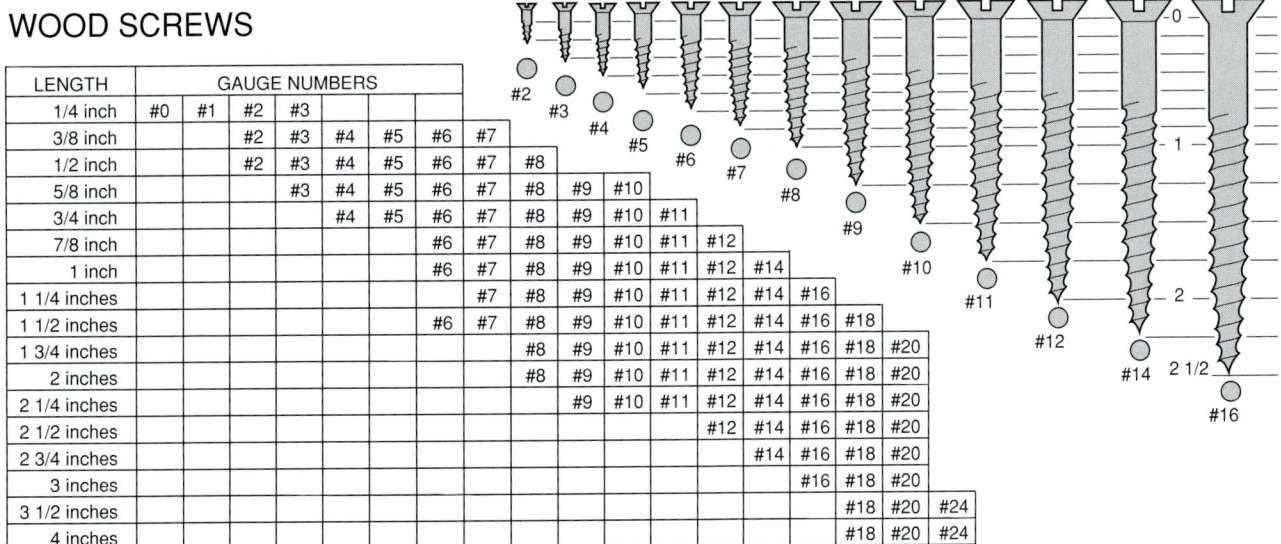

When buying screws, specify the following: (1) length; (2) gauge number; (3) type of head—flat, round, or oval; and (4) material—brass, bronze, hot-dipped galvanized, or stainless steel.

# fasteners

When you purchase wood screws by the box, it is important to understand the labeling. This box contains #8 flat head screws, 1 1/2 inches long.

For example, a 1-inch screw is available in gauge numbers of 3 through 20. The #3 would be a thin screw, while the #20 would have a large diameter. From one gauge number to the next, the diameter of the screw changes by 13 thousandths (0.013) of an inch.

Wood screws are sold by the box. The designation of length, gauge number, and type appears on the container. For instance, if the box is labeled "1 1/2-8-F.H.," it means #8 flat head wood screws, 1 1/2 inches long.

As a general rule, the screw used should be 1/4 to 1/2 inch less than the combined thicknesses of the pieces being joined—depending on whether it is to be countersunk or counterbored. In cases where this formula does not work, such as when screwing into the end grain of wood, use a screw that is twice as long as the top piece of the two materials being joined. The screw diameter should always be in proportion to the parts being assembled; large screws will split thin wood, while small screws will not hold large pieces.

Without a pilot or starting hole, screws tend to follow the grain of the wood and are difficult to drive straight. A pilot hole eliminates this problem and helps prevent splitting. For softwoods, drill a hole only half as deep as the threaded part of the screw. For hardwoods, drill a hole as deep as the entire screw. Use the chart below as a reference guide for drilling pilot holes.

### PILOT HOLE DEPTHS

| Screw Length | Hardwoods | Softwoods |
|---|---|---|
| 1/4" | 1/4" | 1/16" |
| 3/8" | 3/8" | 3/32" |
| 1/2" | 1/2" | 1/8" |
| 5/8" | 5/8" | 3/16" |
| 3/4" | 3/4" | 1/4" |
| 7/8" | 7/8" | 5/16" |
| 1" | 1" | 11/32" |
| 1 1/4" | 1 1/4" | 7/16" |
| 1 1/2" | 1 1/2" | 1/2" |
| 1 3/4" | 1 3/4" | 9/16" |
| 2" | 2" | 5/8" |
| 2 1/4" | 2 1/4" | 3/4" |
| 2 1/2" | 2 1/2" | 13/16" |

Countersinking wood screws means to sink them flush with—not below—the surface of the wood. A countersink drill bit makes this job easy. First drill the pilot hole, then use the bit to drill the countersink. Remember to allow for the depth of the countersink when calculating how long a screw should be.

Counterboring involves drilling a hole deep enough to recess the head of the screw so that it can be covered with wood putty or a plug. To do this, first drill a hole equal to the length of the screw plus the depth of the counterbore. (If you are filling the hole with putty, a 1/4-inch counterbore is adequate; if installing a wood plug, make the counterbore depth 1/2 inch.) The hole diameter should equal that of the shank without the threads. Then use a bit the same diameter as the screw head to drill the counterbore.

While counterbores are most often used to hide screws, they also make it possible to attach thick or wide stock with short screws. For example, to attach a 3/4-inch thick piece to a 2 1/2-inch rail, you would normally need a screw more than 3 inches long. Use of a counterbore can reduce the screw length by at least 50%.

To make counterboring easier, screwmates are available. These bits drill the pilot hole, shank hole, and counterbore all in one operation. If working with #10 x 1 1/4-inch screws, for example, simply buy a screwmate of the same size.

To completely conceal screw heads, wood plugs are ideal. Plugs can be cut with a plug cutter, a device that fits onto a drill. Plug cutters are available in various sizes to match the counterbore bit used. Cut plugs from the same type of wood in which they will be inserted, and make sure the grain matches as closely as possible. Coat the plug with glue and insert it

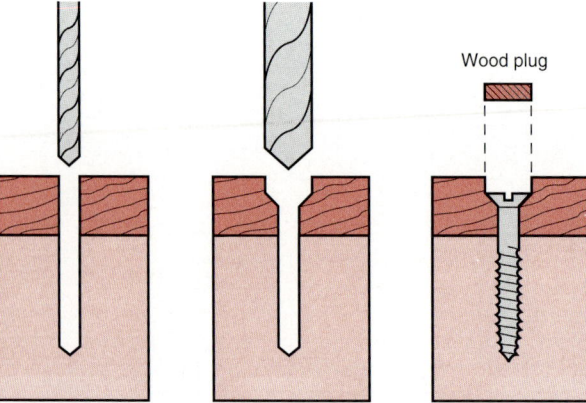

Counterboring requires drilling a hole equal to the length of the screw plus the depth of the counterbore (left), following up with a bit the same diameter as the screw head (middle), then covering the screw head with wood putty or a plug (right).

# fasteners

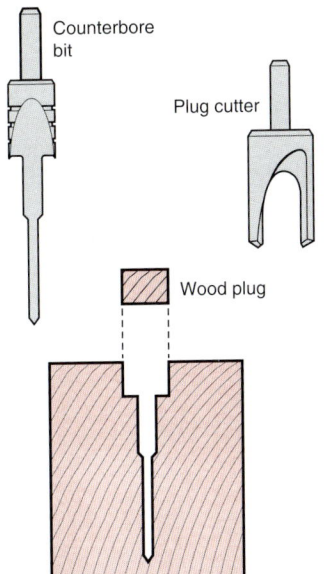

Use a plug cutter to make perfectly formed wood plugs for covering counterbored screws.

in the counterbored hole with the grain direction matching the wood. After the glue dries, the excess can be sanded with abrasive paper.

## CONNECTORS

Beam clips provide an attractive appearance and, more importantly, structural strength for anchoring the top of a post or column to a beam. Usually made of 16-gauge stamped steel, beam clips are plated with gold-zinc dichromate to resist weathering. They can be painted. The nail holes are staggered to provide greater holding power.

To install the beam clip, nail it onto the post or column, position the overhead beam, then nail it in place. For best results, use barbed nails.

Joist hangers ensure that ceiling and floor joists are properly attached to headers. The hanger's built-in nailing and positioning tabs allow for rapid installation. The single joist hanger, which is the type used in the "Elevated Playhouse," is usually made of 18-gauge zinc-coated steel and comes in 2 x 4 inch to 2 x 14 inch sizes.

To install, nail the joist hanger to the joist, position it on the header, and drive in a few nails to hold it in place. Then, drive additional nails to secure the installation. In most instances, common nails are sufficient for use with joist hangers.

Storm clips eliminate wind uplift problems by anchoring trusses or rafters securely to plates and studs. Most designs come in three sizes and are made from 18-gauge zinc-coated steel. Storm clips can be installed in a fraction of the time usually required by conventional methods.

To install storm clips, use two per truss or rafter, one on each end. Position and install them using barbed or decking nails.

While face brackets may seem out of place in this book, their efficient method of connection comes in handy when assembling the "Elevated Playhouse." Fence brackets enable the railing to be nailed to the posts without the need for special cutting, notching, or other fitting. Use barbed nails to secure the fence bracket to the post, insert the rail, and drive additional barbed nails to attach the rail.

Truss clips are usually made of 18-gauge zinc-coated steel. Available in several sizes, they can be installed quickly by hand with a hammer. Their holding power is about 50 pounds per tooth. To install a truss clip, simply place it over the truss joint and hammer it into place.

Post base ties offer fast, adjustable installation of 4 x 4 posts of concrete. The slotted base can be attached even when the anchor bolts are bent. The base can also be attached with nails through the bottom holes. The termite- and rot-proof base cover has weep holes to allow moisture to escape. The base itself is generally made of 16-gauge stamped steel with gold-zinc dichromate finish that resists weathering and can be painted. The spacer plate keeps the post protected from surface moisture.

To install a post base tie, first secure the base with an anchor bolt. Then put the spacer in place, put the 4 x 4 post on the spacer, wrap-up the slotted base, and nail it with barbed nails.

White not a conventional connector, a metal "L" brace of the proper size can be used to support two pieces of wood attached at a 90° angle. Designed for use on inside corners, "L" braces can be attached with regular wood screws or with small lag screws where

## CONNECTORS

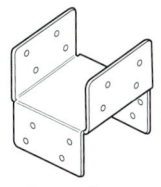
Beam clip

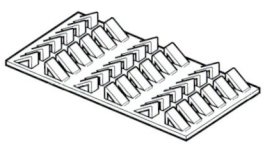
Truss clip

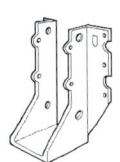
Joist hanger

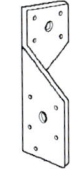
Storm clip

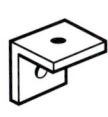
"L" brace

Fence bracket

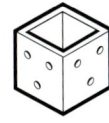
Post base tie

25

# fasteners

additional strength is required. They can also be bent with pliers to fit wood set at angles other than 90°.

## GLUING AND CLAMPING

Selecting the right glue for the projects in this book is not hard at all. Since all of them are intended for outdoor use, resorcinol is the best choice. This two-part glue (liquid resin and powdered hardener) produces a very strong bond and is absolutely waterproof. Drying time is long; it can take up to 16 hours. Urea-resin is another highly water-resistant wood glue, though it has a tendency to become brittle if the glue joint fits poorly.

A proper gluing job depends on four key factors. First, the surfaces to be glued must be absolutely clean. Second, the adhesive must be applied in the precise manner described in the label directions. Third, clamping must be done until the glue has dried. Finally, the glue must be given time to dry completely. It is worth noting that very humid conditions can more than double the recommended drying time for adhesives.

Contrary to what many people believe, a lot of glue does not hold better than a little glue. In fact, the opposite is true. Too much glue weakens a joint, because glue in itself is not a strong substance. By applying a thin coating of glue to each of the mating surfaces and clamping them firmly until the glue

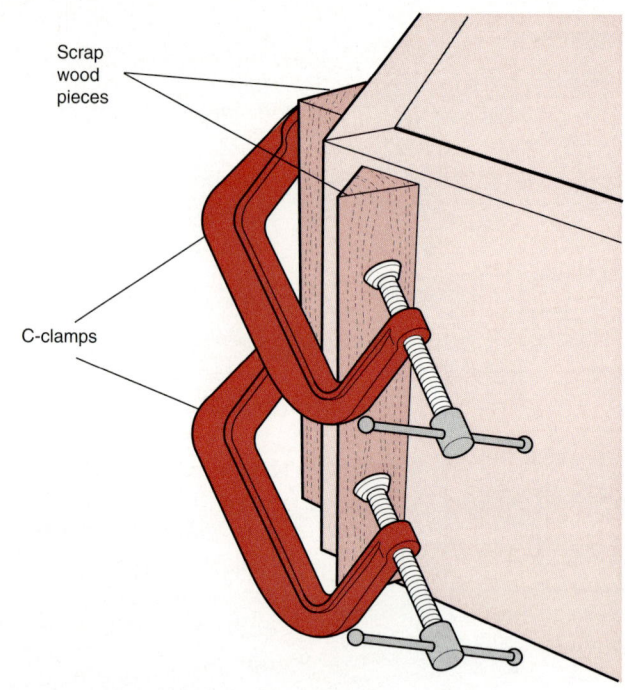

C-clamps are ideal for holding wood joints together while the glue dries.

has dried, the resulting joint will be stronger than the wood itself. If you try to break the joint apart, the wood on either side of the joint will likely fracture before the joint does.

The specific clamping time for a particular glue can always be found in the label instructions. While not absolutely necessary, in most cases overnight drying is suggested for maximum strength. Depending on the size and shape of the joint, several devices can be used for clamping, including C-clamps, spring clamps, and bar clamps (both wood and metal).

The clamp does not have to be overly tight; a firm, snug hold will do. In some cases, it may be necessary to protect the work by inserting small blocks of wood under the jaws of the clamps.

Masking tape makes an excellent "clamp," especially when gluing small parts, as in the "Red Wagon" project. Hold one end of the tape against one side of the joint with the thumb of one hand and pull across the joint with the other hand, using slight pressure, and press the tape firmly against the wood.

# play yards, play things
# Woods

All of the projects in this book call for hardwood, softwood, plywood, or, in some instances, combinations of the three. Before purchasing the materials for any of these projects, familiarize yourself with the basics of wood and how to order the correct sizes and grades.

The nominal size of wood (1 x 4, 1 x 6, etc.) is not the actual size. Nominal is simply the size of the wood before it is planed down at the lumber mill. The chart below shows nominal and actual wood sizes; it is essential that you be aware of the difference when planning a project.

## WOOD DIMENSIONS

| NOMINAL SIZE (WHAT YOU ORDER) | ACTUAL SIZE (WHAT YOU GET) |
|---|---|
| 1 x 1 | 3/4" x 3/4" |
| 1 x 2 | 3/4" x 1 1/2" |
| 1 x 3 | 3/4" x 2 1/2" |
| 1 x 4 | 3/4" x 3 1/2" |
| 1 x 6 | 3/4" x 5 1/2" |
| 1 x 8 | 3/4" x 7 1/2" |
| 1 x 10 | 3/4" x 9 1/4" |
| 1 x 12 | 3/4" x 11 1/4" |
| 2 x 2 | 1 3/4" x 1 3/4" |
| 2 x 3 | 1 1/2" x 2 1/2" |
| 2 x 4 | 1 1/2" x 3 1/2" |
| 2 x 6 | 1 1/2" x 5 1/2" |
| 2 x 8 | 1 1/2" x 7 1/4" |
| 2 x 10 | 1 1/2" x 9 1/4" |
| 2 x 12 | 1 1/2" x 11 1/4" |
| 4 x 4 | 3 1/2" x 3 1/2" |
| 4 x 6 | 3 1/2" x 5 1/2" |

## HARDWOODS AND SOFTWOODS

Lumber is sold in different grades and with different surface treatments. The best grade is clear, meaning that it is free of knots and other blemishes. The next grade is select; this grade is divided into #1, #2, and #3. No. 1 select has minimal blemishes, and as the numbers get higher the blemishes increase, while the cost of the wood decreases. The lowest grade, though still perfectly acceptable, is common. This wood will have more than a few blemishes and is ordinarily used in projects where it will be painted or covered in some way, such as the framing lumber for the playhouses.

The hardwoods used most in these projects are oak, birch, and ash. Commonly used softwoods include pine, Douglas fir, and redwood. While each project includes a recommendation for a specific type of wood, keep in mind that these are only suggestions; your own personal preference may lead you to choose a different type. For example, though the "Red Wagon" project calls for using a hardwood (oak), you may want to use a softwood, such as cedar or spruce. Availability and cost can also affect your selection of wood for a given project.

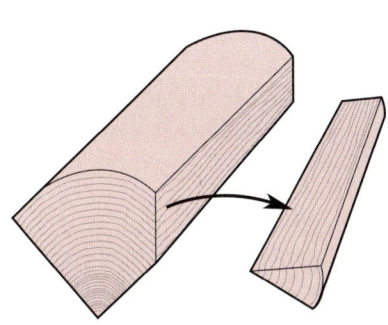
Quarter-sawn

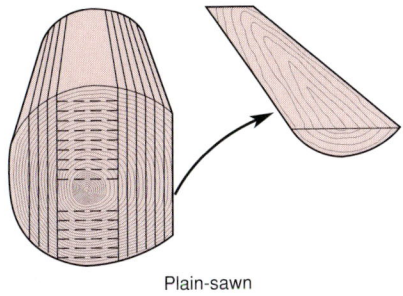
Plain-sawn

Quarter-sawn wood has a tight, parallel grain pattern, while wood that has been plain-sawn has a characteristic loop.

The grain pattern of a wood depends on whether it has been quarter-sawn or plain-sawn. Quarter-sawn wood produces a tight, parallel grain pattern, while plain-sawn wood has a characteristic loop. If the grain makes a difference in a project, make sure all the wood you purchase has been sawn in the same way.

For outdoor projects like these, pressure-treated softwoods are highly recommended because of their excellent weathering properties. Pressure-treated lumber is classified as either LP-2 (above-ground use) or LP-22 (below ground use). A dust mask is an absolute necessity when sanding pressure-treated lumber.

## PLYWOOD

Plywood commonly comes in 4 x 8 sheets, in thicknesses of 1/4-, 3/8-, 1/2-, 5/8-, and 3/4-inch. One major distinction between plywood and regular wood is that for plywood the nominal size is also the actual size. That is, a 1/2-inch-thick panel is really 1/2-inch thick. Plywood is faced with softwood or hardwood in different grades. Exterior softwood plywood is made to withstand the elements, and they should be used for the projects in this book.

Softwood plywood is available in a variety of grades, according to the veneer on the face and back of the panel. Grade A plywood has only minimal blemishes, Grades B and C have an increasing number of defects, and Grade D has large knotholes. A-C and A-D plywood are sometimes referred to as good-one-side; A-A is good-two-sides. A good rule of thumb is to use a better grade when the project will be finished naturally, and a lower grade when you plan to paint it.

*play yards, play things*

# SANDING AND FINISHING

Sanding and finishing operations affect more than just how a project looks. Children rarely take the time to examine a toy before grabbing it or jumping on it, so make sure that all rough surfaces have been sanded smooth beforehand. And the right finish, properly applied, provides an extra measure of protection against weathering.

## SANDING

The two basic aims of sanding are to remove sharp edges, a very important point where children are concerned, and to shape and smooth the pieces for handling and prepare them for finishing.

Sandpaper—or abrasive paper, as it is more properly called—is available in many different materials and weights. The two best types for wood are garnet and aluminum oxide. Use a D weight 80 (medium) grit for initial sanding and shaping, a C weight 120 (fine) grit for follow-up sanding, and an A weight 220 (very fine) grit for final sanding.

While the heavier papers work well with sanding blocks and power sanders, the lighter weight papers are best in tight places. Abrasive papers have either a closed grain or an open grain. Closed-grain papers work faster, but are more likely to clog.

The most basic sanding tool is the sanding block. In its simplest homemade form, this is a rectangular block of wood around which you wrap a piece of abrasive paper. If you buy one, make sure it has some type of clamp to hold the paper, and built-in felt padding to cushion the paper and prevent uneven sanding.

Always sand with the grain of the wood, not across it. Move the sanding block in a straight back-and-forth motion; never in circles.

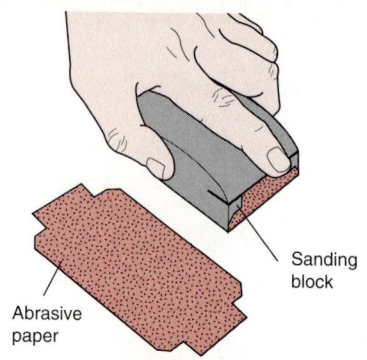

Sanding blocks are shaped to fit the hand and come with abrasive paper cut to size.

Keep the sanding surface level and the pressure on the block even to avoid tapering the work. This is particularly important as you approach the edge of the piece. Be sure to tap the sawdust out of the paper periodically.

Power-sanding aids include drum sanders and disc sanders that can be used in a drill for shaping and sanding curved surfaces. The flat surface of a finishing or orbital sander makes it ideal for final sanding. With any power-sanding operation, let the sander do the work. Do not put undue pressure on the tool; just guide it in a straight line with the grain of the wood. A power sander should never be operated in a back-and-forth motion.

Wear a dust mask when sanding any type of wood. A pair of work gloves is also helpful. After sanding, use a brush to remove sanding dust. Follow up with a good wiping with a tack cloth.

## FINISHING

The finish to use is dictated by the type of wood. Hardwoods such as birch and oak are best suited to clear finishes, as are some softwoods. Some parts of projects, like the body of the "Teeter-Totter," are best left unfinished. Regardless of whether stain or paint is used, any toys that could end up in a child's mouth should have a nontoxic finish.

The projects that will constantly be exposed to the elements must be painted first with an exterior primer, then an exterior-finish paint. Projects that will not be painted should be given a coating of water-repellent sealer. It is a good practice to spray all external hardware with an exterior metal primer, then with an exterior-finish metal paint.

Several light coats of finish, each thoroughly sanded down, are better than one or two heavy coats. Be sure the surface is clean and dry before you start. If the initial coats pick up any dust while drying, touch up the finish with very fine sandpaper before applying the last coat. Avoid getting paint on any surface that will be glued.

Finishing plywood edges presents a special challenge, because the end grain absorbs and loses moisture rapidly. For this reason, plywood panels should be edge-sealed. Use primer to seal plywood panels to be painted, and use a paintable water-repellent preservative for panels that will be stained. For maximum grain show-through on plywood, a semi-transparent stain is a good choice. If you want to hide the grain and color of the wood surface, but not its texture, an acrylic latex solid color is best.

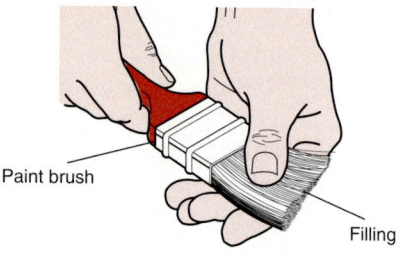

A good quality brush is vital to successful finishing. Fan the brush to check that the filling is firmly set and bound securely.

*play yards, play things*

# PLANNING YOUR PLAY YARD

The design of a play yard is based on the needs and interests of the children who will be using it, and the space available. Since most homeowners have a limited area with which to work, following are some suggestions to help you make the best use of the space available. Regardless of the size of the play yard, the well-being of the children must always be of utmost concern. To this end, some guidelines designed to promote safe play are also presented.

## DESIGN FACTORS

The best scenario for designing a play yard would be to take a 1/4 acre or more of wide-open land, build all or most of these projects, and scatter them over the grounds for your children to pick and choose as they please. Obviously, for most people this is not realistic. More likely is a backyard area of 1/16 acre or less, possibly irregular in shape, with built-in obstructions such as walkways, clotheslines, and patios.

Since enlarging the yard itself is usually not feasible, you need to concentrate on making the most of your existing space. There are more ways to expand the usable area within the boundaries of your property than you might think. For example, trees and shrubbery can be removed or relocated, swampy land can be drained and filled, and tool sheds and other outbuildings can be located so that they do not take up prime "play space." You can even use retaining walls to terrace sloping ground and create level play areas.

You and the children will have to choose the projects you want in your play yard. The aim should be to accommodate as many projects as possible without overcrowding or compromising on safety. Start by deciding which of the "permanent" projects you want to include, then use this as the foundation around which the play yard is designed. Permanent projects are those which are either anchored to the ground or simply too heavy to be moved freely. These include: "Jungle Gym," "Teeter-Totter," "Carousel," "Adjustable Chinning Bar," "Six-Sided Garden Plot," "Sandbox," and of the "Playhouses." The "Balance Beam" is not included in this group, since you have the option of anchoring it on a temporary basis, rather than cementing it into the ground.

The permanent projects take up the most space, with the biggest being the "Jungle Gym" and "Elevated Playhouse"; each one is over 20 feet wide. In a 1/16-acre play yard, either of these two would take up about one-eighth of the available area. Since both projects serve as an all-purpose exercise center, choose one as the centerpiece of your play yard. If space is really at a premium, the "Elevated Playhouse" is best because it combines an exercise center and playhouse into one. If you have the room, the "Jungle Gym" and any playhouse is an ideal starting point.

When deciding which projects to include, the aim is not to see how many things you can cram into your backyard. Aside from the clutter this would create, such a setup fails to take into account one crucial element: a play yard is for children. Children need a certain amount of open space for running, tumbling, and playing catch. The sample layouts on pages 31 and 32 were designed with this in mind.

The best play yards are planned in advance. Take a look at your yard from inside the house, and pay attention to the views from the windows; this will help you avoid blocking an attractive view with one of the large projects. Decide from which room you will most often be supervising your children, and lay out the play yard accordingly. Take note of which doors will be used to gain access to the outside, and whether dirt might be tracked in where it will be most conspicuous. Always keep the convenience factor in mind. For instance, locating the outdoor play area near the indoor play space can save a lot of effort when it's time to bring the toys in for the night.

## PLAY YARD SAFETY

It is essential to provide adequate space around each piece of play yard equipment. Your planning should take into account each project's "use zone"; that is, any activity or movement which can be expected around it. For example, sufficient space is needed for the swings on the "Elevated Playhouse" and "Jungle Gym" to accommodate the largest arc through which the swings travel, including a child's extended legs. Adequate room must be provided for children to jump from swings, exit slides, and spin off the "Carousel." Garages, walkways, gates and fences, trees, and other play areas should be located at least 8 feet away from the estimated use zone associated with a piece of equipment.

Separation of play spaces promotes play yard safety. Equipment should be arranged to accommodate the traffic of children at play. For example, the "Elevated Playhouse" and "Jungle Gym" should be placed away from areas where running children may acci-

## planning your play yard

dentally move in front of swings or into exit areas of slides. Also, young children can be protected from the more active play of older children by situating sedentary projects like the "Sandbox" in a corner of the play yard, away from the action equipment.

An important consideration is to keep the play yard free from visual barriers that can hamper supervision of any part of the play area. Every parent knows how important it is to keep an eye on children, so do not place projects behind shrubbery that will block your view. Set up the "Jungle Gym" and the playhouses near the back of the yard or along the side. Placing them in the front will obscure your view of the children playing behind them.

### EQUIPMENT SAFETY

Safety was the overriding factor in the design of each of the projects in this book. Careful consideration was given not to create any openings or angles that could trap a child's head or any other part of the body. With this in mind, if you add swinging exercise rings to the "Jungle Gym" or "Elevated Playhouse," choose their size carefully. Rings with diameters of 5 to 10 inches invite children to put their heads through them, an obvious entrapment hazard.

Do not leave any exposed bolts or other fasteners that could puncture skin or catch on clothing. A good way to avoid this is by using recessed counterbores whenever possible. Where counterbores are not part of the design, any bolt threads extending beyond the nut should be sawed off and filed smooth. Avoid open-ended "S" hooks because they can also catch on clothing.

A free swinging, empty swing seat can cause serious injury if it hits a child in the head. To reduce the risk of injury, swing seats should be made of light-weight material such as plastic, canvas, or rubber. To prevent cuts and scrapes, the seats on the "Teeter-Totter" (and any other wooden seats) should have smoothly finished or rounded edges.

Metal or aluminum slides sitting in the sun can cause burns, so they should be placed in shaded areas or, if possible, installed so that the sliding surface faces north. Placing slides in a shaded location will also prevent them from reflecting the glare of the sun and interfering with children's vision.

The projects in this book are intended for use on one surface above all others: grass. Professional athletes prefer natural grass playing fields, and with good reason. Its inherent natural beauty aside, grass has a softness and springiness that makes it far superior to any ground covers you can buy. There's no better protective surface for small children.

### PREVENTIVE MAINTENANCE

While the projects in this book are all designed to withstand the test of time, periodic inspections and some old-fashioned preventive maintenance are still warranted. Even the best-built projects will suffer if neglected. By regularly checking the equipment in your play yard, you'll also help prevent possible injury to your children.

Look for cracked or broken concrete footings, and make any necessary repairs. Nothing compromises safety more than a weakened foundation. Check for any damaged wood members, and replace with pressure-treated lumber. While special attention should always be given to structural members, any broken piece of wood is potentially harmful to children.

Look for splinters and serious checking in the wood, and resand where needed. Inspect all nuts and bolts for tightness; normal usage can loosen fasteners and hardware over time. To make sure that the structural integrity of each project is as good as the day it was built, apply your weight, or the weight of another adult, to the equipment; if it can withstand such a load, it can handle the weight of children.

Depending on how hard the equipment is used, you may have to refinish it after a period of time. The climate in which you live is also a factor; high acid-rain content can take a heavy toll on wood finishes. Periodic applications of high-quality exterior paints and stains will minimize the weathering of the wood. When refinishing ladder rungs, use a clear, natural finish that will penetrate the wood without creating a surface film that can become slippery.

Preventive maintenance should also extend to your lawn; it needs to be in the best possible condition to withstand the heavy use children subject it to. Letting air into the soil about once a year helps alleviate soil compacting that is caused by the constant pounding of feet, which in turn leads to worn, thin grass. This process of letting air into the soil is best done with a power-driven aerator, which can be rented from most lawn and garden stores.

Grass in a play yard should be mowed slightly higher than other lawns. Naturally, the areas of heaviest use will be prone to worn spots. These can be repaired either by reseeding or by patching with sod lifted from another area of the yard. Spots that have been worn low can be filled with topsoil before patching.

An alternative to an all-grass play yard is to frame out a portion of your yard and lay down a bed of wood chips. This technique is especially helpful if your grass is having a difficult time withstanding the heavy foot traffic.

*planning your play yard*

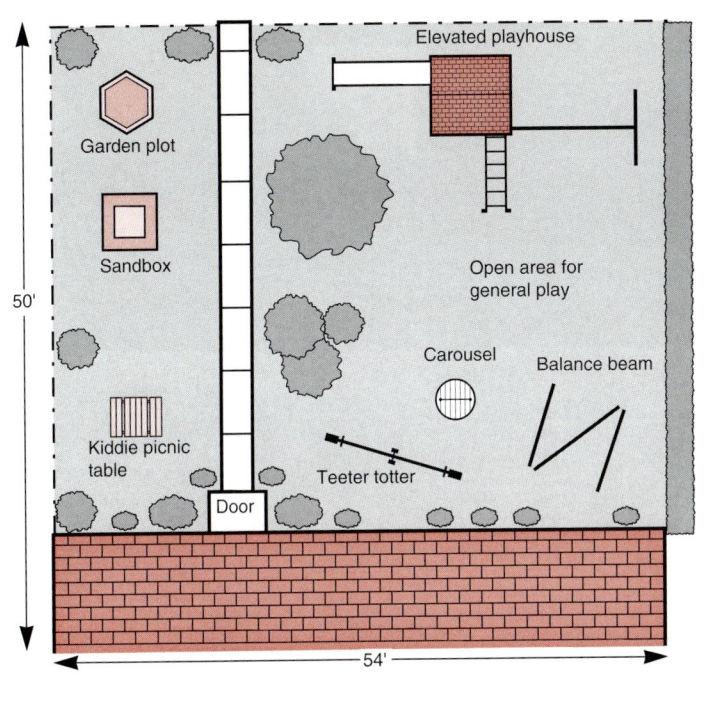
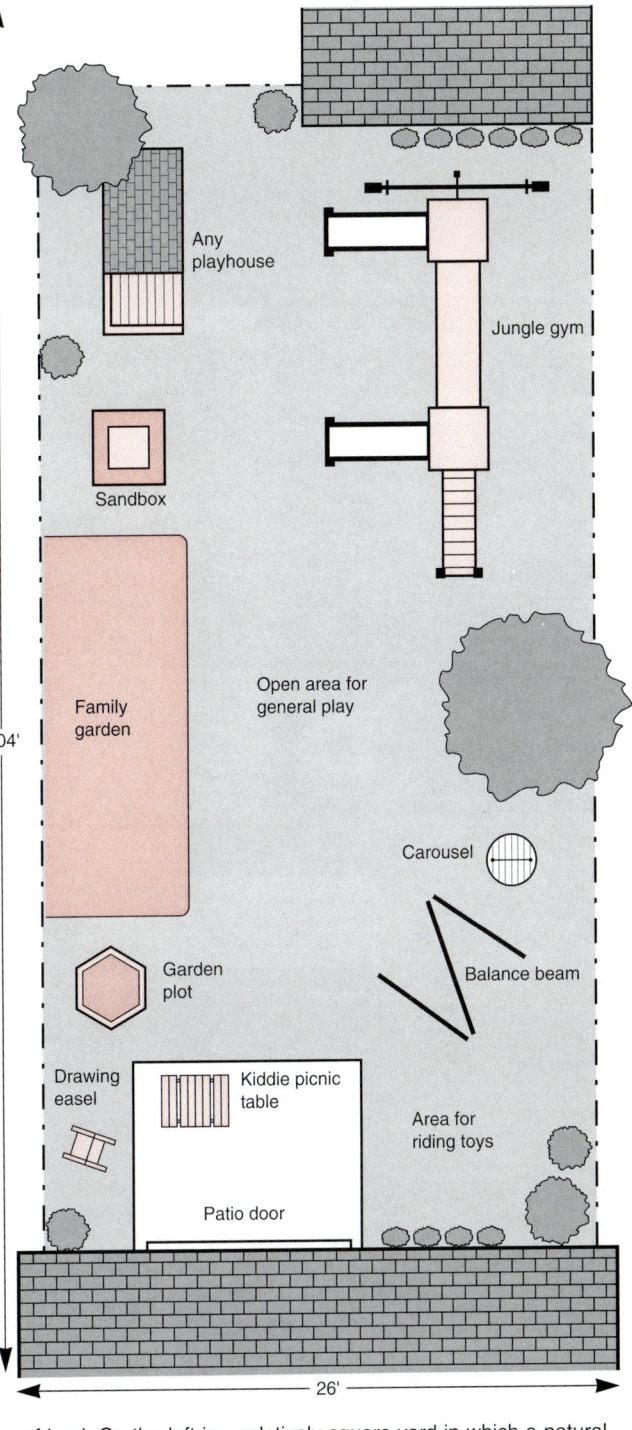

## RECOMMENDED USE ZONES*

| PROJECT | AREA |
|---|---|
| Jungle Gym | 25 feet length and 14 feet width |
| Teeter-Totter | 14 feet length and 10 feet width |
| Balance Beam | 12 feet length and 11 feet width |
| Carousel | 8 feet length and 8 feet width |
| Adjustable Chinning Bar | 7 feet length and 10 feet width |
| Rocking Horse | 6 feet length and 7 feet width |
| Frontier General Store | 8 feet length and 8 feet width |
| Framed Playhouse | 13 feet length and 8 feet width |
| Log Cabin | 10 feet length and 8 feet width |
| Elevated Playhouse | 27 feet length and 16 feet width |
| Play Castle | 17 feet length and 11 feet width |
| Kiddie Picnic Table | 7 feet length and 8 feet width |
| Sandbox | 10 feet length and 10 feet width |
| Drawing Easel | 6 feet length and 6 feet width |
| Game Table and Stools | 8 feet length and 7 feet width |
| Adirondack Chair | 6 feet length and 7 feet width |
| Six-Sided Garden Plot | 7 feet length and 8 feet width |
| Window Box Planter and Stand | 6 feet length and 6 feet width |
| Bad-Guy Bean Bag Game | 6 feet length and 15 feet width** |
| Basketball Backboard | 10 feet length and 15 feet width |

* When used in conjunction with the layout planning grid on page 33, these measurements will ensure that the projects are placed safe distances from each other in the play yard. Projects that can be moved around freely, such as the Red Wagon and Wheelbarrow, are not included in this chart.

** The extra width is required for adequate bean-bag tossing distances.

These examples of play yard designs are based on approximately 1/16 acre of land. On the left is a relatively square yard in which a natural obstruction (in this case, the walkway from the house) is used to advantage; it becomes a dividing line separating the quiet activities from those involving action. Note that no equipment was placed behind the shrubbery where the children would be hidden from view when the parents are inside the house. The large exercise project is in the back of the yard, but far enough away from the tree so as not to tempt children to try to leap from the top of the structure into the tree—a potentially dangerous situation. The design on the right puts all of the action equipment along one side of the long, narrow yard. This layout creates an open path down the center of the yard so that people can reach the garage without disrupting the children's activities. The patio is a perfect spot for the "Kiddie Picnic Table," and the "Six-Sided Garden Plot" is situated next to the full-size family garden so that the children can tend their own crops alongside a family member. The playhouse was built right next to some shrubs, thus lending a natural hiding place when playing Cowboys and Indians. In both designs, a generous open area remains for general play activities.

# planning your play yard

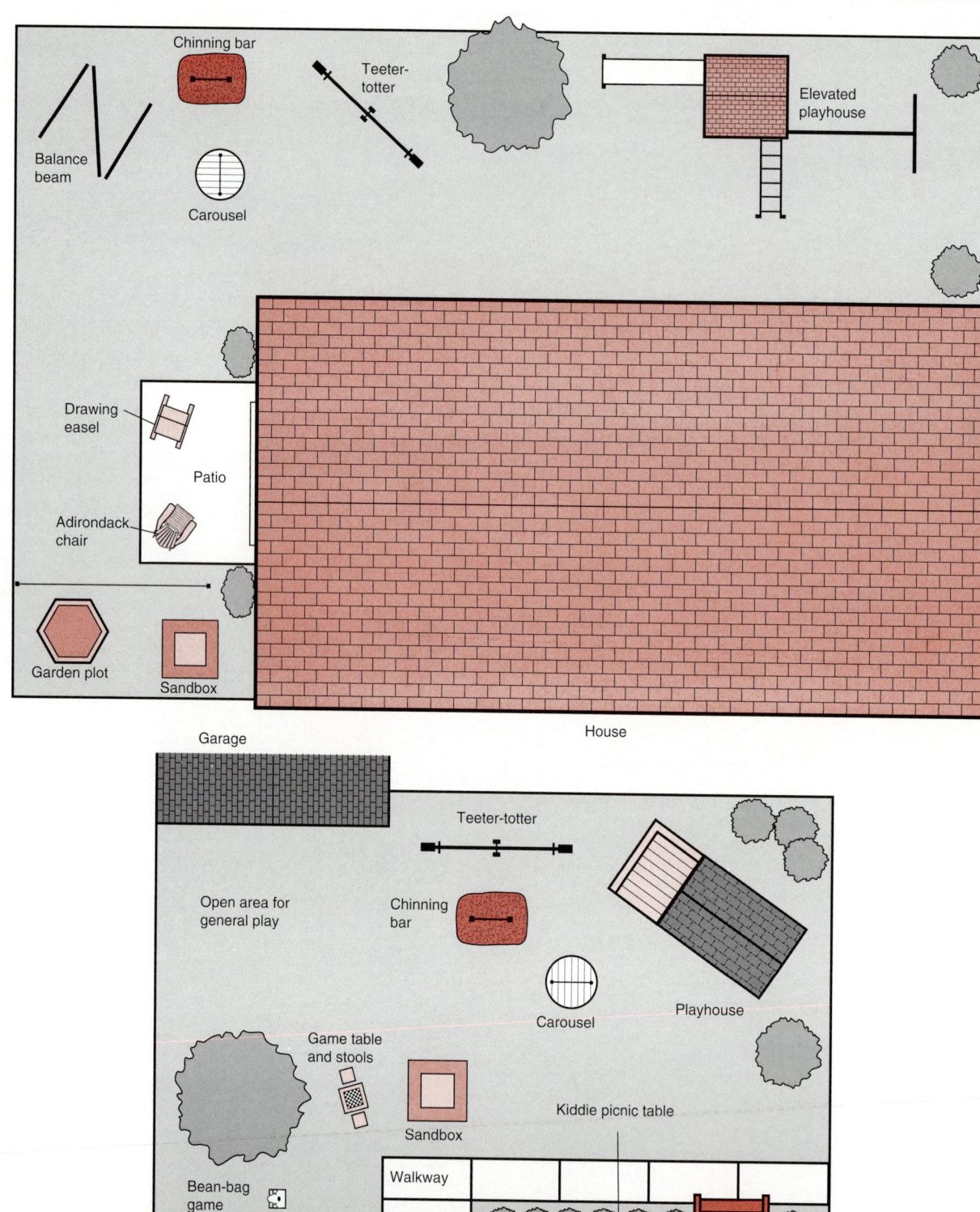

Here are two additional play yard designs. The design on the top, because of its relatively small amount of play space, does not have an open area for general play. However, omitting the "Balance Beam" will provide a generous open area in the corner. The design on the bottom makes good use of the narrow space between the house and the tree by placing the "Bad-Guy Bean Bag Game" there. In neither design is any project hidden from view by trees or shrubbery.

*planning your play yard*

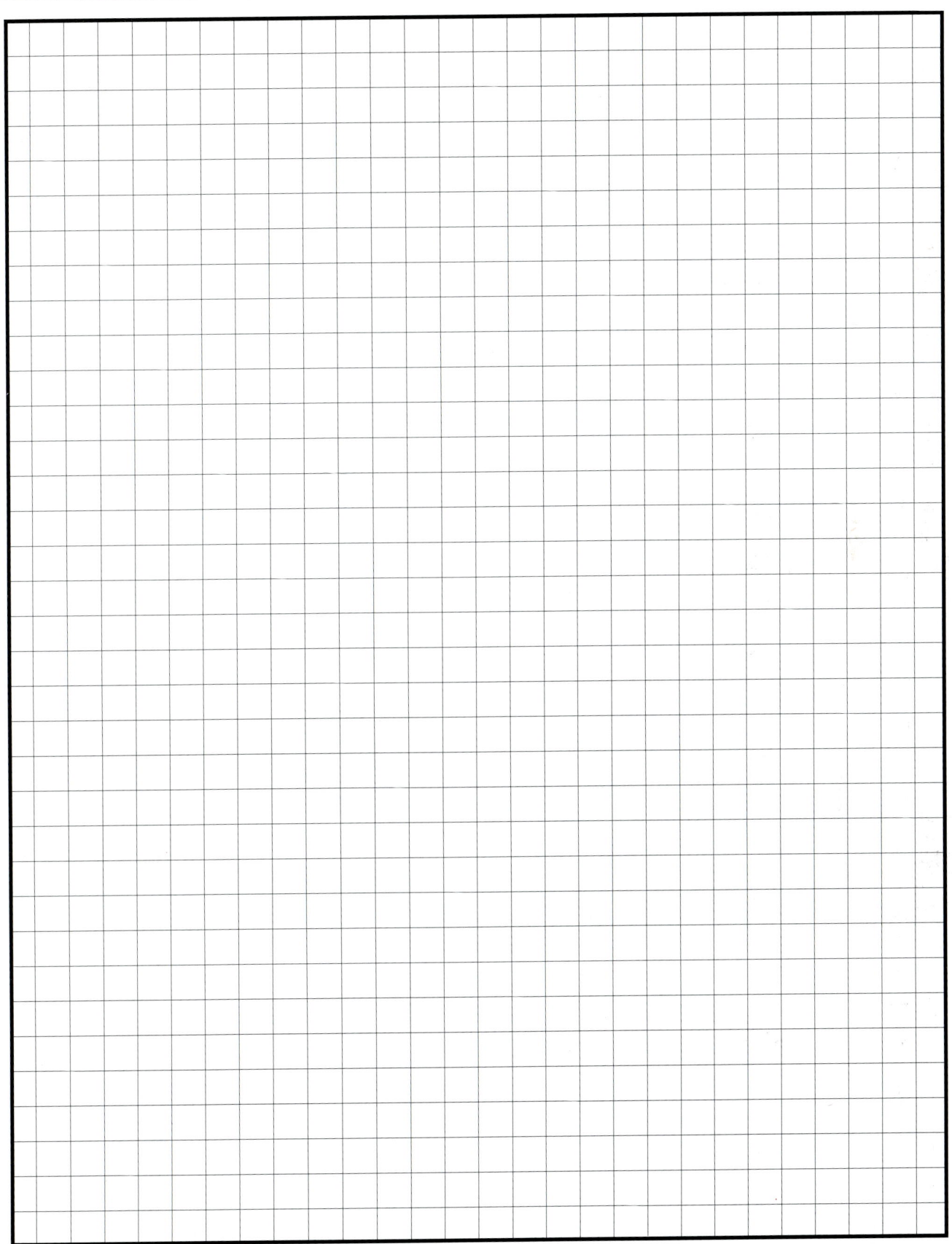

When planning the layout of your play yard, let each square equal 2 feet.

## projects for exercise
# JUNGLE GYM

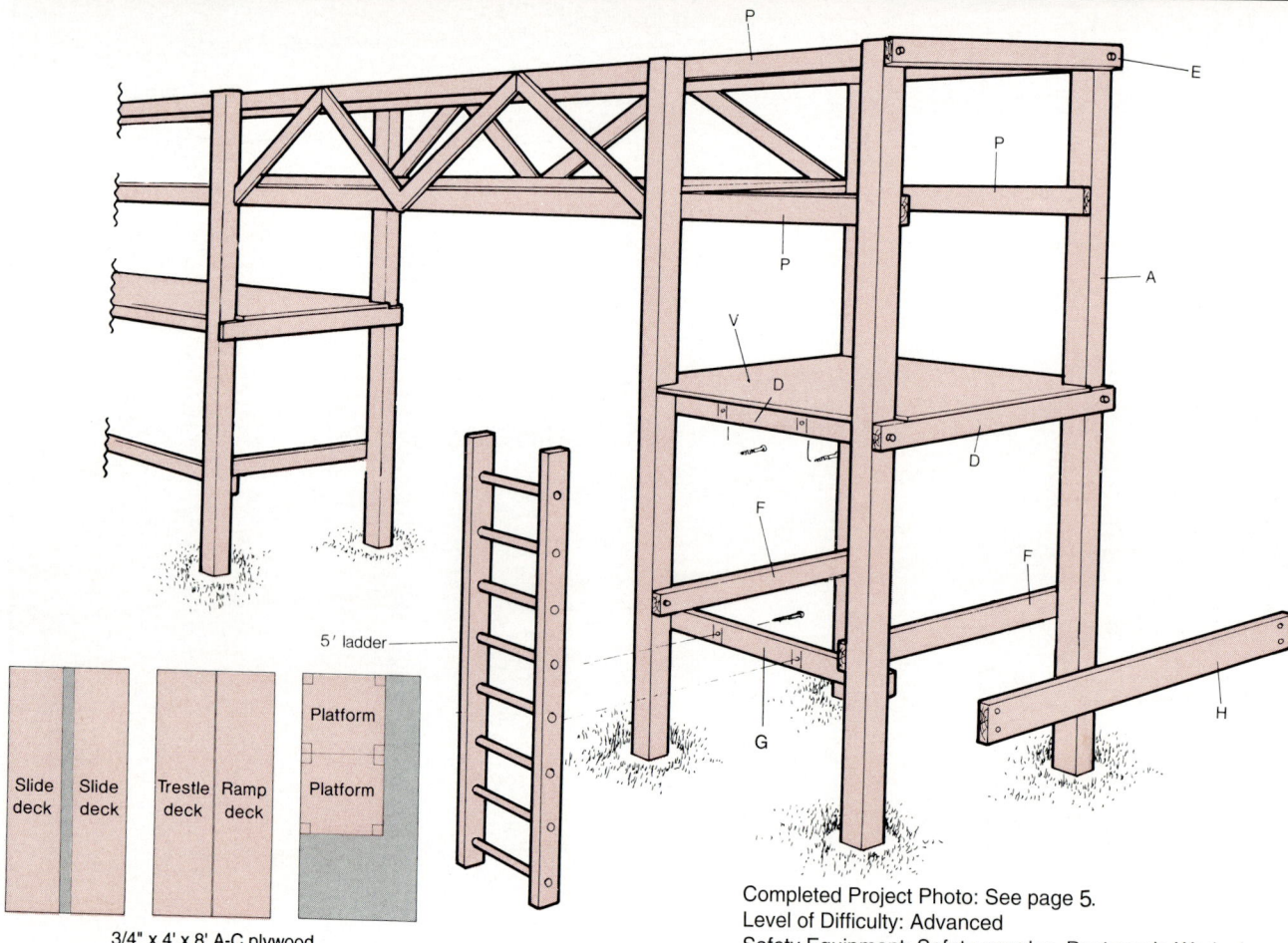

Completed Project Photo: See page 5.
Level of Difficulty: Advanced
Safety Equipment: Safety goggles, Dust mask, Work gloves

Children will get unparalleled enjoyment out of this backyard playground combination. Without a doubt, a well designed and carefully constructed jungle gym is the crown jewel of any play yard. The possibilities are endless, with two slides, one cleated ramp, one seesaw, four ladders, two platforms, and an overhead trussed walkway. You can also install climbing ropes, rings, or swings beneath the walkway.

The jungle gym is built with standard, readily available lumberyard wood and hardware. It is

**MATERIALS, PARTS, AND CUTTING LIST**

| Material/Part Name | Qty. | Size |
|---|---|---|
| Pressure-treated #2 select oak | 1 | 5/4" x 4 x 9' |
| (K) Ramp cleats | 9 | 1 1/16" x 1 1/16" x 23" |
| Pressure-treated #2 select Douglas fir | 5 | 2 x 4 x 8' |
| (C) Temporary cross-members | 8 | 1 1/2" x 3 1/2" x 31" |
| (G) Lower 5' ladder supports* | 2 | 1 1/2" x 3 1/2" x 31" |
| (I) Ramp rails | 2 | 1 1/2" x 3 1/2" x 96" |
| (AA) 3' ladder top supports* | 2 | 1 1/2" x 3 1/2" x 21" |
| (BB) 3' ladder spacers* | 2 | 1 1/2" x 3 1/2" x 8" |
| Pressure-treated #2 select Douglas fir | 6 | 2 x 4 x 10' |
| (L) Slide rails | 4 | 1 1/2" x 3 1/2" x 120" |
| (S) 5' ladder sides | 4 | 1 1/2" x 3 1/2" x 60" |
| Pressure-treated #2 select Douglas fir | 6 | 2 x 4 x 12' |
| (E) Upper cross-members | 2 | 1 1/2" x 3 1/2" x 31" |
| (F) Lower cross-members | 4 | 1 1/2" x 3 1/2" x 31" |
| (X) Seesaw adjustment cleats | 6 | 1 1/2" x 3 1/2" x 108" |
| Pressure-treated #2 select Douglas fir | 7 | 2 x 4 x 14' |

| Material/Part Name | Qty. | Size |
|---|---|---|
| (P) Trestle beams | 4 | 1 1/2" x 3 1/2" x 158" |
| (Q) Trestle bracing** | 8 | 1 1/2" x 2 3/4" x 36 3/8" |
| (U) 3' ladder sides | 4 | 1 1/2" x 3 1/2" x 36" |
| (W) Seesaw | 1 | 1 1/2" x 3 1/2" x 108" |
| Pressure-treated #2 select Douglas fir | 1 | 2 x 8 x 14' |
| (D) Platform supports | 8 | 1 1/2" x 1 1/2" x 31" |
| (H) Inner seesaw trunnion support | 1 | 1 1/2" x 5 1/2" x 31" |
| Pressure-treated #1 select pine | 3 | 2 x 4 x 8' |
| (Y) Feet, slide, and ramp | 6 | 1 1/2" x 3 1/2" x 48" |
| Pressure-treated #1 select pine | 1 | 4 x 4 x 6' |
| (B) Seesaw post | 1 | 3 1/2" x 3 1/2" x 72" |
| Pressure-treated #1 select pine | 4 | 4 x 4 x 12' |
| (A) Tower posts | 4 | 3 1/2" x 3 1/2" x 144" |
| Common pine half round molding | 1 | 3/4 x 8' |
| (N) Slide deck nosing | 4 | 3/4" half round |
| Hardwood dowel | 7 | 1 x 36" |

## projects for exercise

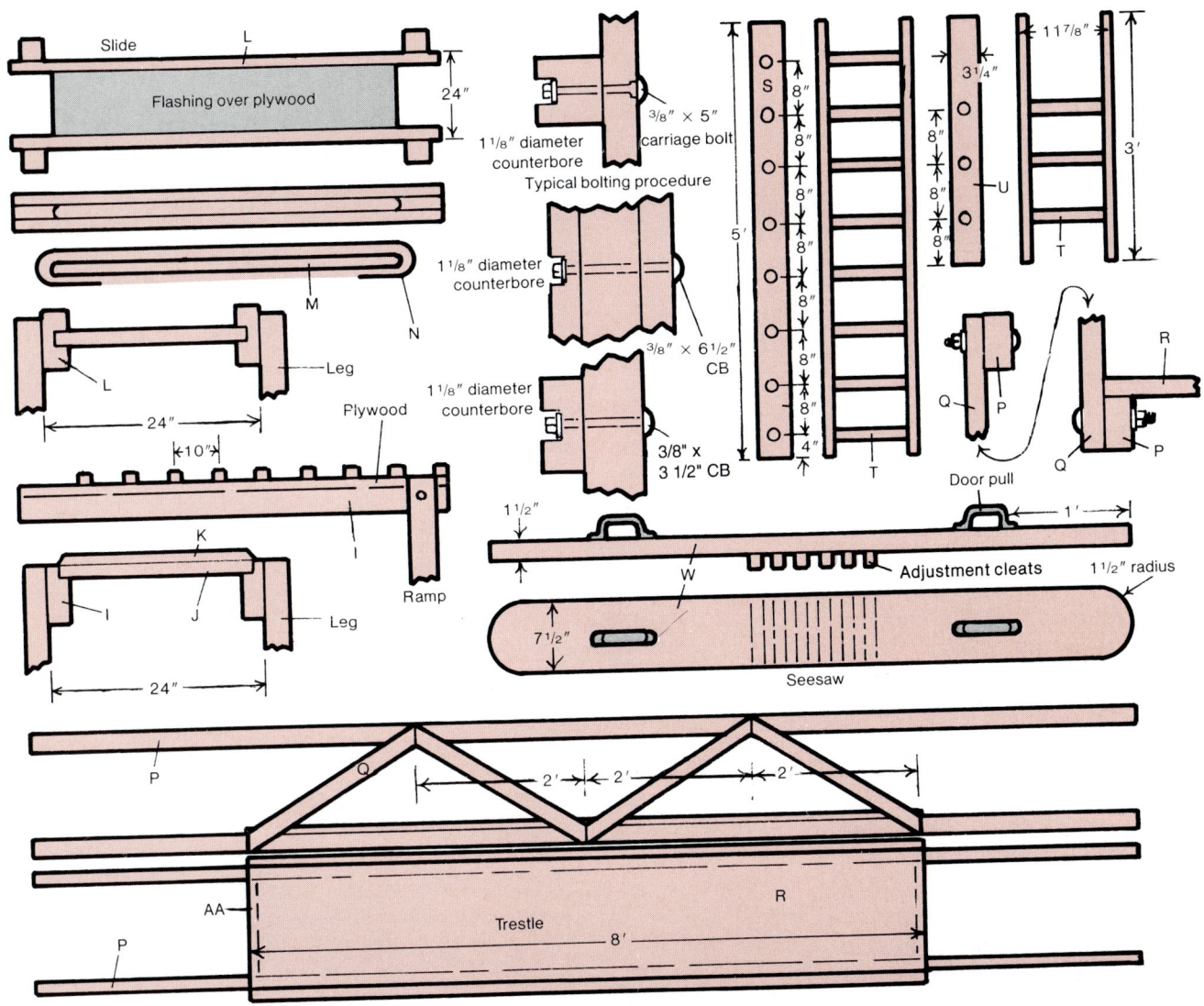

basically two towers, constructed of 4 x 4s and 2 x 4s, connected by a trussed walkway. The entire structure rests on concrete footings and is stabilized by the slides, which are bolted to it at each end. The slide feet also rest on concrete footings.

With the "use zone" figured in, the jungle gym requires an area at least 22 feet long and 14 feet wide for optimum safety.

## 1 BUILDING THE TOWERS

Build up each tower on saw horses, one side at a time, to limit the amount of heavy lifting you have to

### MATERIALS, PARTS, AND CUTTING LIST (CONTINUED)

| Material/Part Name | Qty. | Size |
|---|---|---|
| (T) Rungs | 20 | 1"-dia. x 11 7/8" |
| A-C exterior grade plywood | 3 | 3/4 x 4' x 8' |
| (J) Ramp deck | 1 | 3/4" x 23" x 96" |
| (M) Slide deck | 2 | 3/4" x 22 1/2" x 96" |
| (R) Trestle deck | 1 | 3/4" x 24" x 96" |
| (V) Platform | 2 | 3/4" x 31" x 34" |
| 24-inch wide aluminum flashing | 1 | 18' length |
| (O) Slide surface | 2 | 22 1/2" x 108" |
| Galvanized NPT pipe | 1 | 1/2 x 16" |
| (Z) Seesaw trunnion | 1 | 18" wide overall with flanges, 1/2"-dia. |
| Door pulls | 2 | #4 |
| Floor flanges (NPT) | 2 | 1/2" |
| Galvanized carriage bolts/washers/nuts | 22 | 3/8 x 3 1/2" |
| Galvanized carriage bolts/washers/nuts | 56 | 3/8 x 5" |
| Galvanized carriage bolts/washers/nuts | 4 | 3/8 x 6 1/2" |

| Material/Part Name | Qty. | Size |
|---|---|---|
| Galvanized flat head and Phillips head, hardened assembly screws | 120 | #8 x 2" |
| Galvanized oval head nails | — | 10d |
| Galvanized oval head nails | — | 8d |
| Galvanized flat head wood screws | 4 | #12 x 1" |
| Galvanized flat head bolts/washers/nuts | 4 | 1/4 x 2" |
| Galvanized lag bolts/washers | 14 | 5/16 x 3" |
| 1 x 2 furring (eight 8' pieces) | 1 | bundle |
| Dry concrete mix | 15 | 80-lb. bags |
| 5/8-3/4" stone | 5 | 5-gal. buckets |

\* Make from temporary cross-members after towers are installed.
\*\*Rip 2 3/4" wide pieces from 2 x 4 dimensional lumber. Fit exact length and miter angle to trestle beams, with beams laid out parallel at exact spacing.

35

## projects for exercise

do. To begin this assembly, position the two 12-foot-long posts (A) on the horses, parallel to each other, and 24 inches apart from inside face to inside face. In this position, the post faces that are up will be the inside faces when the assembly is complete.

There are three 31-inch-long 2 x 4s needed for each pair of posts: one temporary cross-member (C) flush with the top; one temporary cross-member (C) whose bottom edge is 24 inches down from the top; and one platform support (D) whose top edge is 48 3/4 inches down from the top.

Mark the locations for these pieces on the posts. Then clamp or tack-nail them in place, while checking that the assembly is square. Next, drill 3/8-inch-diameter bolt holes. Turn the assembly over, and counterbore the holes in the posts 3/4 inch deep, using a 1 1/8-inch spade bit. Doing this will keep the hardware flush and out of harm's way. Secure the pieces with 3/8" x 3 1/2" carriage bolts. Nail scrap cross-bracing between the posts on the opposite ends.

Repeat the entire procedure just described, making three more subassemblies. Then set two of these subassemblies on edge on the horses, with the insides facing each other.

Join the two subassemblies by adding, in the same manner as be-fore, the upper cross-member (E) at the top and the third platform support (D) and lower cross-member (F) to the frame. The lower cross-member's top edge should be 82 inches from the top. Then rotate the complete assembly, and add the last platform support (D) and lower cross-member (F).

Add scrap cross-bracing to the remaining two planes not yet braced, and nail the platform (V) to the platform supports to stabilize the assembly. Now, install one of the lower ladder supports (G), with its top edge flush with the bottom edges of the lower cross-members.

Repeat the entire operation to build the second tower. Note that in the final assembly the towers will be facing each other, so both lower ladder supports (G) should be installed at the rear, directly opposite the slides.

### BUILDING THE TOWERS

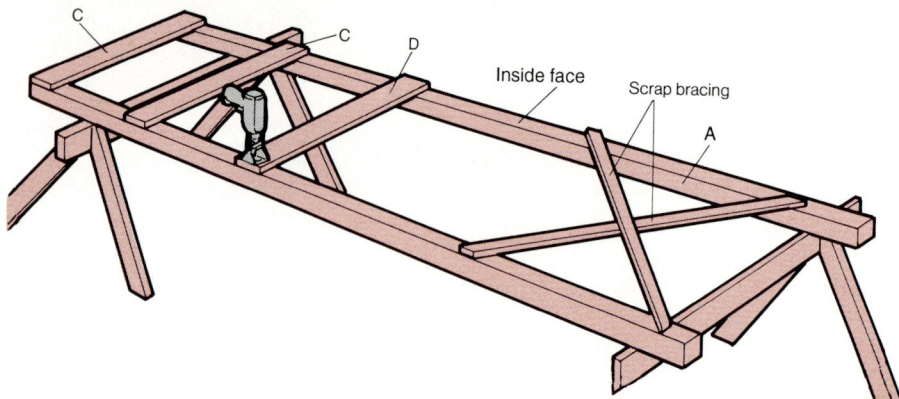

Build the towers half at a time. Place a pair of posts on saw horses, parallel to each other, with the ends squared up. Then mark, position, clamp, drill, and bolt the cross-members and supports in place. Add the scrap cross-bracing.

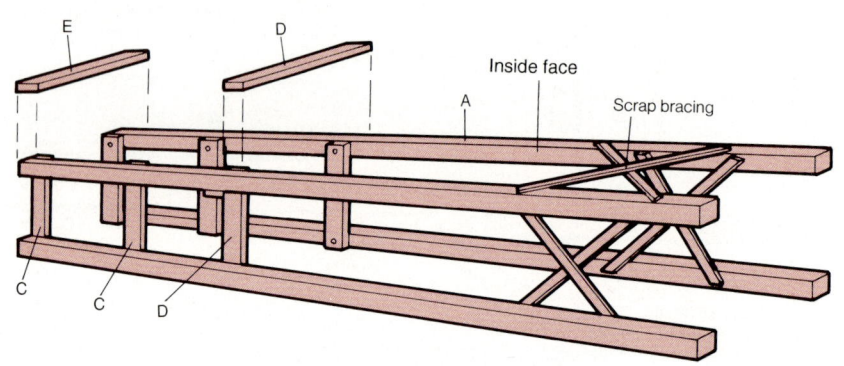

Place the halves on edge on the horses, two at a time, parallel to each other, and with the ends squared up and the insides facing each other. Mark, clamp, drill, and bolt the joining members in place. Stabilize the assembly with scrap cross-bracing.

### BUILDING THE TRESTLE

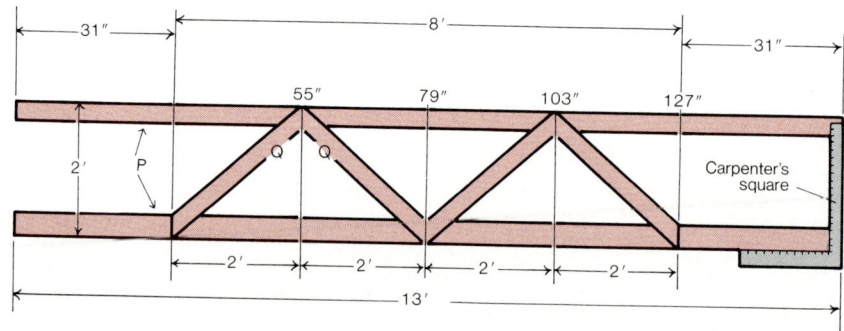

Place two beams on horses, parallel to each other and with their ends squared up. Mark off the positions of the trestle bracing on both beams. Then fit, clamp, drill, and bolt the bracing to the beams.

36

*projects for exercise*

## BUILDING THE TRESTLE (CONTINUED)

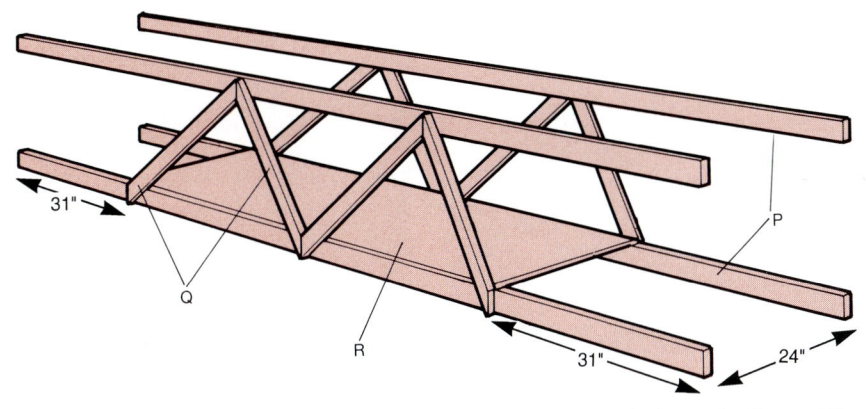

Stand a pair of trestle sides on edge on the horses with the insides facing each other and the ends squared up. Place the trestle deck between them and on top of the lower beams. Nail the deck to these beams.

## MAKING THE RAMP

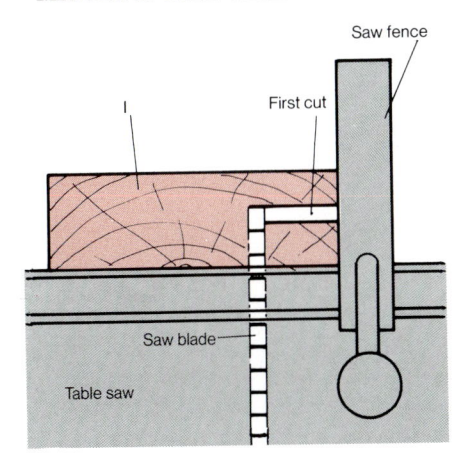

The ramp deck sits in rabbets machined in the rails. Cut these rabbets in two passes on the saw for each rail.

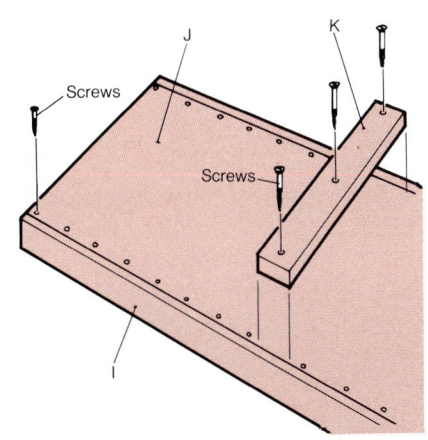

Place the deck in the rabbets, and center it. Assemble the screws. Position the cleats on the deck, and screw them in.

## MAKING THE SLIDES

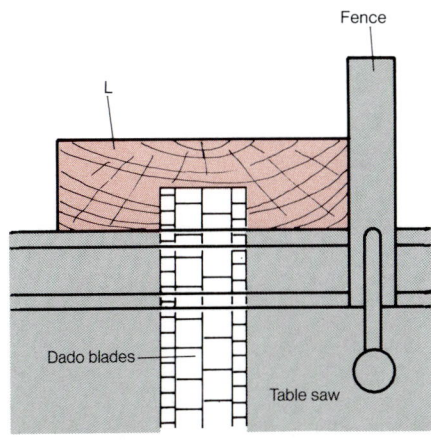

Machine the grooves in the slide rails using a dado blade. Keep the depth as accurate as possible.

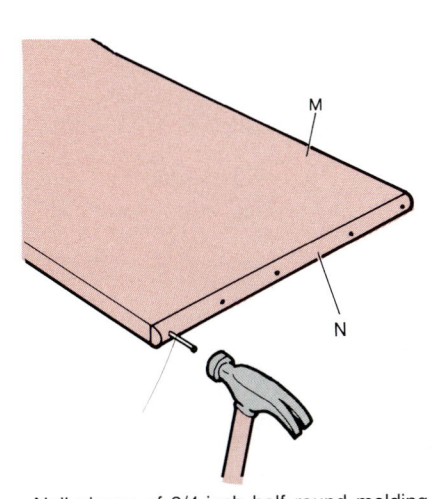

Nail pieces of 3/4-inch half round molding to the ends of the slide deck. Trim these nosing ends flush.

## 2 BUILDING THE TRESTLE

Position a pair of trestle beams (P) on the horses, parallel to each other and 24 inches apart from outer edge to outer edge. Square up the ends, and mark off 2-foot increments on the beam faces, starting 31 inches in from either end. When completed, the 31-inch beam sections will be bolted between the tower posts.

Rip 12 feet of 2 x 4 to a width of 2 3/4 inches. Then cut this into four lengths of trestle bracing (Q) that are approximately 36 inches each. Set the miter gauge on the table saw at 40 1/2°, and trim both ends of each piece so that the miters are parallel. (If a table saw is not available, the miters can, of course, be cut with a circular saw.) Then fit each piece in the triangular truss pattern by trimming it back with the miter gauge at the same setting. This should occur at about 33 7/8 inches overall length. When satisfied with the fit, clamp, drill, and assemble the trestle sides with 3/8 x 3 1/2-inch carriage bolts, nuts, and washers. Make another trestle side in the same way. Nail the trestle deck (R) to the upper edges of the lower trestle beams with 10d nails, lining up the deck ends with the 31-inch marks.

## 3 MAKING THE RAMP

Cut 1-inch-wide by 7/8-inch-deep rabbets in the rails (I). Screw the deck (J) to the rails. Saw out the cleats (K) and bevel their ends. Mark the cleat locations on the ramp deck, and position the cleats. Finally, drill through them into the deck with a combination bit, and screw the cleats in place using #8 x 2-inch flat head screws.

Cut a pair of feet (Y) to length from pressure-treated #1 select pine, and clamp them to the lower ends of the rails. Drill holes and install the feet using 3/8 x 3 1/2-inch carriage bolts, nuts, and washers.

*projects for exercise*

Note that the overall width of the ramp from outer rail face to outer rail face must be 24 inches so that it will fit between the posts of the tower.

## 4 MAKING THE SLIDES

As with the ramp, the total width of the slides from outer rail face to outer rail face must be 24 inches to fit between the posts of the towers; the slide deck itself is 22 1/2 inches wide. Therefore, cut dadoes in the slide rails (L) 3/4 inch deep and 13/16 inch wide.

Next, nail pieces of 3/4-inch half round molding (N) to the top and bottom edges of the plywood slide decks (M). Since the slide decks are to be surfaced with 23 1/2-inch-wide aluminum flashing (O), order the flashing 24 inches wide, and cut 1/2 inch off one edge with a utility knife, guided by a straightedge.

Align the flashing with the slide deck, and roll 5 to 6 inches of it around one end on to the back side; then staple or tack it in place. Stretch it out, roll it around the other end, and staple it.

Now, with one end of the slide rails laying flat on a work surface and dado facing up, start the slide deck into the dado, and advance it until it is centered on the rail. Do the same with the second rail, and compress the rails in place with bar or pipe clamps.

Next, drive galvanized, oval head nails into the rail edge, through the slide deck, and into the rail on the other side of the dado, locking the assembly together. Add the feet as you did before for the ramp. Repeat this entire procedure to build the second slide.

## 5 MAKING THE LADDERS

There are two 5-foot ladders and two 3-foot ladders; both sizes are constructed in exactly the same

### MAKING THE SLIDES (CONTINUED)

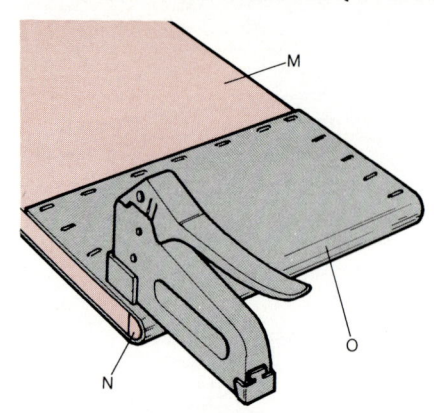

Place the precut flashing on the deck, and roll it around the ends. Nail or staple it in place on the underside.

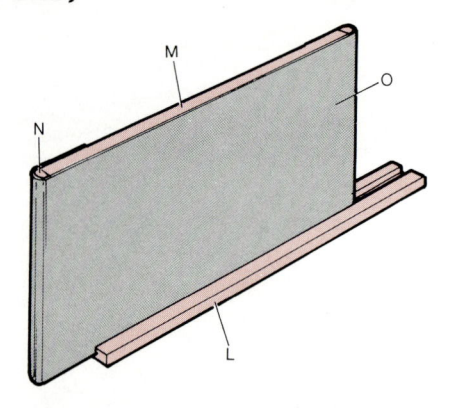

Slide the combined deck and aluminum flashing into the machined grooves in the slide sides.

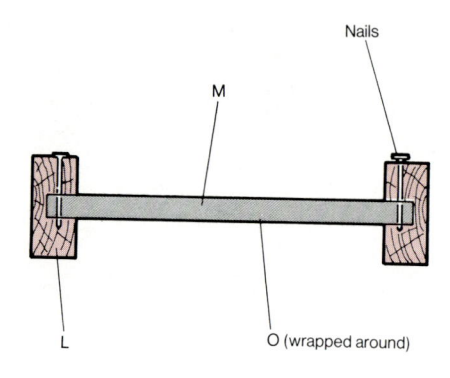

This cross-section view shows how nails driven through the rail edge and deck lock these parts together in an assembly.

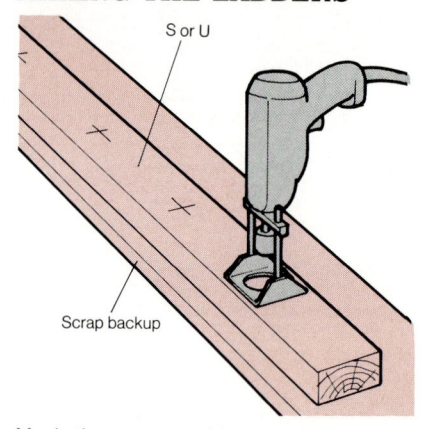

### MAKING THE LADDERS

Mark the rung positions on the ladder sides. Mount a drill in a guide and, against scrap backup, drill the holes.

### MAKING THE LADDERS (CONTINUED)

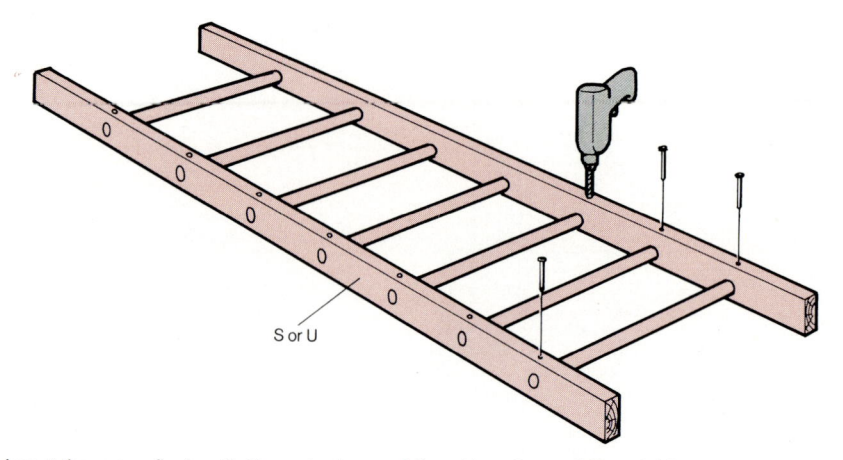

Insert the rungs flush with the outer faces of the sides. Cross drill and drive nails to lock the rungs in place.

38

# projects for exercise

## STARTING THE INSTALLATION

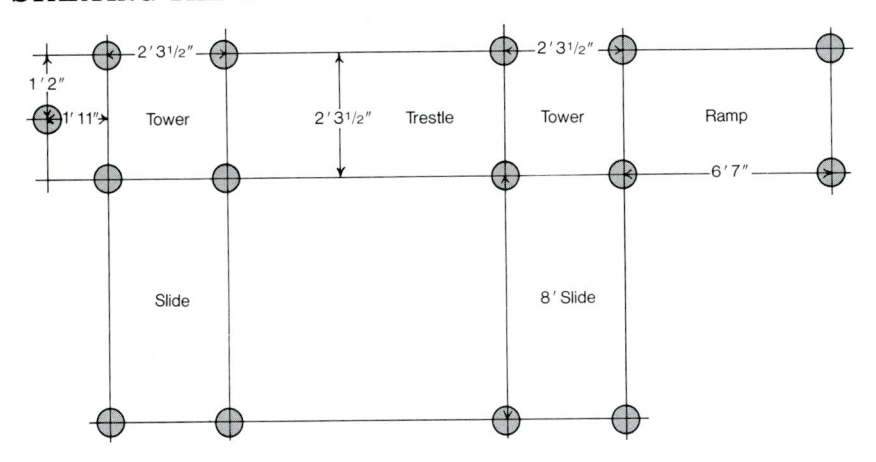

Use stakes and mason's cord to lay out the locations of the postholes. Use the 3-4-5 triangular method to ensure square, true corners. Drive a stake in the ground at each intersection, marking the hole centers.

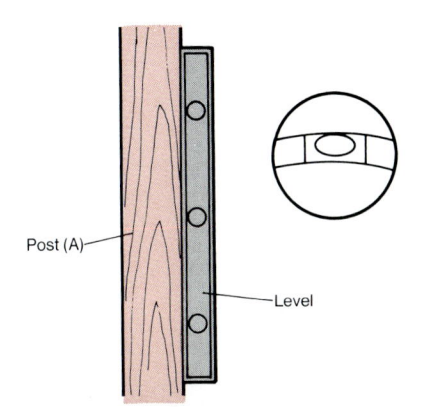

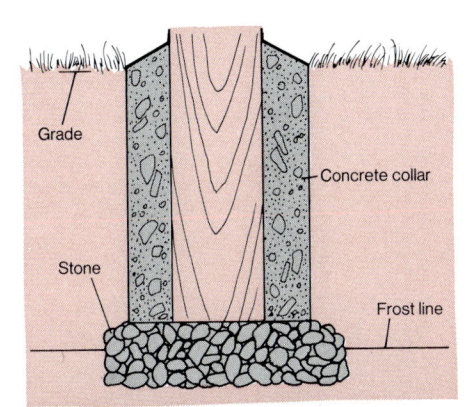

Place posts in holes on top of 6 inches of stone. Check for plumb on adjacent faces with a level, and brace the posts in place.

Backfill the plumbed and braced posts with concrete. The collars should taper at the top to shed water.

## INSTALLING THE SECOND TOWER

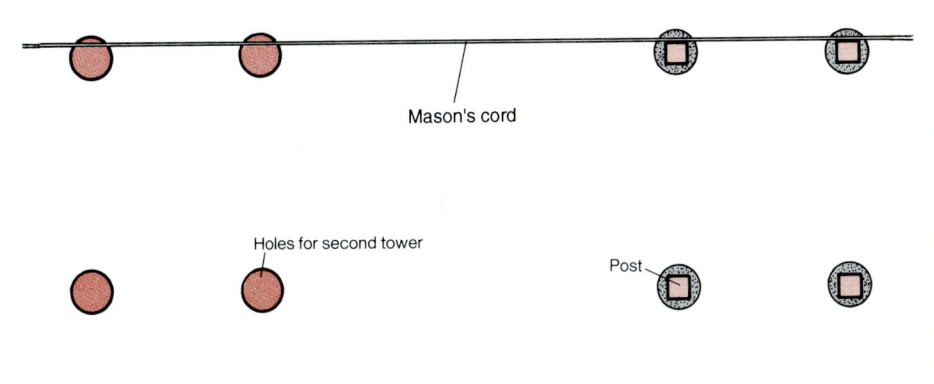

To align the tower posts, stretch a mason's cord from the farthest tower post, past and just touching the second post, and on past the other tower locations. This will let the trestle fit between the towers without bending the beams.

way. Lay out the hole centers for the rungs on all ladder sides (S, V) as follows: (1) on the 5-foot ladder, make the first hole center 4 inches from the end and the other hole centers every 8 inches; (2) on the 3-foot ladder, make the hole centers every 8 inches.

Drill these holes using a 1-inch-diameter bit, assisted by a drill guide to keep the holes perpendicular to the surface. Cut the rungs (T) from dowel, and assemble the ladders. The 11 7/8-inch rung length allows three rungs to be made from each 3-foot dowel.

Then drill 1/8-inch-diameter pilot holes through the sides at each rung, and drive in galvanized, oval head nails to lock the rungs in place.

## 6 BUILDING THE SEESAW

The seesaw can be made of Doug-las fir or 6 x 4 or 8 x 4 oak, depending on the size of the people who will be using it. For large kids or adults, use the oak and switch to 3/4-inch NPT (normal pressure and temperature) pipe and flanges for the trunnion (Z). But for small kids (60 pounds or less), the fir and 1/2-inch NPT pipe and flanges should be fine.

Round off the ends of the seesaw (W). If you wish, customize the shape by slightly necking down the area where the small child will sit. Be sure to break all corners (sand and/or plane the edges smooth for handling), and sand the surface smooth to remove splinters.

Saw out the adjustment cleats (X) from 5 x 4 oak. Then, lay the seesaw on a work surface, face up, and mark the locations for the cleats. Three cleats are attached to the seesaw on either side of the centerline, separated by a 7/8-inch gap (larger if using 3/4-inch pipe).

Clamp the cleats in position, drill holes with a combination bit,

# projects for exercise

and insert the #8 x 2-inch screws. Finish up by installing door pulls for handholds.

Note that both the trunnion and its flanges are supported by a separate post (B) on the outboard side and a trunnion support (H) on the inboard side. Fitting these parts is best done after the towers, trestle, ramp, and slides have been installed.

## 7 STARTING THE INSTALLATION

Drive stakes, and stretch mason's cord between them so that the intersections of the cords are over the post-hole centers. Then drive a stake into each of these centers and remove the cords.

Dig each of the fifteen holes down to the frost line. Depending on the depth of the frost line where you live, the posts may need to be shorter or longer than the dimensions listed. (To make the job of digging the postholes easier, consider renting a post-hole digger). Drop about 6 inches of 5/8-inch stone into each hole, and keep a bucket of stone handy in case you need to adjust the post height.

Remove the scrap bracing from one of the towers, and, with some help, place the bottoms of the posts into the first four-hole group. Check the posts for plumb by placing a level in the vertical position against adjacent faces on the posts, while your helpers add or remove stone to accommodate the adjustment.

The top ends of the slide and ramp rails may need minor changes in length or miter trimming in order to fit neatly between the posts before bolting. The feet may also require some trimming to adjust the heights of the slide or ramp over them.

When the tower is plumbed and all slide and ramp adjustments have been made, backfill the appropriate holes with concrete

## INSTALLING THE SECOND TOWER (CONTINUED)

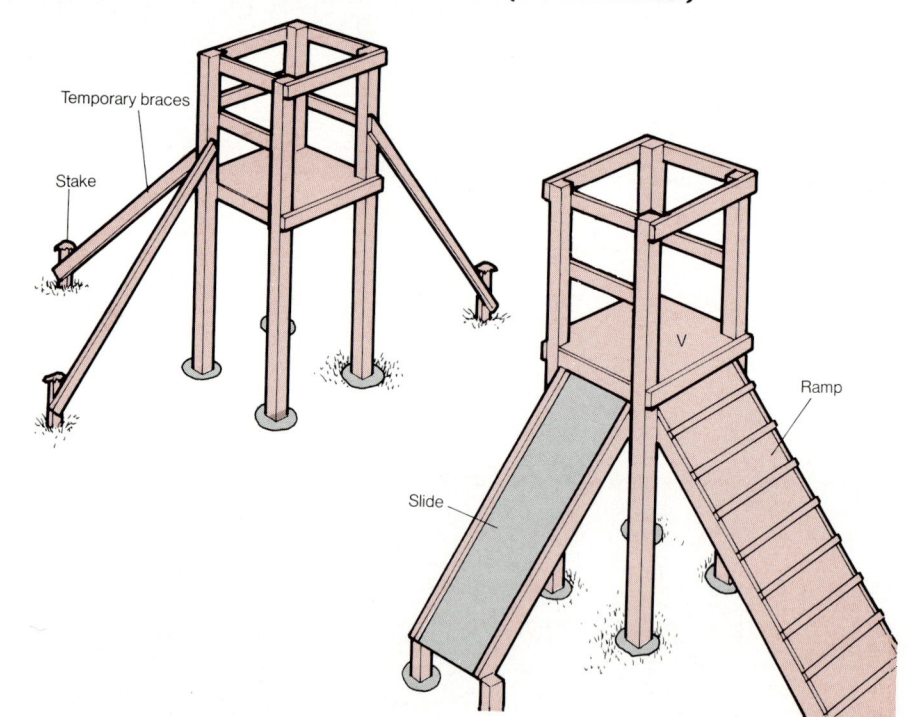

Stabilize the first tower with the ramp and the slide assemblies. Then adjust the second tower for alignment, height, plumb, and distance from the first tower. Brace it in position, recheck it, and backfill the holes with concrete.

## INSTALLING THE TRESTLE, SECOND SLIDE, SEESAW, AND LADDERS

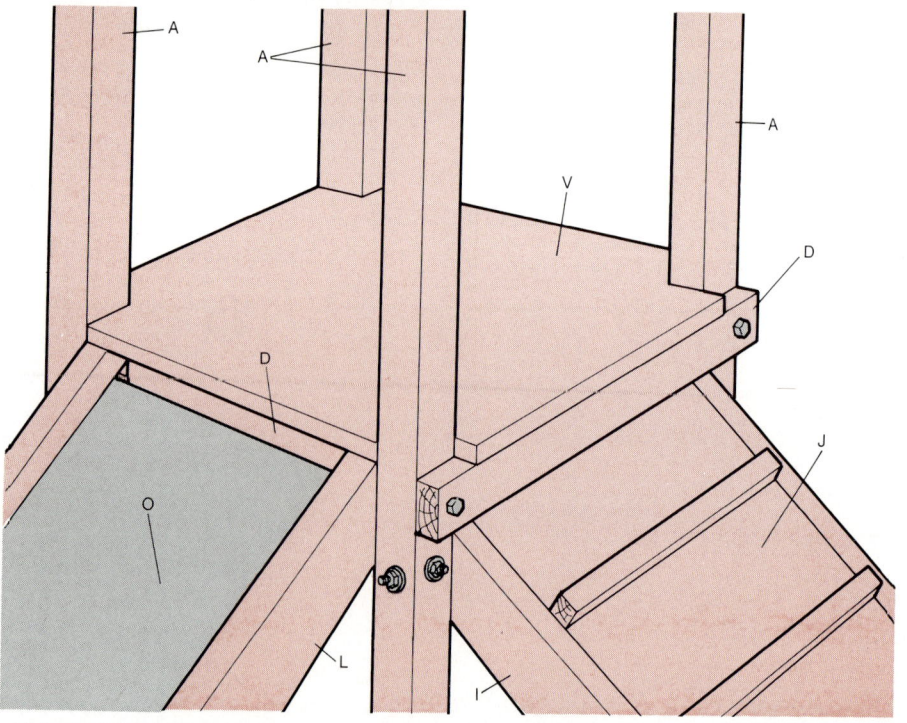

This close-up shows how the slide and ramp are joined to the first tower just underneath the platform. After fitting these parts and bolting them to the posts, trim back the ends of the rails that protrude past the posts.

**projects for exercise**

### INSTALLING THE TRESTLE, SECOND SLIDE, SEESAW, AND LADDERS (CONTINUED)

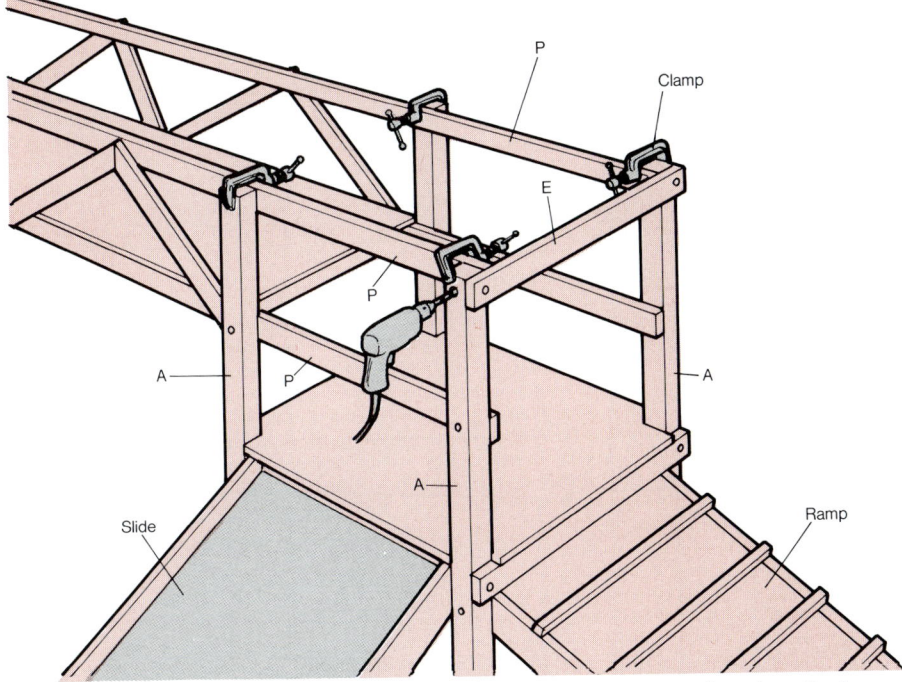

When the concrete footings have set, remove the temporary cross-members from the tower tops. With a helper, lift the trestle assembly, and clamp it in the spot vacated by the temporary cross-members. Drill and bolt the beams to the posts.

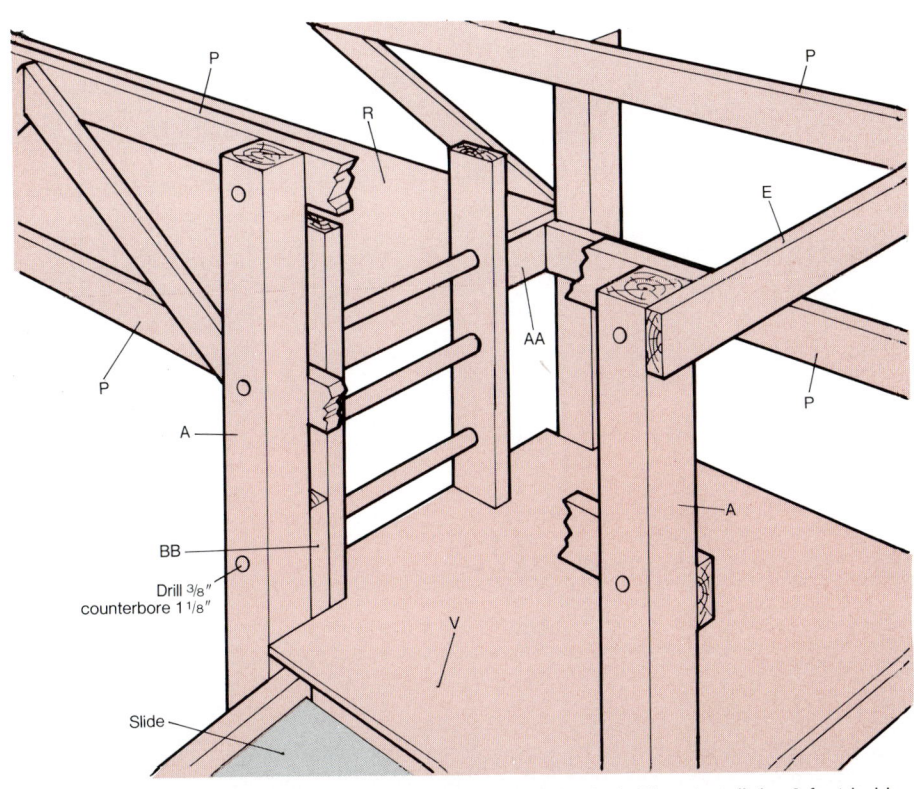

Install the upper ladder support at the end of the trestle deck. Then install the 3-foot ladder and its spacer. Lag-bolt the ladder support and the platform to the ladder. Carriage-bolt the ladder side and its spacer to the post.

collars. These collars should taper up at grade to shed water. Allow all concrete to cure for 2 to 3 days.

## 8 INSTALLING THE SECOND TOWER

Erecting the second tower is a bit more difficult because it must conform to the position, height, and orientation of the first. Now, with your helpers, set the second tower in place. Check its alignment relative to the first tower with a mason's cord, as shown in the drawing. Check and correct the stone level to accommodate the plumb attitude of the tower posts. Hang a line level on the cord between the towers to check that they are at the same height. Finally, make sure that there are exactly 8 feet between the towers at the 7- and 9-foot levels for fitting the trestle. Do this critical work slowly and carefully. Then lock the second tower in place with stakes and braces, and backfill the holes with concrete. Allow the concrete to cure for 2 to 3 days.

## 9 INSTALLING THE TRESTLE, SECOND SLIDE, SEESAW, AND LADDERS

Install the second slide, making trim and height adjustments as before. Bolt on the inner seesaw trunnion support, and install the seesaw post, pipe, and floor-flange assembly. Backfill the post and the second slide's feet with concrete. Allow sufficient curing time.

Before lifting up the trestle to the towers, remove the temporary cross-members from the tower tops. Then trim two of these cross-members to 21-inch lengths. These are now the upper ladder supports (AA). Screw them in place under both trestle deck ends, between the beams.

You will need some help to raise the trestle into position; once it is in

## projects for exercise

place, clamp the beams to the posts in exactly the same position that the temporary cross-members occupied. Drill through the beams from the existing holes in the posts, and bolt the beams to the posts.

Lag-bolt the 5-foot ladders to the lower ladder supports at the bottom and to the platform supports at the top. Set the 3-foot ladder side ends on the platform, and sandwich a spacer (BB) between the post and the ladder side. Drill and bolt them together using 3/8- x 6 1/2-inch carriage bolts, washers, and nuts. Then, lag-bolt the upper parts of the 3-foot ladders to the upper ladder supports, and run a lag bolt up through the platform into the end of the other ladder side.

If larger children will be playing on the jungle gym, include a pair of vertical posts for extra-firm support under the trestle center. Then, set the posts in concrete and bolt them to the trestle at the top. Sand all surfaces where fingers might pick up a splinter or cut. Paint or stain the entire structure as desired. When sanding or staining/painting, always be sure to wear the proper safety aids. Before the kids try out the slide for the first time, rub it down with a piece of waxed paper; this will make the slides much faster.

Rings, knotted ropes, landing nets, and swings are available in the larger toy-store chains. Attach this additional equipment to the trestle according to the instructions provided by the manufacturer; they usually call for eyebolts or screw eyes.

### INSTALLING THE TRESTLE, SECOND SLIDE, SEESAW, AND LADDERS (CONTINUED)

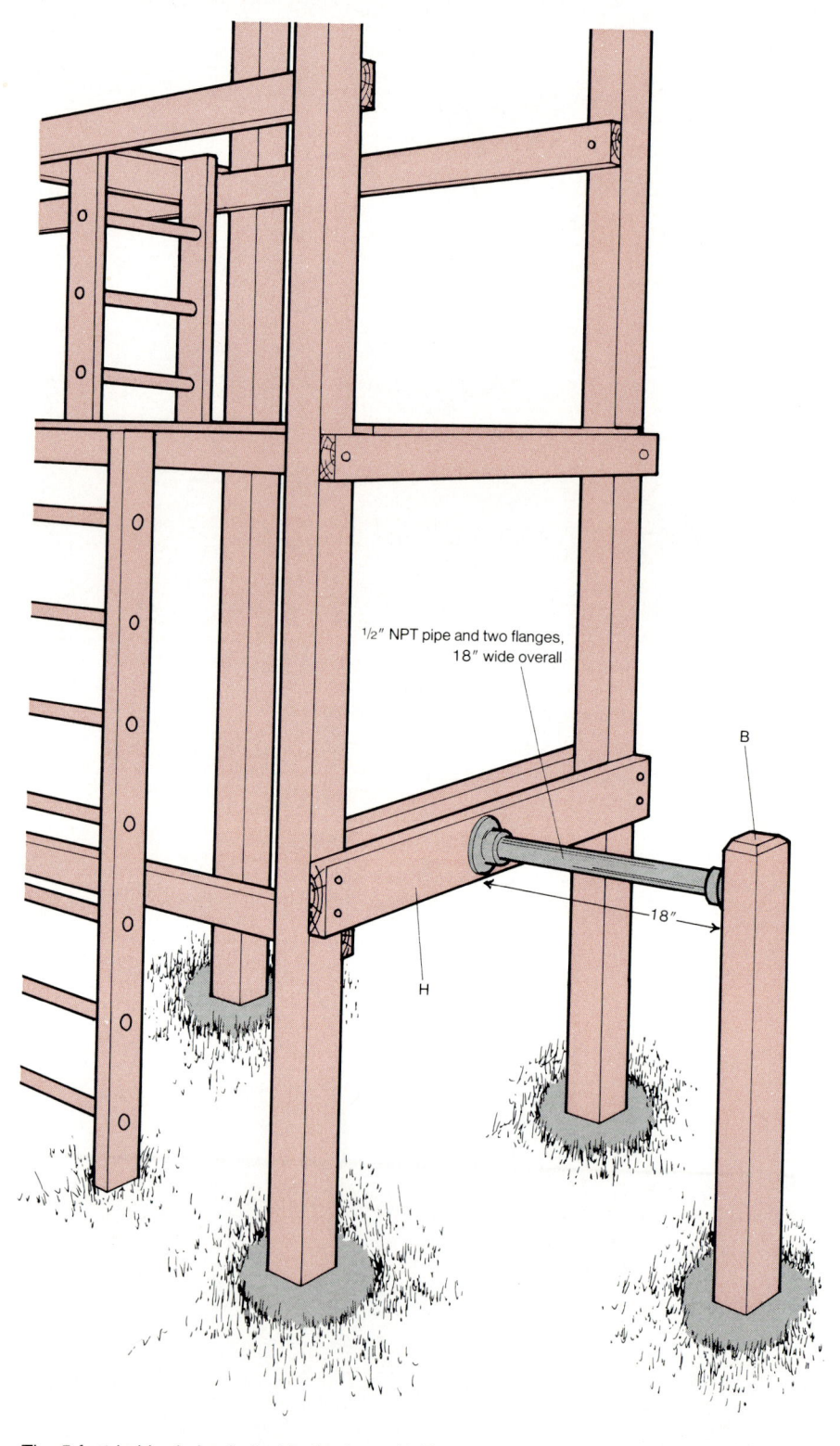

The 5-foot ladder is lag-bolted to the lower ladder support near the bottom and to the platform support at the top. The seesaw trunnion pipe and flange assembly is attached to the outboard post and to the trunnion support on the tower.

## projects for exercise

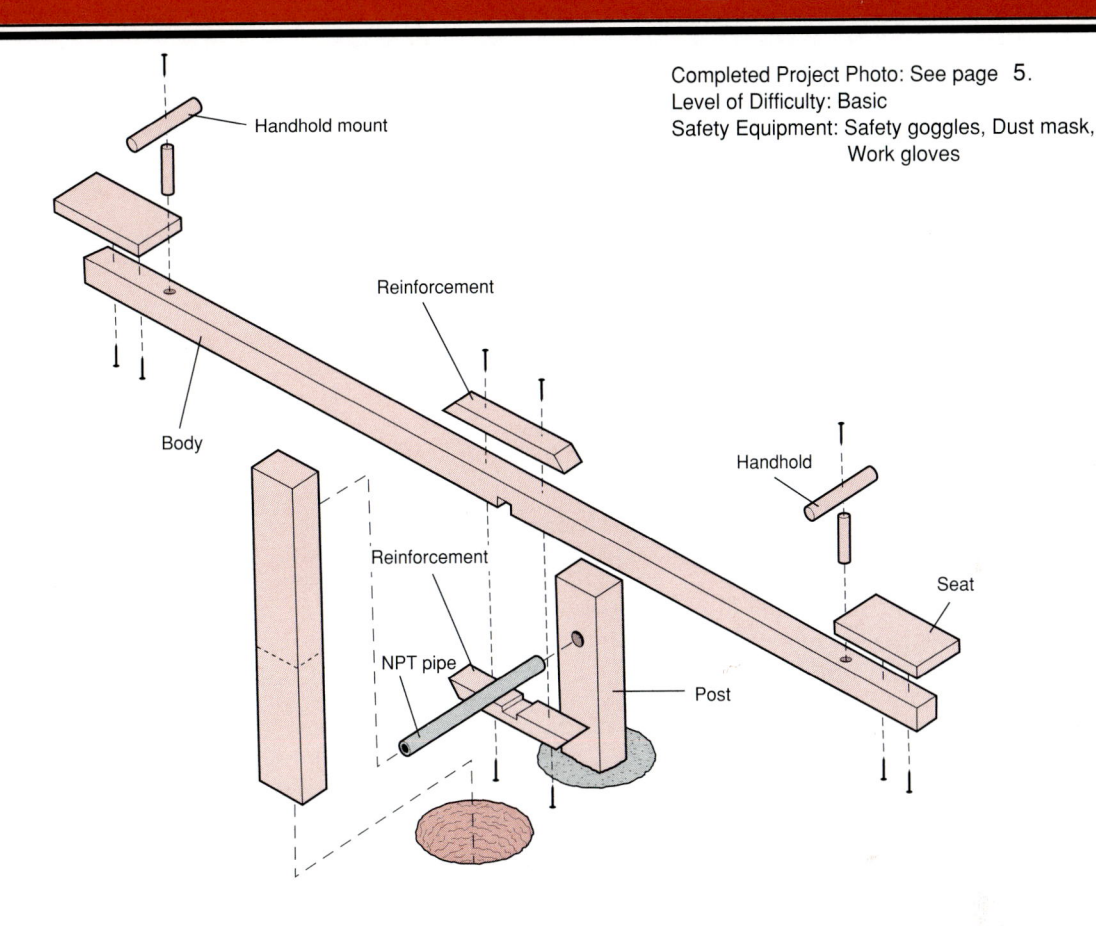

# TEETER-TOTTER

Completed Project Photo: See page 5.
Level of Difficulty: Basic
Safety Equipment: Safety goggles, Dust mask, Work gloves

*Labels on diagram:* Handhold mount, Body, Reinforcement, Reinforcement, NPT pipe, Post, Handhold, Seat

Teeter-totters, or seesaws, have long been a playground favorite. It is little wonder why, since few experiences are as exhilarating for a child as a ride on a teeter-totter. With this project, your children will not have to go to the playground for their ride. This teeter-totter is built with pressure-treated pine to withstand the elements, so it is sure to be a source of enjoyment for years to come. With the "use zone" figured in, the teeter-totter requires an area at least 14 feet long and 10 feet wide for optimum safety.

## 1 CUTTING THE PIECES

When cutting the posts, keep in mind that they must be buried to the local frost line for stability, and must extend at least a full 2 feet aboveground. For these reasons, it may be necessary to cut them slightly longer than the recommended 3-foot, 6-inch length. Cut the rest of the pieces to the dimensions given in the Materials, Parts, and Cutting List. Note that the two reinforcements in this example were beveled 2 inches on each end for a more attractive look. This optional beveling can be done with a portable circular saw. For purposes of safety, round off the edges of the seats.

### MATERIALS, PARTS, AND CUTTING LIST

| Material/Part Name | Qty. | Size |
|---|---|---|
| Pressure-treated #1 select pine | 1 | 2 x 4 x 3' |
| Reinforcements | 2 | 1 1/2" x 3 1/2" x 16" |
| Pressure-treated #1 select pine | 1 | 2 x 8 x 3' |
| Seals | 2 | 1 1/2" x 7 1/4" x 14" |
| Pressure-treated #1 select pine | 1 | 4 x 4 x 12' |
| Body | 1 | 3 1/2" x 3 1/2" x 138" |
| Pressure-treated #1 select pine | 1 | 4 x 6 x 8' |
| Posts | 2 | 3 1/2" x 5 1/2" x 42" |
| Hardwood dowel | 1 | 1"-dia. x 2' |

| Material/Part Name | Qty. | Size |
|---|---|---|
| Handhold mounts | 2 | 1"-dia x 8" |
| Hardwood dowel | 1 | 2"-dia. x 2' |
| Handholds | 2 | 2"-dia. x 10" |
| Galvanized NPT pipe | 1 | 1 13/4" OD x 20" |
| Galvanized flat head wood screws | 4 | #18 x 4" |
| Galvanized flat head wood screws | 8 | #12 x 3" |
| Galvanized flat head wood screws | 2 | #6 x 2 1/2" |
| Premixed concrete | 2 | 50-lb. bags |
| OD = outside diameter | | |

43

*projects for exercise*

## 2 INSTALLING THE POSTS

Mark a spot 6 inches down from the top of each post, then drill a hole 2 inches in diameter and 2 1/2 inches deep, in each post. When marking off for the post-hole excavation, keep in mind that there must be 16 inches between inside post edges. Dig the holes to the frost line. Mix one of the bags of concrete, install the first post, and pour the concrete around its base. It is a good idea to brace the post temporarily until the concrete sets so that it remains plumb. Insert the galvanized NPT pipe into the drilled hole in the post. Mix another bag of concrete and install the second post in the same way. When the pipe is inserted in both posts, it should be square to the posts and perfectly level.

## 3 NOTCHING THE BODY AND BOTTOM REINFORCEMENT

Both the body of the teeter-totter and the bottom reinforcement must be notched in order to accommodate the galvanized NPT pipe. Make a mark 5 feet 9 inches from one end of the body; this is the exact center of the piece. From

### INSTALLING THE POSTS

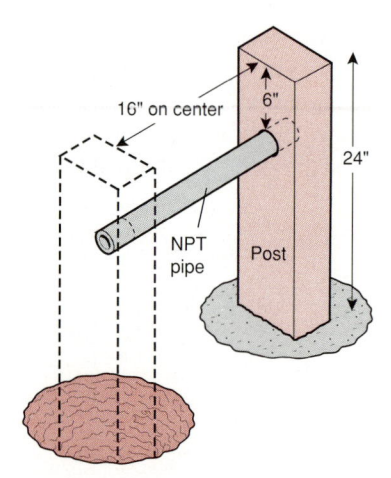

Do not cement the second post in place before making sure that the galvanized NPT pipe is level and square to both posts.

### NOTCHING THE BODY AND BOTTOM REINFORCEMENT

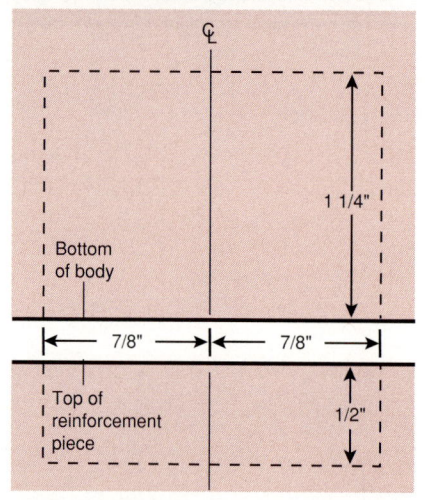

Notch the body and bottom reinforcement carefully. If either notch is cut incorrectly, the safety of the project may be compromised.

this point, measure 7/8 inch in both directions and make two more marks. The resulting 1 3/4-inch section must be dadoed to a depth of 1 1/4 inches on the bottom of the body. Using a circular saw, make the first cuts on the end marks. Made additional cuts every 1/4 inch between those marks. A chisel can be used to remove any remaining material. An identical 1 3/4-inch dado is then cut in the top of the bottom reinforcement; however, this dado is cut only to a depth of 1/2 inch.

## 4 ADDING THE SEATS AND HANDHOLDS

Install the seats on the body by driving #12 x 2 1/2-inch flat head wood screws from the bottom of the body into the seats. Note that each seat overhangs the end of the teeter-totter approximately 4 inches. Install the handhold mounts by first drilling a 1-inch-diameter hole approximately 1-inch deep in the body directly in front of each seat. Apply glue to the ends of the handhold mounts, and press-fit them in the holes

### FINAL ASSEMBLY

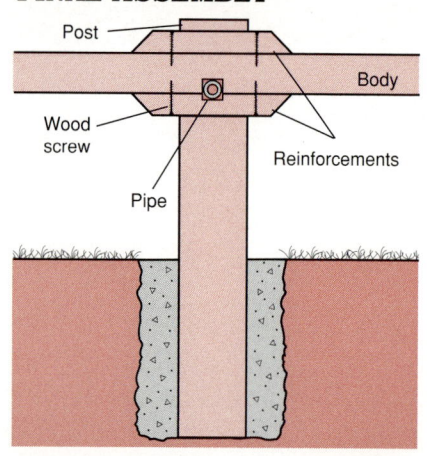

For maximum holding power, drive the 3-inch screws into the flat part of the reinforcements, never the beveled ends.

using a mallet. Then drill a 1-inch-diameter hole in the handholds on the mounts. A spade bit is the best choice for drilling the handholds; clamp them securely in a bench vise before starting to drill. Finally, drive a #6 x 2 1/2-inch flat head wood screw into the top of each handhold to secure them to the mounts.

## 5 FINAL ASSEMBLY

When assembling the teeter-totter, use the notches cut in the body and bottom reinforcement to fit these pieces over the pipe. With the body resting on the pipe and a helper holding the bottom reinforcement in place, drive #18 x 4-inch flat head wood screws up through the bottom reinforcement and into the body. Drive the screws into the flat portion of the reinforcement, not the beveled ends. Add the top reinforcement by centering it directly over the bottom piece and driving screws down into the body. Be sure to sand all over to prevent splinters and cuts. With the assembly complete, paint or stain the seats, handholds, and handhold mounts as desired.

*projects for exercise*

# BALANCE BEAM

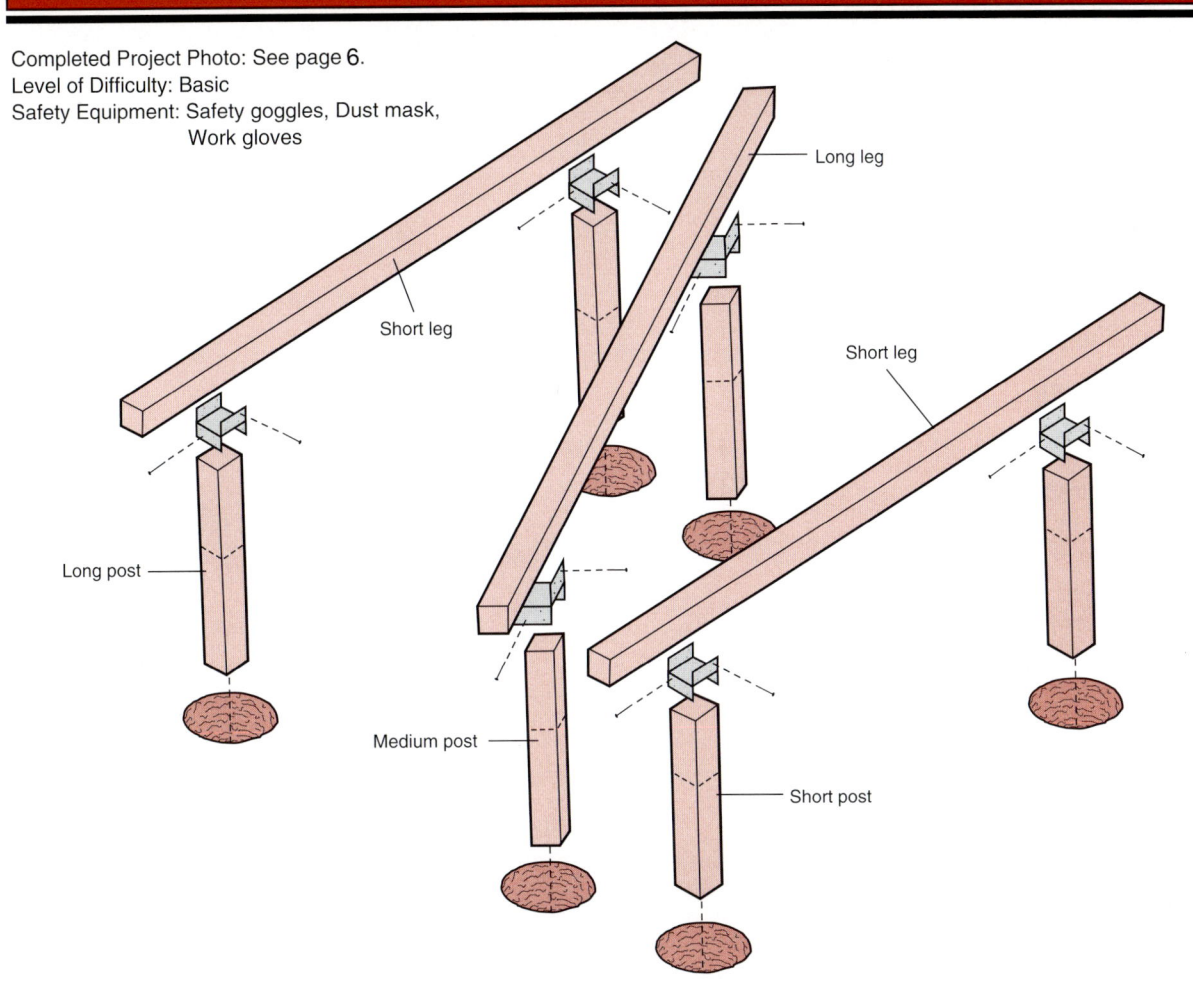

Completed Project Photo: See page 6.
Level of Difficulty: Basic
Safety Equipment: Safety goggles, Dust mask, Work gloves

- Long leg
- Short leg
- Short leg
- Long post
- Medium post
- Short post

This "Z"-shaped balance beam is challenging fun for children. It helps improve balance and coordination, while providing friendly competition, as each child attempts to stay on the beam longest without falling off. As an added challenge, the height of each leg is different; one short leg is 10 inches aboveground, the long leg is 12 inches aboveground, and the other short leg is 14 inches aboveground.

The balance beam is made from 4 x 4 pressure-treated pine. To ensure permanence, concrete is used to secure the posts. However, if space is at a premium in your play yard, you may wish to keep the balance beam for only a few years, then remove it when your children are a bit older and the space can be better used for other projects. In this case, just tamp dirt around the posts instead of cementing them in place.

With the "use zone" figured in, the balance beam requires an area at least 12 feet long and 11 feet wide for optimum safety.

Note: If you are building the balance beam for older children, you may wish to incline the legs as shown in the photograph on page 5. This can be done by simply cutting one post in each pair shorter than the other. Since this feature is probably too challenging or dangerous for younger children, how-

**MATERIALS, PARTS, AND CUTTING LIST**

| Material/Part Name | Qty. | Size |
|---|---|---|
| Pressure-treated #2 select pine | 2 | 4 x 4 x 5' |
| Short posts | 2 | 3 1/2" x 3 1/2" x 28" |
| Medium posts | 2 | 3 1/2" x 3 1/2" x 30" |
| Pressure-treated #2 select pine | 1 | 4 x 4 x 6' |
| Long posts | 2 | 3 1/2" x 3 1/2" x 32" |
| Pressure-treated #2 select pine | 2 | 4 x 4 x 8' |

| Material/Part Name | Qty. | Size |
|---|---|---|
| Short legs | 2 | 3 1/2" x 3 1/2" x 96" |
| Pressure-treated #2 select pine | 1 | 4 x 4 x 10' |
| Long leg | 1 | 3 1/2" x 3 1/2" x 120" |
| Beam clips | 9 | 3" |
| Galvanized barbed nails | 1 lb. | 1 1/2" - 10 gauge |
| Premixed concrete | 4 | 50-lb. bags |

# projects for exercise

ever, the instructions that follow presume that each leg will be perfectly level.

## 1 CUTTING THE PIECES

The 10-foot 4 x 4 and the 8-foot 4 x 4s are kept as is for the three legs. Cut the long posts from the 6-foot 4 x 4, and cut the medium size and short posts from the 5-foot 4 x 4s.

## 2 DIGGING THE POSTHOLES

Set the three legs on the ground in their exact positions to form the "Z" shape. Each leg uses two posts, one 18 inches from each end. Mark off the post-hole locations on the ground, and dig each hole to a depth of 18 inches—or deeper if the frost line in your area is more than 18 inches. In such cases, the posts will have to be cut proportionately longer. Install the posts two at a time, and use a line level to make sure the tops are level. When satisfied with the position of the posts, use temporary bracing to keep them plumb, then mix and pour concrete around the bases.

## 3 ASSEMBLING THE PARTS

Once the concrete has set and the posts are secure, barb-nail a beam clip onto the top of each post. There are eight predrilled holes in each clip for attaching to the post, and another eight holes for attaching to the legs. Mark the location of the beam clips on the legs, 18 inches from each end. When positioning the legs on the posts, these marks should be centered in the beam clips. Secure the legs to the beam clips with barbed nails to complete the job.

### DIGGING THE POSTHOLES

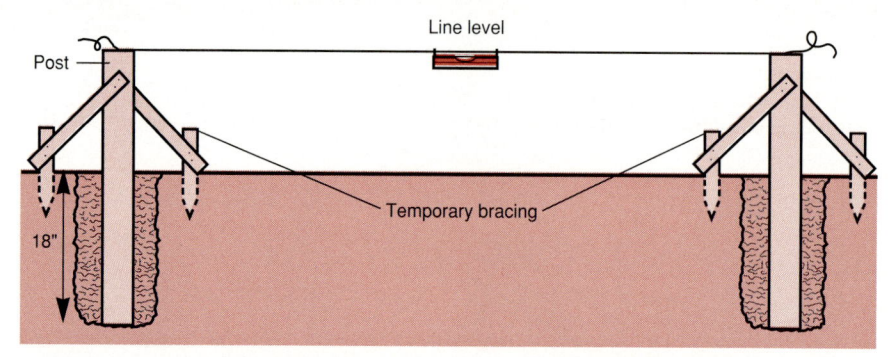

Brace the posts temporarily to keep them plumb while pouring the concrete bases.

### DIGGING THE POSTHOLES (CONTINUED)

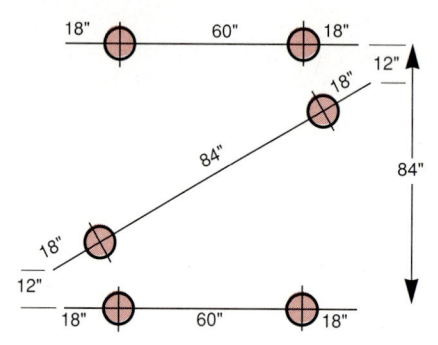

Lay out the locations of the postholes according to this diagram.

### ASSEMBLING THE PARTS

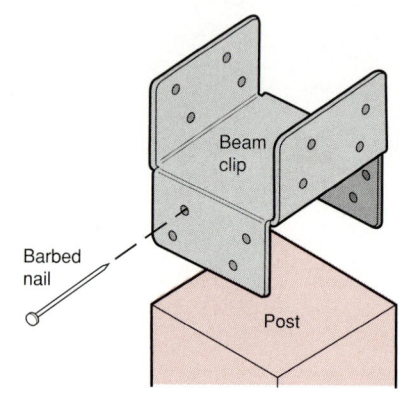

The beam clip is the perfect structural connector for the balance beam.

### ASSEMBLING THE PARTS (CONTINUED)

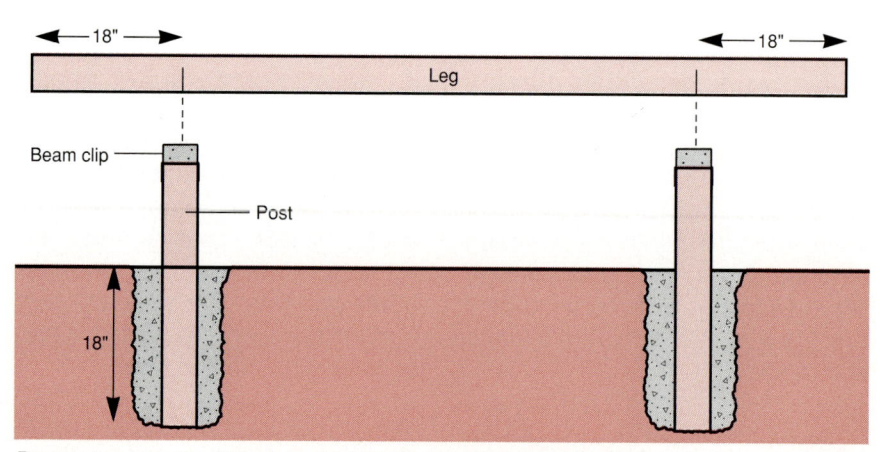

Be sure to center the 18-inch marks in the beam clips when installing the legs.

*projects for exercise*

# Carousel

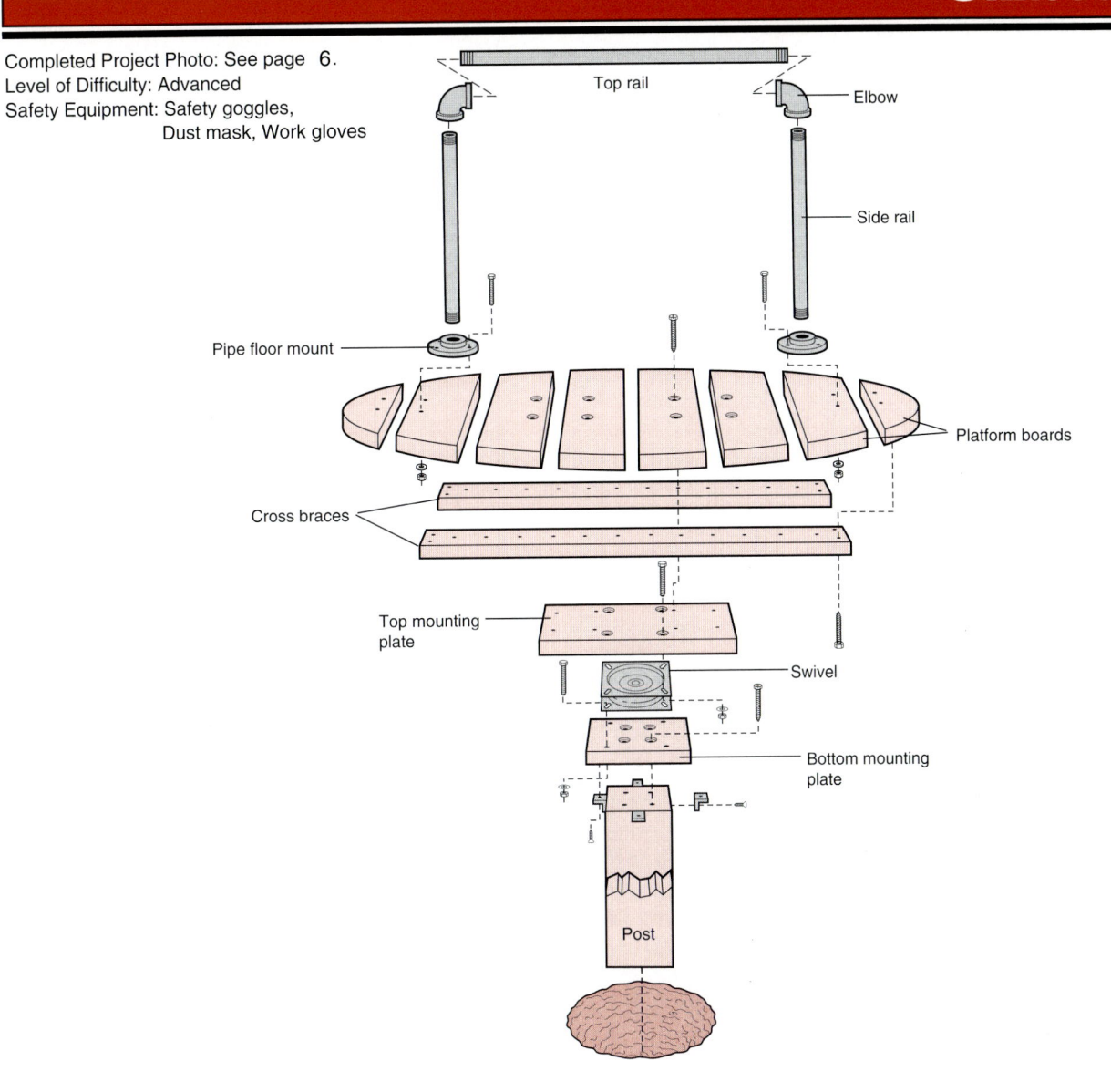

Completed Project Photo: See page 6.
Level of Difficulty: Advanced
Safety Equipment: Safety goggles, Dust mask, Work gloves

Labels on diagram: Top rail, Elbow, Side rail, Pipe floor mount, Platform boards, Cross braces, Top mounting plate, Swivel, Bottom mounting plate, Post

## MATERIALS, PARTS, AND CUTTING LIST

| Material/Part Name | Qty. | Size |
|---|---|---|
| Pressure-treated #2 select pine | 1 | 2 x 4 x 7' |
|     Cross braces | 2 | 1 1/2" x 3 1/2" x 39 1/2" |
| Pressure-treated #2 select pine | 2 | 2 x 6 x 6' |
|     Platform boards | 2 | 1 1/2" x 5 1/2" x 26" |
|     Platform boards | 2 | 1 1/2" x 5 1/2" x 42" |
| Pressure-treated #2 select pine | 2 | 2 x 6 x 8' |
|     Platform boards | 2 | 1 1/2" x 5 1/2" x 35 3/4" |
|     Platform boards | 2 | 1 1/2" x 5 1/2" x 40 1/2" |
| Pressure-treated #2 select pine | 1 | 2 x 8 x 3' |
|     Top mounting plate | 1 | 1 1/2" x 7 1/4" x 18" |
|     Bottom mounting plate | 1 | 1 1/2" x 7 1/4" x 7 1/2" |
| Pressure-treated #2 select pine | 1 | 4 x 6 x 3' |
|     Post | 1 | 3 1/2" x 4 1/2" x 36" |
| Galvanized NPT pipes | 2 | 1 1/2"-dia. x 17" |
|     Side rails | 2 | 1 1/2"-dia. x 17" |
| Galvanized NPT pipe | 1 | 1 1/2"-dia. x 36" |
|     Top rail | 1 | 1 1/2"-dia. x 36" |
| Galvanized pipe elbows | 2 | 1 1/2"-dia. |

| Material/Part Name | Qty. | Size |
|---|---|---|
| Galvanized pipe floor mounts | 2 | 1 1/2"-dia. |
| Galvanized roller bearing swivel | 1 | 5"- to 6"-dia. |
| Galvanized "L" braces | 4 | 1" x 2" |
| Galvanized flat head screws | 40 | #8 x 2 1/2" |
| Galvanized round head screws | 8 | #8 x 1 1/2" |
| Galvanized flat head screws | 4 | #8 x 4" |
| Galvanized round head bolts/ (dia. sized to floor mount holes) nuts/washers | 8 | 1" long |
| Galvanized machine bolts/ washers/nuts | 8 | 2" long* |
| Premixed concrete | 3-6 | 50-lb. bags |

*The exact length and diameter of the bolts/washers/nuts will depend on the swivel used. The diameter should match the swivel mounting hole diameter. The exact length will depend on the clearance between the top and bottom sections of the swivel.

47

## projects for exercise

Young children love to spin and turn, so this compact carousel will receive quite a workout in any backyard play area. It is designed for young children with a combined maximum weight limit of 150 pounds.

The round carousel platform measures 42 inches in diameter and is equipped with a metal push rail that doubles as a holding rail for young riders. The platform is bolted to a swivel that is mounted to the top of a 4 x 6 post anchored in the ground.

The swivel is a rather unique hardware piece that many stores may not carry in stock. But if you show these plans to a salesperson at any reputable hardware store, he or she will be able to order one for you. Be sure there are adequate mounting holes in the top and bottom of the swivel body. There should also be sufficient clearance between the top and bottom swivel sections for the nuts and washers of the mounting bolts. Study the illustrations in this project before purchasing any hardware.

With the "use zone" figured in, the carousel requires an area at least 8 feet long and 8 feet wide for optimum safety.

### 1 CONSTRUCTING THE PLATFORM

Begin by cutting all 2 x 4, 2 x 6, and 2 x 8 pieces to size. Arrange the 2 x 6 pieces with the best side face down as shown. Connect the 2 x 6 pieces together by mounting the two 2 x 4 cross braces and the 2 x 8 top mounting plate to the underside of the platform using #8 x 2 1/2-inch galvanized screws.

Drill pilot holes for all screws. Pilot holes should extend through the 2 x 4 or 2 x 8 and about 3/4 inch into the 2 x 6. Be careful not to pierce through the top of the platform. A piece of tape wrapped around the drill bit is an easy, accurate way to set pilot hole depth.

### CONSTRUCTING THE PLATFORM

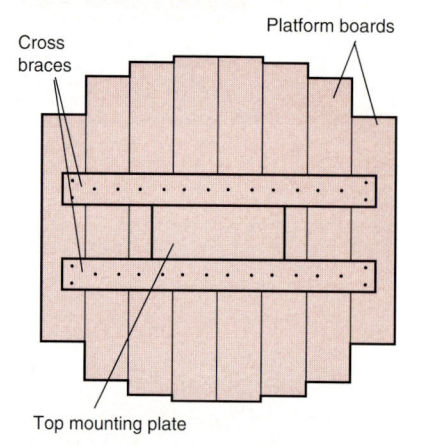

Attach the two cross braces to the underside of the platform. The top mounting plate is not attached at this time. It is simply used to set cross brace spacing.

### 2 MARKING OUT THE CIRCLE CUTTING LINE

The finished platform is a true circle, measuring 42 inches in diameter. To mark this circle accurately, turn the assembled platform best side up and locate its center point by measuring in from the edge 21 inches along the joint between the two 42-inch center 2 x 6s. Tap the small finishing nail into the joint at this point. Using any piece of light, straight lumber, drill two holes in it 21 inches apart, on center. An inexpensive wooden yardstick is great for this purpose. You can be absolutely certain your 21-inch measurement is accurate.

Place one hole in the stick over the finishing nail, and lay the stick flat on the platform. Insert the tip of a pencil into the other hole in the stick and rotate it around to mark out the diameter of the circle.

### 3 CUTTING OUT THE PLATFORM

The simplest way to cut out the circular platform is with a portable saber saw. Make certain the entire platform is very well supported and that there is sufficient clearance under the platform for the saw blade. Cut slowly and carefully, keeping the blade perpendicular to the cutting line.

An alternate and extremely accurate method of cutting out a circle is to use a router and homemade circular cutting jig. As shown, the jig is simply a long strip of 1/4-inch hardboard or plywood that is attached to the router in place of its regular base. A hole in the opposite end of the jig allows it to be pivoted around the center pivot nail. The pivot hole in the jig must be located 21 inches from

### MARKING OUT THE CIRCLE CUTTING LINE

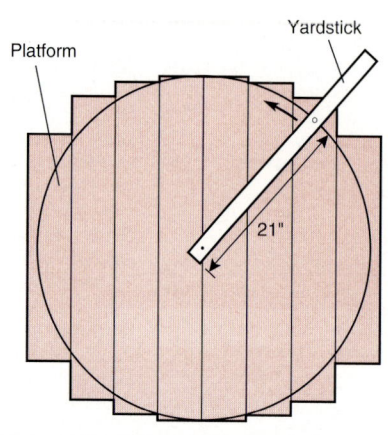

Mark out the 42-inch-diameter platform.

### CUTTING OUT THE PLATFORM

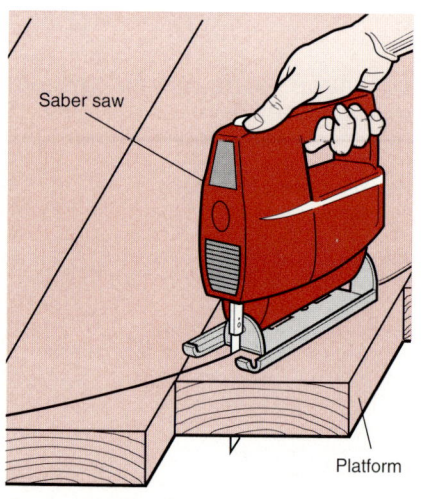

For a true edge, keep the saber saw blade perpendicular to the surface of the platform.

*projects for exercise*

## CUTTING OUT THE PLATFORM

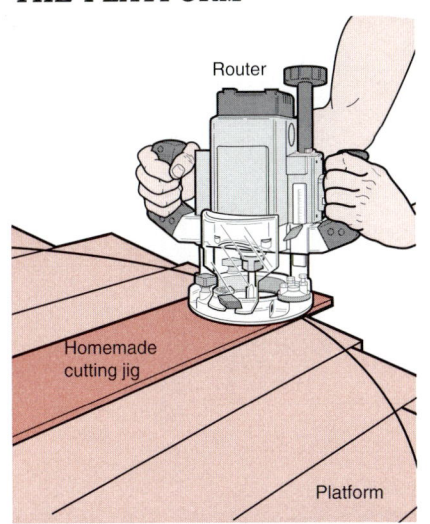

Make the router trim cuts in several passes to avoid overloading the router or bit.

the inside cutting edge of the router bit. During the cut, the router will exert a great deal of outward force on the pivot nail, so secure the nail by driving it through the joint between the center 2 x 6s and into a scrap piece of lumber located beneath the platform.

Mount a straight edge stagger tooth cutting bit in the router. Make the cut in four passes, each about 1/2 inch deep. Support the waste side of the cut during the last two passes so it does not break off and splinter the finished edge.

## 4 CONSTRUCTING THE POST ASSEMBLY

The 7 1/4- x 7 1/2-inch bottom mounting plate is anchored to the top of the 4 x 6 post using four #10 x 4-inch galvanized flat head screws driven down from the top. For added strength at this joint, "L" braces are attached to the post and bottom mounting plate using #8 x 1 1/2" round head screws.

The swivel is then centered on the bottom mounting plate and its bottom mounting holes marked. Bolt holes are drilled at these

## CONSTRUCTING THE POST ASSEMBLY

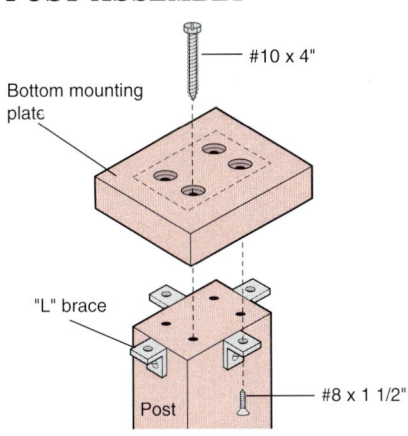

Predrill all screw holes and position the screws so they will not cross paths inside the wood when constructing the post assembly.

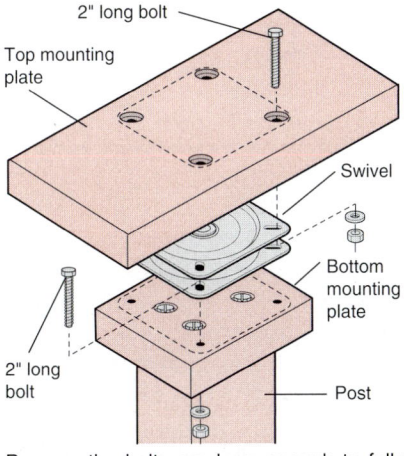

Be sure the bolts are long enough to fully engage the washer and nut when mounting the swivel to the bottom and top mounting plates. Tighten securely.

points and the swivel is bolted to the post assembly using machine bolts, washers, and nuts. The bolt length will be approximately 2 to 2 1/4 inches, based on swivel clearances. The bolt diameter is based on the swivel mounting hole diameter.

The 2 x 8 x 18-inch top mounting plate is then centered on the top of the swivel. Remember, this top plate will fit between the platform cross braces. The platform will screw to the top mounting plate.

Mark out and drill the top plate mounting holes. Bolt the top plate

## SETTING THE POST

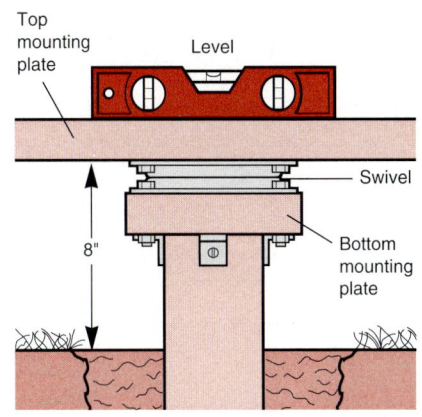

The top mounting plate should be 8" aboveground. Before securing, make sure it is level.

to the swivel using bolts installed from the top. Countersink the top of the bolt flush with the surface of the top mounting plate.

## 5 SETTING THE POST

Locate the carousel on level ground. The top of the post assembly should be located at least 8 inches aboveground to provide adequate clearance. This clearance is also needed when mounting the platform, so do not set the post too low.

The post should extend a minimum of 2 1/2 feet into the ground or below local frost line levels, whichever is greater. Dig the hole with a post-hole digger. Keep it as narrow as possible to reduce the amount of concrete needed to set the post. Position the post in the center of the hole and fill in around it with concrete. Use a level to check and recheck the post several times during installation. Brace the post as needed so it cannot move. Remember, the post must be set plumb with the top of the swivel absolutely level. If the post is cocked or not level, the swivel may bind, or the carousel may strike the ground or wobble excessively as it turns.

*projects for exercise*

**MOUNTING THE PLATFORM**

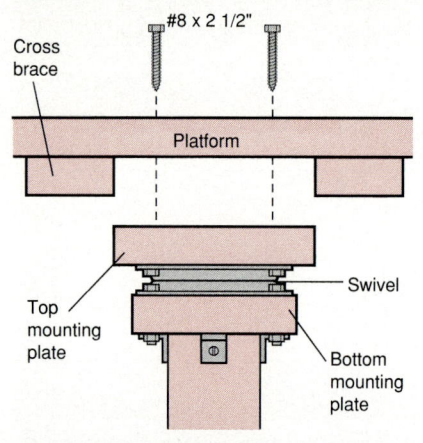

**MOUNTING THE PUSH RAIL**

Center the platform on the top mounting plate and screw it in position.

## 6 MOUNTING THE PLATFORM

This step requires a helper. After the concrete cures for at least 48 hours, lift the platform onto the 2 x 8 x 18-inch top mounting plate. The plate should fit between the cross braces. Center the platform on the top plate. Each end of the top plate should be 12 inches from the perimeter of the carousel platform when the platform is perfectly centered.

Secure the platform to the top mounting plate using eight #8 x 2 1/2-inch flat head screws.

## 7 INSTALLING THE PUSH RAIL

Assemble the push rail by attaching the two 17-inch lengths of 1 1/2-inch galvanized NPT pipe to the 36-inch galvanized NPT pipe using threaded pipe elbows. Thread the two pipe floor mounts onto the bottoms of the 17-inch side rails. If you plan to paint the push rail and/or carousel platform, do so before installing the rail to the carousel.

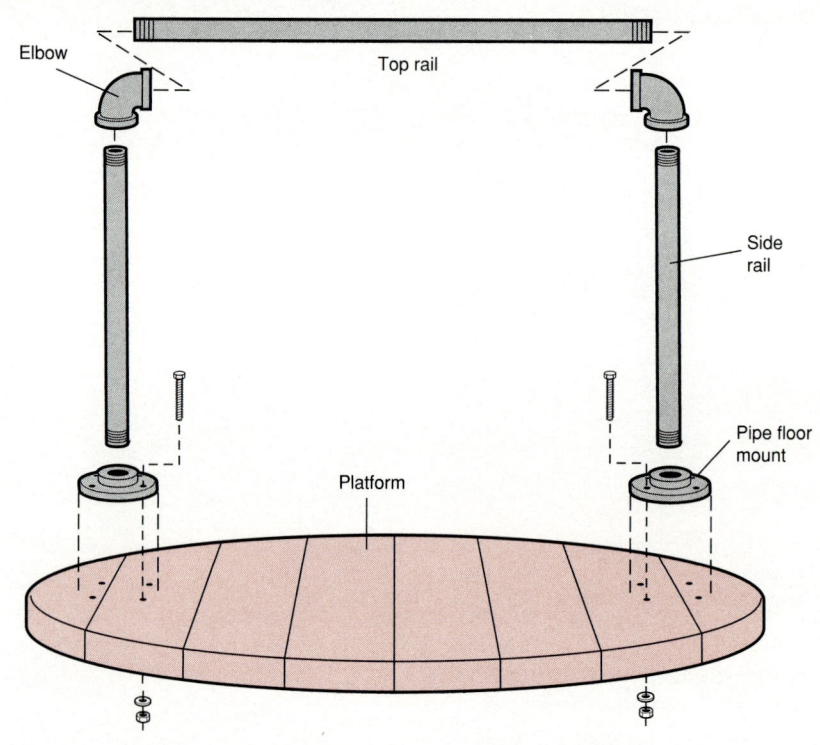

Pipe floor mounts are used to secure the metal push rail to the platform.

## 8 MOUNTING THE PUSH RAIL

Center the push rail on the carousel platform with the pipe floor mounts equidistant from the edge of the platform. Mount the pipe floor mounts to the platform using four 1-inch long round head bolts, nuts, and washers sized to fit the mounting holes in the pipe floor mounts. Mark out the bolt hole positions and drill proportionally sizes holes through the platform. Install the bolts down through the top of the mount and platform and install the washers and nuts from below.

50

*projects for exercise*

# Adjustable Chinning Bar

Completed Project Photo: See page 6.
Level of Difficulty: Basic
Safety Equipment: Safety goggles, Dust mask

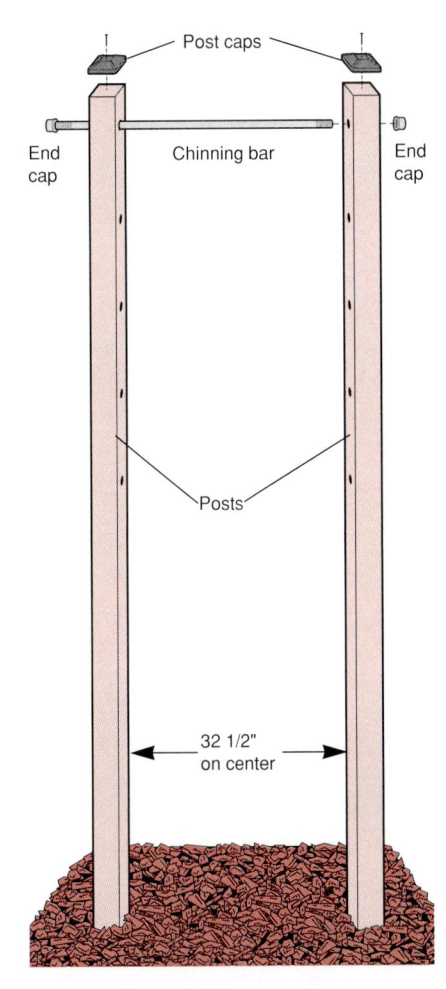

Chinning bars can't be beat when it comes to providing good arm and shoulder strengthening exercises for children. This particular one adjusts easily, so you can change the height to fit the size of the child using it. This is not a difficult project, and renting a posthole digger will make your work even easier.

With the "use zone" figured in, the adjustable chinning bar requires an area at least 7 feet long and 10 feet wide for optimum safety.

## 1 PREPARING THE POSTS

Locate the postholes so that the posts will be set 32 1/2 inches, on center. Holes should be dug to a minimum depth of 18 inches; with 8-foot posts, this will leave 6 1/2-foot posts above-ground for chinning. For taller children, you may want to consider using 10-foot posts and burying them 2 feet, for a full 8 feet aboveground.

Drill 1 5/16-inch-diameter holes (to account for the slightly larger outside diameter of the pipe) all the way through the posts, with the first hole approximately 3 to 4 inches from the top. Use a tape measure to make sure that each set of holes is an equal distance from the top of the post. The number of holes and amount of spacing between them is up to you; in this example, there are five sets, with 14 inches between the holes.

## 2 ASSEMBLY

Set the first post in its hole, mix one of the bags of concrete, and pour the concrete around the base by filling the entire hole. Install the second post in the same manner, then check to make sure the posts are level. Brace the posts temporarily until the concrete has had time to set.

Install the chinning bar. To prevent it from slipping through the posts, use threaded NPT pipe. The bar should be square to the posts and perfectly level. Threaded end caps help secure the bar to the posts while also providing a measure of protection. You may also wish to top off the posts with some sort of decorative cap, as was done in this example.

For extra protection, spread a layer of wood chips underneath and around the chinning bar.

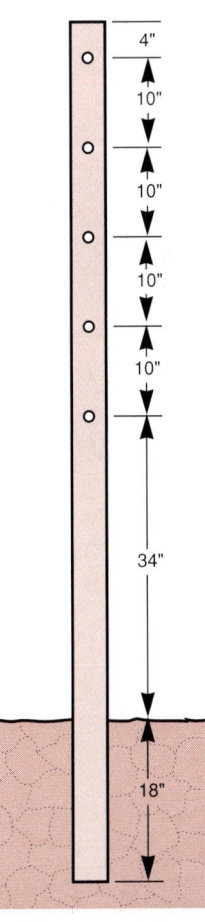

Here is one way to space the holes for the chinning bar; the spacing you use will depend on the height of your children.

### MATERIALS, PARTS, AND CUTTING LIST

| Material/Part Name | Qty. | Size |
|---|---|---|
| Pressure-treated #2 select pine | 2 | 4 x 4 x 8' |
|     Posts | 2 | 3 1/2" x 3 1/2" x 96" |
| Galvanized NPT pipe | 1 | 1"-dia. x 42" |
|     Chinning bar | 1 | 1"-dia. x 42" |
| Threaded end caps | 2 | 1"-dia. |
| Post caps | 2 | 3 1/2" x 3 1/2" square |
| Galvanized common nails | 2 | 8d |
| Premixed concrete | 2 | 50-lb. bags |

*projects for riding toys*

# Red Wagon

Completed Project Photo: See page 7.
Level of Difficulty: Basic
Safety Equipment: Safety goggles, Dust mask

## MATERIALS, PARTS, AND CUTTING LIST

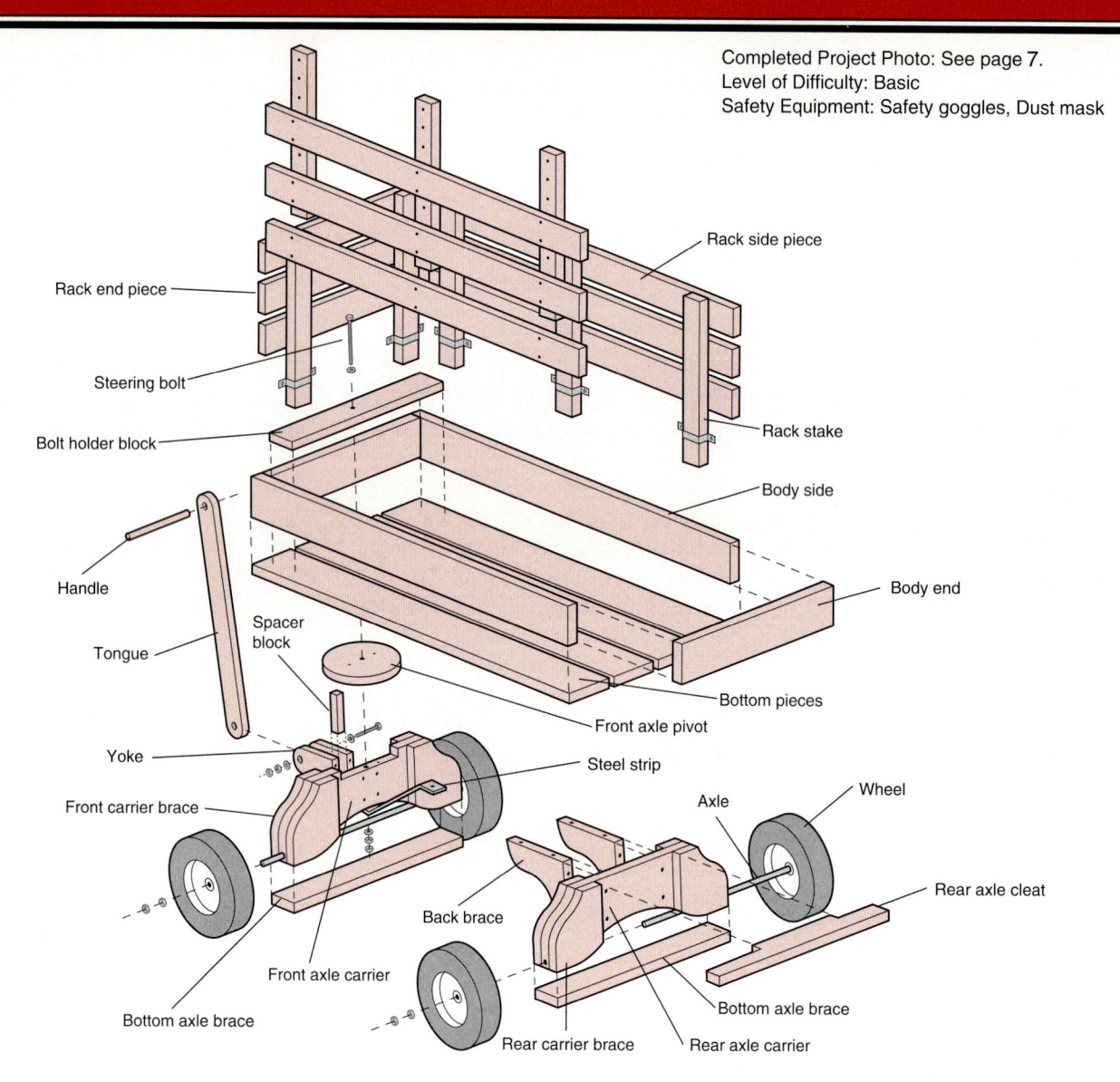

| Material/Part Name | Qty. | Size |
|---|---|---|
| Common oak | 2 | 1 x 2 x 4' |
|     Rack stakes | 6 | 3/4" x 1 1/2" x 16" |
| Common oak | 3 | 1 x 2 x 5' |
|     Rack stakes | 2 | 3/4" x 1 1/2" x 16" |
|     Spacer block | 1 | 3/4" x 1 1/2" x 3" |
|     Tongue | 1 | 3/4" x 1 1/2" x 24" |
| Common oak | 1 | 1 x 3 x 6' |
|     Rear axle cleat | 1 | 3/4" x 1 3/4" x 15" |
|     Yoke pieces | 2 | 3/4" x 2 1/2" x 4" |
|     Bottom axle braces | 2 | 3/4" x 2 1/4" x 16" |
| Common oak | 3 | 1 x 4 x 8' |
|     Bolt holder block | 1 | 1/2" x 3" x 14 1/2" |
|     Rack end pieces | 3 | 3/4" x 3" x 15 1/2" |
|     Rack side pieces | 6 | 3/4" x 3" x 31 1/2" |
|     Rear carrier braces | 4 | 3/4" x 3 1/2" x 5" |
| Common oak | 4 | 1 x 5 x 6' |
|     Body ends | 2 | 3/4" x 4" x 14 1/2" |
|     Body sides | 2 | 3/4" x 4" x 33" |
|     Bottom pieces | 4 | 3/4" x 3 15/16" x 33" |

| Material/Part Name | Qty. | Size |
|---|---|---|
|     Back braces | 2 | 3/4" x 3 3/4" x 5" |
|     Front carrier braces | 4 | 3/4" x 4 1/2" x 5" |
| Common oak | 1 | 1 x 6 x 3' |
|     Front and rear axle carriers | 2 | 3/4" x 5" x 16" |
| Common oak | 1 | 1 x 8 x 2' |
|     Front axle pivot | 1 | 3/4" x 6"-dia. |
| Hardwood dowel | 1 | 1/2"-dia. x 1' |
|     Handle | 1 | 1/2" dia. x 5" |
| Flat stainless steel strip | 1 | 1/8" x 1" x 10" |
| Threaded stainless steel rods | 2 | 1/2"-dia. x 21" |
| Bolt | 1 | 1/2" x 3" |
| Bolt | 1 | 1/2" x 5 1/2" |
| Nuts and washers | 4 | 1/2" |
| Lawn mower wheels | 4 | 8" dia. |
| Galvanized flat head wood screws | | #8 x 1 1/4" |
| Galvanized flat head wood screws | | #8 x 1" |
| Wood plugs | | 1 1/4" |
| Angle irons | | 4" |

52

## projects for riding toys

Amid all the changing trends in toys, the old red wagon still has great appeal. Children will use it to haul everything from dolls to cats and dogs to rocks, so it must be well-built to withstand punishment, with all pieces joined securely. The wagon shown here was made almost entirely from 3/4-inch common oak stock. This project also includes instructions for adding an enclosing rack to the completed wagon. If you decide not to add the rack, remember to subtract the necessary amount of stock from the materials.

### 1 ASSEMBLING THE AXLE CARRIERS

Enlarge the graph drawings shown in Details A and B. Double the drawings as indicated to make patterns for the front and rear axle carriers and carrier braces. Transfer them to 3/4-inch oak stock. Cut both axle carriers to size. Take care to make the upper notch in the front axle carrier exactly 5/8 inch deep and 6 inches wide. This notch accommodates the front axle that serves as a large washer allowing the front wheels to steer. Cut the front and rear carrier braces with the grain turned 90° to that of the axle carriers (see Front View); this will give the axle carriers greater strength. Attach the carrier braces, with glue and #8 x 1 1/4-inch flat head wood screws, to both sides of both ends of the axle carriers. Clamp tightly and allow to dry overnight.

### 2 DRILLING THE AXLE HOLES

Use a 1/2-inch paddle bit or forstner bit to bore the axle holes through the center of each end of the axle carriers, 1/2 inch from the bottom as seen in the Front View. A drill press makes this job easy, but a portable drill will do if the pieces are fixed tightly in a vise. Make sure to keep the drill bit square up and down and side to side or the axles won't align properly. Sand the glued ends of the axle carriers.

### 3 FITTING THE AXLES

Slip the 1/2-inch threaded axle rods through the axle holes; if they bind, it may be necessary to rebore the holes slightly. Position each axle so that one end protrudes from the axle carrier just enough to accept the washer, wheel, and nut; fasten the wheel in position. Then slip the other washer and wheel over the long end of the axle and screw on the nut. With both wheels now in place, cut off the long end of the axle just outside the nut with a hacksaw. The wheels must be fit in place before trimming the axle because it may be impossible to thread the nut onto the cut end; removing the nut over the cut rethreads the axle. When both axles have been trimmed, remove the nuts, wheels, and washers.

### 4 COMPLETING THE FRONT AXLE CARRIER AND BUILDING THE YOKE

Cut a 6-inch diameter circle from 3/4-inch oak stock to make the front axle pivot; sand it smooth. Check to be sure that it fits in the notch on the front axle carrier. Enlarge the yoke graph drawing (Side View), transfer the pattern to the stock, and cut out the two yoke pieces and the spacer block. Use glue and #8 x 1 1/4-inch flat

## ASSEMBLING THE AXLE CARRIERS

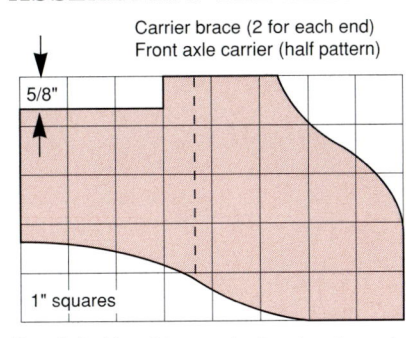

Detail A: Use this graph drawing to make the front axle carrier and accompanying carrier braces.

Carrier brace (2 for each end)
Front axle carrier (half pattern)
5/8"
1" squares

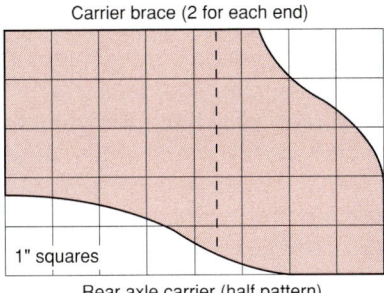

Detail B: Use this graph drawing to make the rear axle carrier and accompanying carrier braces.

Carrier brace (2 for each end)
1" squares
Rear axle carrier (half pattern)

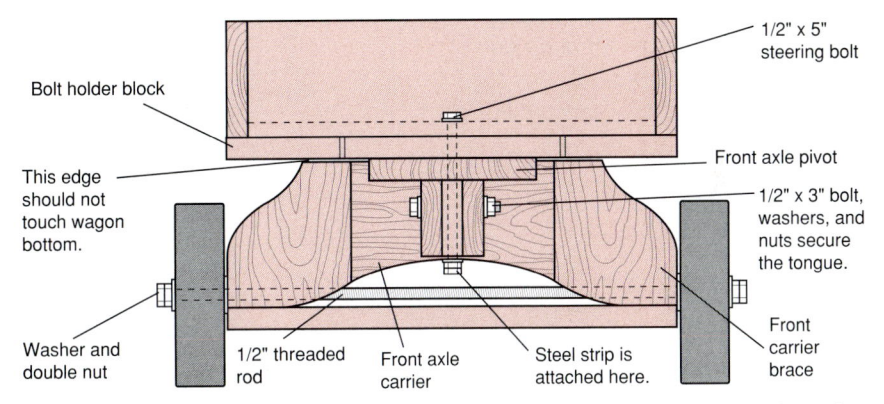

As seen in this Front View, turn the grain of the carrier braces 90° to that of the axle carriers for greater strength.

- 1/2" x 5" steering bolt
- Bolt holder block
- This edge should not touch wagon bottom.
- Front axle pivot
- 1/2" x 3" bolt, washers, and nuts secure the tongue.
- Washer and double nut
- 1/2" threaded rod
- Front axle carrier
- Steel strip is attached here.
- Front carrier brace

53

## projects for riding toys

head wood screws to attach the yoke pieces with the spacer block between them. Clamp and dry overnight, then drill 1/2-inch holes for the 3-inch tongue-securing bolt where marked. Attach the yoke to the center of the front axle carrier with the top edge flush with the bottom of the notch; use glue and #8 x 1 1/4-inch wood screws driven in from the back of the axle carrier. When the glue is dry, use glue and the same-sized screws to attach the front axle pivot to the front axle carrier and yoke. The front axle pivot should be centered in the middle of the axle carrier. Countersink the screws so that they will not rub against the wagon body.

### 5 BORING THE CENTER BOLT HOLE

When the front axle pivot is in place, bore a 1/2-inch hole through its center and down through the axle carrier. Be sure to drill straight down to avoid boring through the side of the axle carrier.

### 6 MAKING THE TONGUE AND HANDLE

Cut the tongue to size from 3/4-inch stock. Round both ends and sand thoroughly; then bore 1/2-inch holes through the tongue 3/4 inch from each end, as shown in the Side View. Glue a 1/2-inch dowel, 5 inches long, through the top to act as the handle.

### 7 BUILDING THE BODY

Cut the body sides and ends to size from 3/4-inch stock. Fasten the ends between the sides with glue and #8 x 1 1/4-inch flat head wood screws counterbored and covered with wood plugs. Glue the plugs in place; then cut them flush and sand them off. Cut the bottom pieces to size, sand them, and fasten them to the sides and ends with flat head wood screws, leaving 1/8-inch gaps between the bottom pieces as shown in the Rear View. Countersink these screws, but do not bother to plug them. Check to make sure that the body is squared up as you install the bottom.

## BUILDING THE BODY

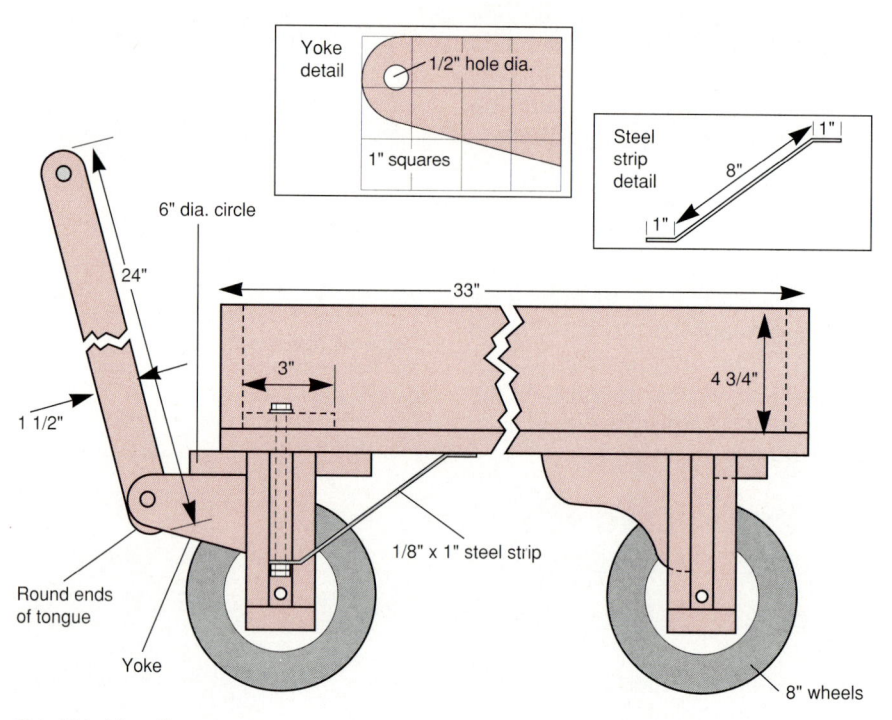

This Side View illustrates how the tongue-and-yoke assembly fits together.

## INSTALLING THE REAR AXLE CARRIER

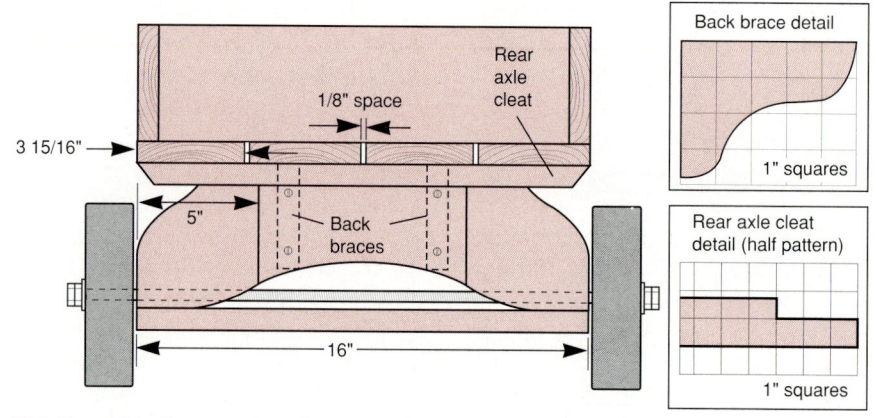

This Rear View illustrates how the wagon bottom is assembled.

### 8 INSTALLING THE BOLT HOLDER BLOCK

Cut the bolt holder block to size and glue and screw it in place inside the wagon body at the front, using countersunk 1-inch flat head wood screws as shown in the Side View. Bore a 1/2-inch hole down through the bolt holder block exactly in the center. Sand the

projects for riding toys

entire wagon body smooth, especially around all edges and corners, and be sure to sand the wooden plugs flush with the surrounding surfaces.

## 9 INSTALLING THE REAR AXLE CARRIER

Transfer the pattern for the rear axle cleat in the Rear View to 3/4-inch stock, cut it out, and sand smooth. Use glue and 1 1/4-inch flat head wood screws to install the cleat on the underside of the wagon body, 2 inches from the back of the wagon, with the notches on the ends facing forward. Then fit the rear axle carrier up against the cleat, as shown in the Rear View. Fasten it to the cleat and the wagon body with glue and 1 1/4-inch flat head wood screws, driving the screws down through the floorboards from the inside. Countersink these screws and be sure that no sharp points remain on the screw heads to scratch an unsuspecting passenger. Enlarge the graph drawing for the back braces that fit on the front of the rear axle carrier (Rear View), transfer the pattern to 3/4-inch stock, and cut out the two braces. Fasten them in place with glue and 1 1/4-inch flat head wood screws driven down through the body and in from the back of the rear axle carrier. Again, countersink the screws and be especially careful about sharp edges.

## 10 INSTALLING THE FRONT AXLE CARRIER

Center the front axle carrier over the hole in the bolt holder block; insert the 5 1/2-inch steering bolt from inside the wagon bed up through the front axle carrier. Fasten the bolt with a washer and nut. Cut the steel strip, bend it to shape, and bore a hole in each end for the steering bolt and screw. Screw one end of the strip to the wagon bed. Slip the other end over the steering bolt and fasten in place with the two nuts tightened together. This provides plenty of brace, but still allows the front axle carrier to turn freely.

## 11 PAINTING THE WAGON

With the wheels removed, paint the entire wagon bright red, giving it several coats of a good enamel. Then reinstall the wheels, insert the tongue in the yoke, and bolt it in place.

## 12 ADDING THE SIDE RACKS

As seen in the Top View and the exploded drawing, you can construct an enclosing rack of 3/4 x 1 1/2-inch stakes held in place with angle iron straps bent to shape and screwed to the inside of the wagon body. The rack itself is made of 3/4-inch oak pieces fastened to the stakes with flat head screws.

*ADDING SIDE RACKS*

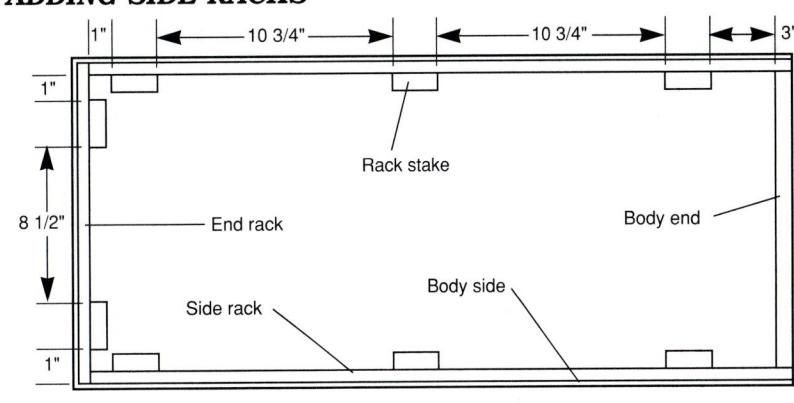

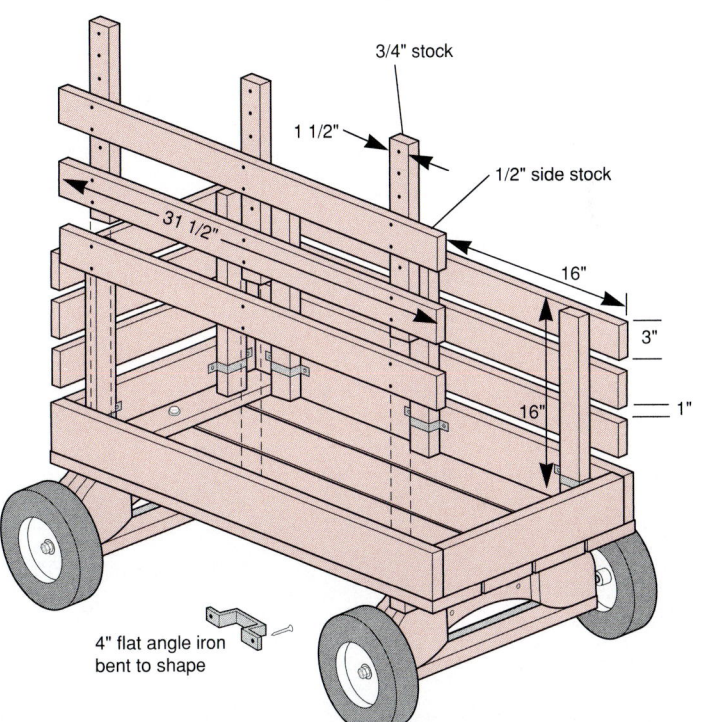

This Top View shows where the rack stakes attach to the wagon body. The rack makes a handsome addition to the red wagon.

## projects for riding toys
# Rocking Horse

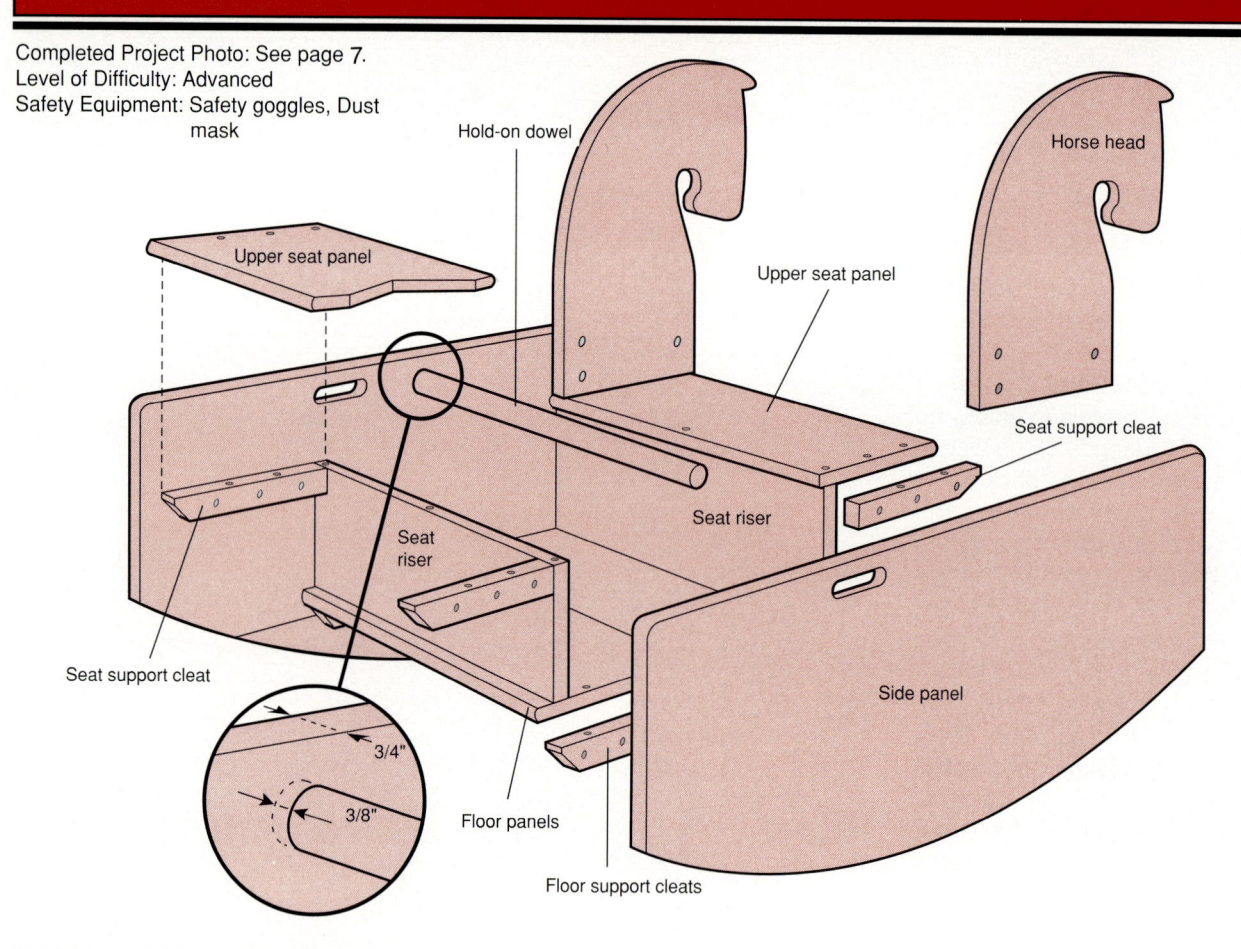

Completed Project Photo: See page 7.
Level of Difficulty: Advanced
Safety Equipment: Safety goggles, Dust mask

### MATERIALS, PARTS, AND CUTTING LIST

| Material/Part Name | Qty. | Size |
|---|---|---|
| Pressure-treated #2 select pine, sanded both sides | 1 | 1 x 12 x 10' |
|     Side panels | 2 | 3/4" x 14" x 36" |
| Pressure-treated #2 select pine | 1 | 1 x 12 x 10' |
|     Horse heads | 2 | 3/4" x 11 1/2" x 16 1/2" |
|     Upper seat panels | 2 | 3/4" x 9 1/2" x 16 1/2" |
|     Seat risers | 2 | 3/4" x 5 1/2" x 16 1/2" |
|     Floor panels | 2 | 3/4" x 9" x 16 1/2" |
|     Seat support cleats | 4 | 3/4" x 1" x 8 1/2" |
|     Floor support cleats | 2 | 3/4" x 1" x 17 1/2" |
| Hardwood dowel | 1 | 1" x 17 1/2" |
|     Hold-on dowel | 1 | 1"-dia. x 17 1/2" |
| Galvanized tee-nuts | 6 | #20 x 1/4" |
| Galvanized flat head wood screws | 58 | #8 x 1 1/4" |
| Waterproof urea resin or resorcinol glue | 1 | can or bottle |

This project requires careful layout work and saber or scroll saw cutting, but otherwise it is fairly simple in its assembly. The result is a riding toy that young children will love. Its sturdy construction makes it suitable for indoor and outdoor use, although it should be protected from inclement weather. With the "use zone" figured in, the rocking horse requires an area at least 6 feet long and 7 feet wide for optimum safety.

Since it is impossible to show the horse head profile and other designs in this book to full size, they are presented on graph drawings of reduced size. Enlarge the pattern to its proper size by drawing a grid (using 1-inch or 1/2-inch squares, as the case may be) on graph paper and transferring the pattern to it. Start by numbering the horizontal and vertical lines on the grid in the book. Put these same numbers on the corresponding lines you have drawn on the full-size grid. Select a starting point on the grid in the book where the outline of the pattern crosses one of the grid lines. Locate this point by means of the numbers on the lines, horizontally and vertically. Transfer this point to its corresponding location on the full-size grid, using the same numbers. Continue in the same manner until you have a point plotted for each intersection where the outline crosses a grid line. Next, connect all the points freehand or with a straightedge, flexible curve, or draftsman's french curve, as necessary. Make as many adjust-

*projects for riding toys*

## GLUING THE SIDE PANELS

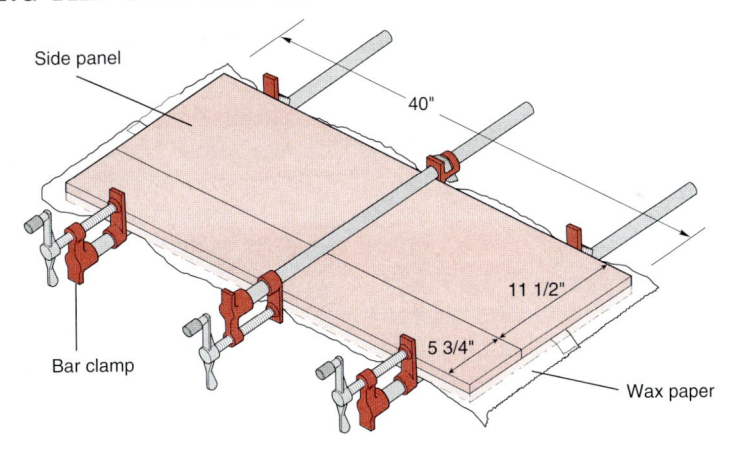

Glue and clamp the side panels.

## 1 GLUING THE SIDE PANELS

Since the boards used to make the side panels actually measure 11 1/2 inches wide, two 3-foot lengths must be glued and clamped to form a board that will accept the 36-inch radius when sized to a 14-inch final width.

It is best to glue the panels a little oversize and then to cut the final length after the glue has set. So begin by cutting three 40-inch lengths of 1 x 12 stock. Rip-cut one of the pieces down its length to create two 5 3/4-inch-wide pieces.

Butt an 11 1/2-inch wide and 5 3/4-inch wide length side by side, and glue together using waterproof resorcinol or urea resin glue. Hold the joint tightly together using at least three 18-inch bar or pipe clamps. If you insert waxed paper between the two boards, you can glue both panels at the same time using three clamps. If

ments as you need to achieve a smooth continuous line.

The pattern can be transferred to the wood with carbon paper, or you can glue the pattern to a stiff paper and cut it out with a sharp scissors or mat knife. This will give you a durable template that you can mark around with a ballpoint pen over and over.

the wax paper is not positioned properly, the panels may glue themselves together. Allow the glue to set up overnight.

## 2 SIZING THE PIECES

Cut all pieces according to the diagrams and templates provided. Crosscut the side panels to their final 36-inch x 14-inch size and layout the 36-inch radius using string or a yardstick and a marking pencil. Cut out the curved portion of the panels using a saber saw or bench top scroll saw.

Drill two 3/4-inch diameter holes in each side panel in the positions shown, and cut out the stock between the holes to create the rear handles.

Cut the upper seat panels, seat risers, floor panels, and support cleats to the dimensions shown in the Materials, Parts, and Cutting List. Cut the cleats from pieces of scrap stock. Miter-cut both ends of the floor cleats and one end of the seat cleats as shown in the exploded view.

## 3 CUTTING THE HORSE PROFILES

The two horse head profiles are cut from separate pieces of 3/4-inch stock measuring at least 16 1/2 inches x 11 1/2 inches. Use the template given to draw up a full-scale template on a large piece

### SIZING THE PIECES

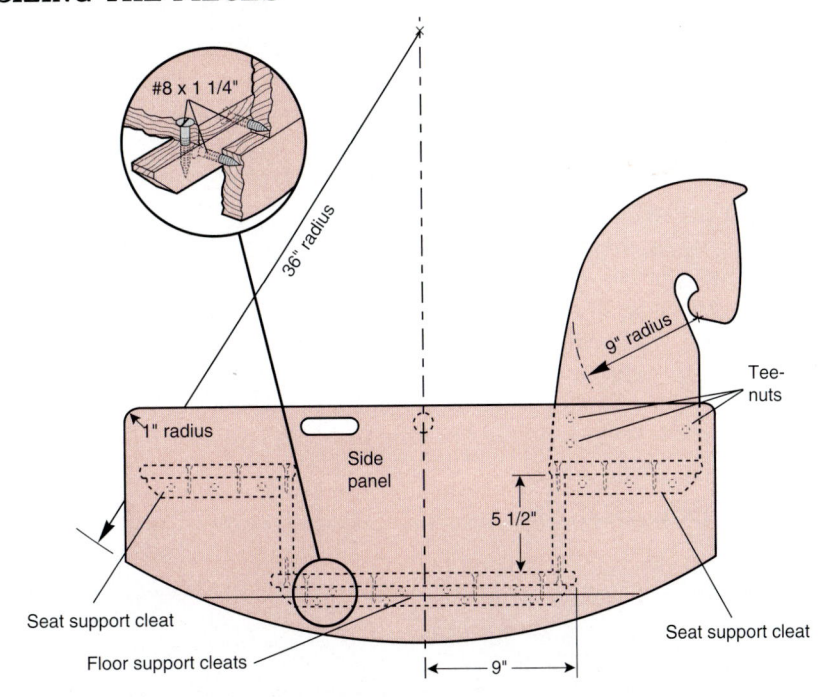

Cross-cut the side panels to their final size and lay out the 36-inch radius using string or a yardstick and a marking pencil.

57

## projects for riding toys

### CUTTING THE HORSE PROFILES

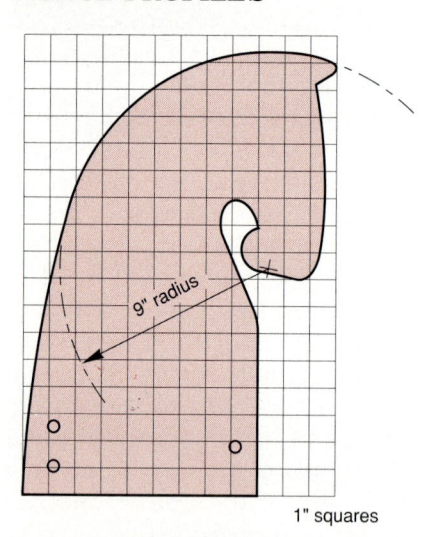

Use this graph drawing to make a pattern for the horse head profiles.

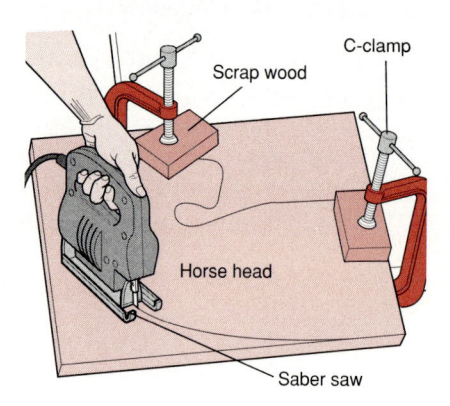

Be sure to clamp the stock securely before attempting to cut with the saber saw.

of graph paper. Transfer the full scale outline to the stock and cut out the head profile using a saber saw or scroll saw. If you are using a saber saw, clamp the stock to a workbench to prevent it from slipping.

### 4 DRILLING THE DOWEL HOLES

Use a 1-inch-diameter spade bit to bore 3/8-inch deep holes in the side panels for installing the 17 1/2-inch dowel. These holes must be aligned with one another, so measure and drill carefully. Drill in short stages until the 3/8-inch depth is reached. Do not risk drilling all the way through to the other side.

### 5 ASSEMBLING THE PARTS

Drill 1/8-inch-diameter pilot holes for all screws. For added strength you can also apply glue to all jointed surfaces before screwing them fast. The screws will act as clamps to hold the glue joint tight as it dries.

Assemble the floor cleats to the side panels using four #8 x 1 1/4-inch flat head wood screws for each cleat. If the side panel is a glued piece, position the cleat over the glue seam as shown in the detail drawing.

Insert the dowel in its mounting holes before positioning the floor panels and screwing them down into the top of the cleats. Use three screws in each panel on each side.

Locate the position of the seat support cleats and attach them to the side panels using two screws in each cleat. Attach the seat risers to the floor panels using three screws from the underside of the floor panel. Mark out and drill these pilot holes carefully so the screw will enter the center of the seat riser bottom. Also screw the top corners of each riser into the seat cleats.

Position each head profile on the forward seat panel and drill three 5/16-inch holes through the horse and side panels. Do not use glue at this connection. Simply slip tee-nuts through the holes, turn on the nut and tighten. Tee-nuts are ideal in this instance because they provide steel threads in lumber and plywood. When a flush installation is required, counterbore a shallow hole to accommodate the flange of the tee-nut.

Sand all corners and rough edges using medium grit sandpaper. Paint or stain the piece as desired.

### ASSEMBLING THE PARTS

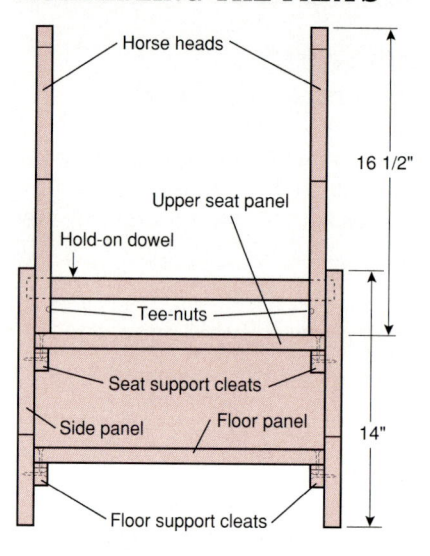

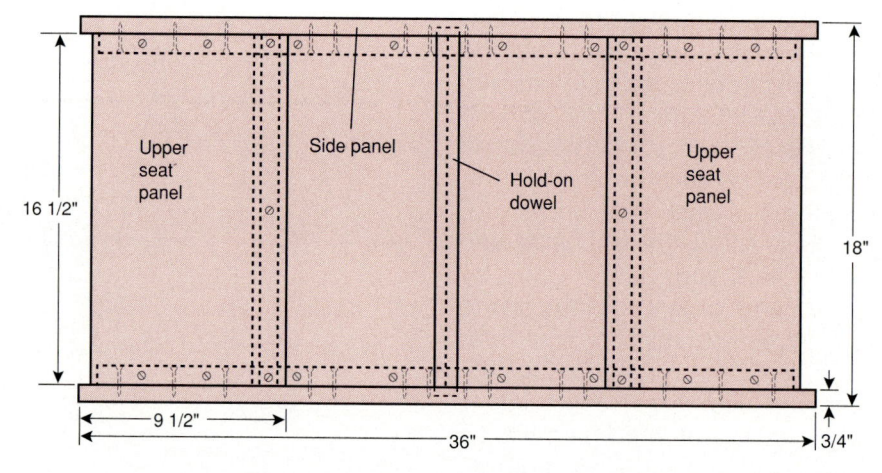

Examine these front and top views of the rocking horse for important assembly details.

projects for riding toys

# TODDLER SLED

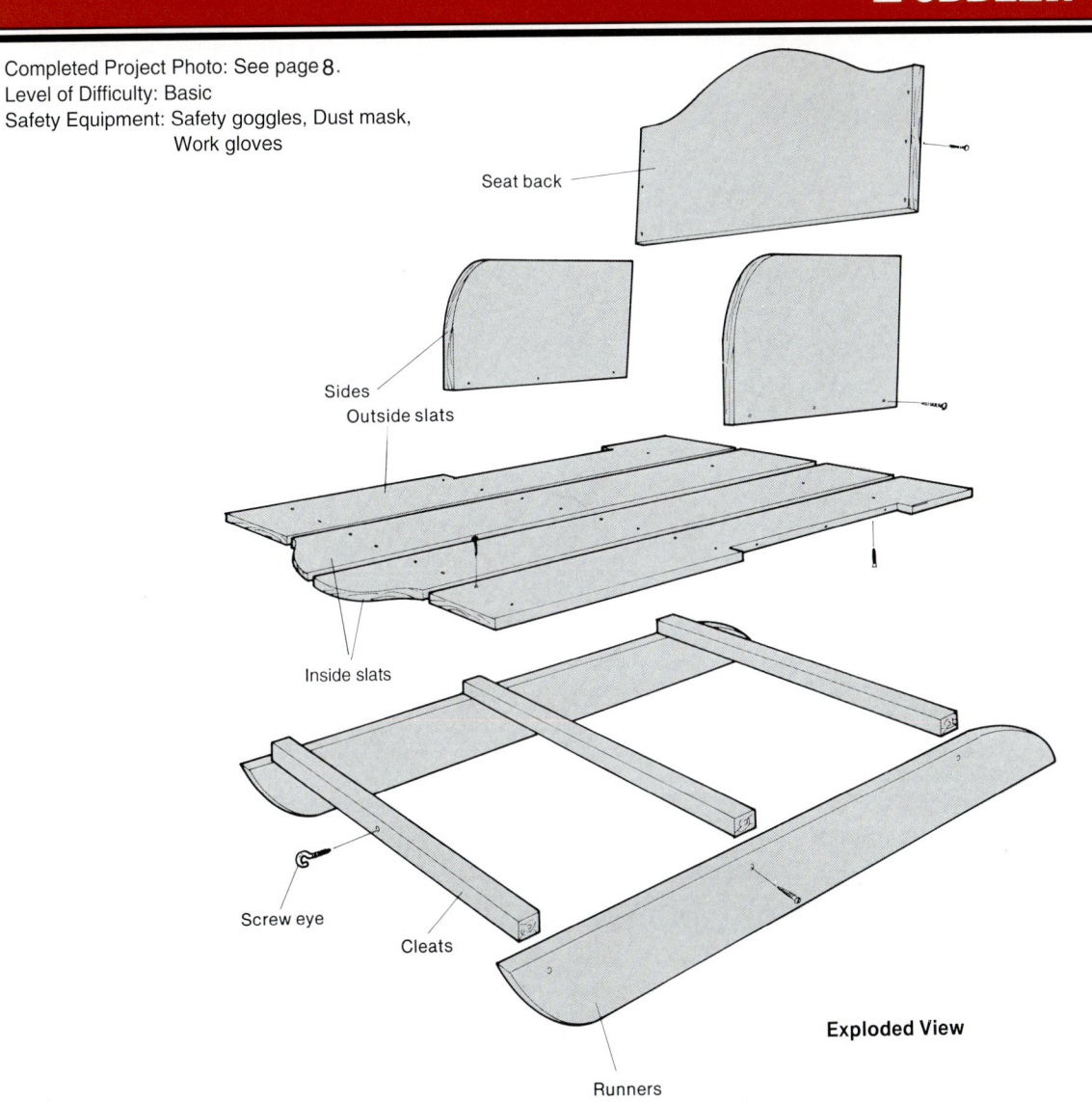

Completed Project Photo: See page 8.
Level of Difficulty: Basic
Safety Equipment: Safety goggles, Dust mask, Work gloves

*Exploded View*

Labels: Seat back, Sides, Outside slats, Inside slats, Screw eye, Cleats, Runners

While the other projects in this book conjure up images of sunshine, warm breezes, and green grass, here is one that is very different. This good-looking sled can easily hold two small children for loads of fun in the snow. The high sides and back provide both safety and comfort. For resilience, use a durable hardwood such as ash. The stock is 1/2-inch thick, which may be hard to find at a lumberyard. However, since not much is needed to build the sled, it might be practical to order the wood from a mail-order supplier.

## 1 CUTTING AND VARNISHING THE PIECES

Enlarge the graph drawings for the sides, seat back, runners, and slats. Mark the given dimensions of the two sizes of slats, transfer the

### MATERIALS, PARTS, AND CUTTING LIST

| Material/Part Name | Qty. | Size |
|---|---|---|
| #1 select ash | 1 | 1 x 2 x 7' |
|    Outside slats | 2 | 1/2" x 2" x 20 1/2" |
|    Cleats | 3 | 3/4" x 1" x 11" |
| #1 select ash | 1 | 1 x 4 x 8' |
|    Runners | 2 | 1/2" x 3 1/2" x 24" |
|    Inside slats | 2 | 1/2" x 3 3/8" x 22" |

| Material/Part Name | Qty. | Size |
|---|---|---|
| #1 select ash | 1 | 1 x 8 x 3' |
|    Sides | 2 | 1/2" x 7 1/4" x 10" |
|    Seat back | 1 | 1/2" x 7" x 10 3/4" |
| Galvanized round head wood screws | 24 | #8 x 1 1/4" |
| Galvanized round head wood screws | 6 | #8 x 1 1/2" |
| Galvanized round head wood screws | 12 | #8 x 1" |
| Screw eye | 1 | |
| Rope | 1 | |

59

## projects for riding toys

### CUTTING AND VARNISHING THE PIECES

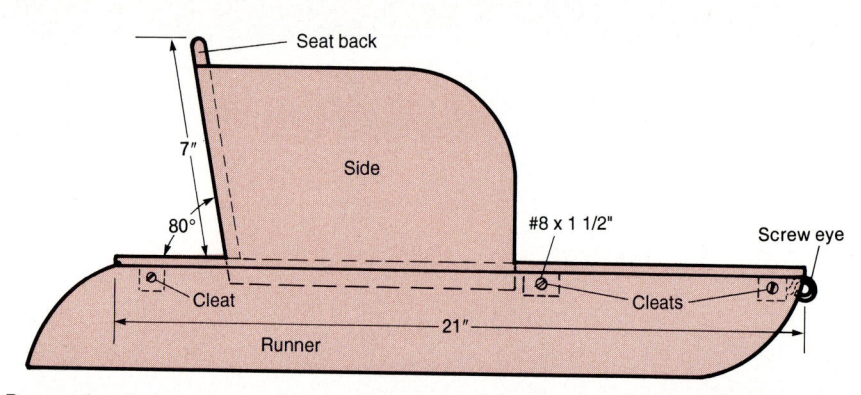

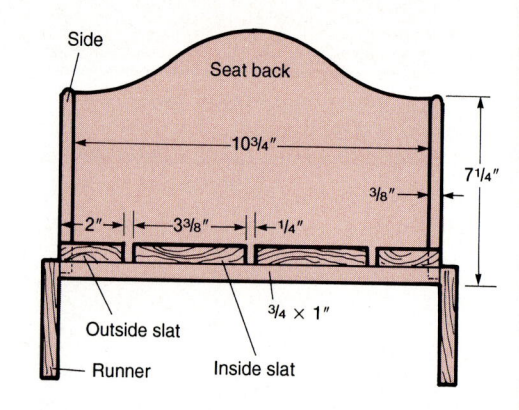

Be sure the cleats are screwed flush against the top edges of the runners. The view to the right shows the placement of the slats on the cleats.

pattern for the ends of the inside slats to the stock, and mark the notches in the outside slats. Mark the dimensions for the seat back and transfer the patterns for the curved top. Transfer the patterns for the runners and sides. Cut out all the pieces with a sharp coping saw or saber saw. Cut the three cleats to the given dimensions. Sand all the pieces thoroughly and finish with several coats of water-repellent sealant or spar varnish.

### 2 ASSEMBLING THE SLED

Fasten the cleats between the runners with #8 x 1 1/2-inch round head wood screws. The cleats should be flush against the top edges of the runners. Use one screw at each end of each cleat. Fasten the slats to the cleats by using #8 x 1 1/4-inch countersunk screws, two screws at each cleat. Position the slats, leaving a 1/4-inch space between them. Then slip the sides of the seat into the notches in the outside slats and fasten 1 inch deep, with 1-inch round head wood screws driven from the inside into the runners. Finally, fasten the seat back between the sides, again with 1-inch round head wood screws. Screw a large screw eye into the front cleat, tie on a pull rope, and the sled is ready to go.

### GLUING SIDE PANELS

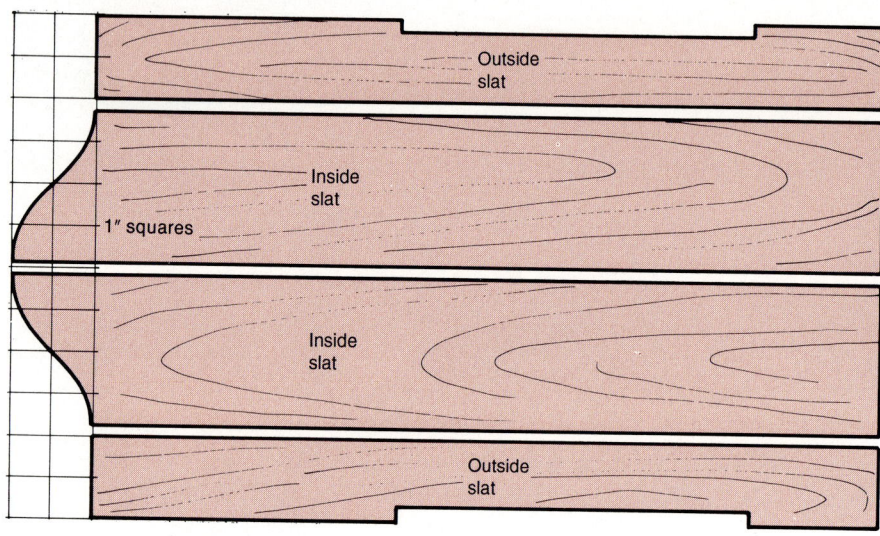

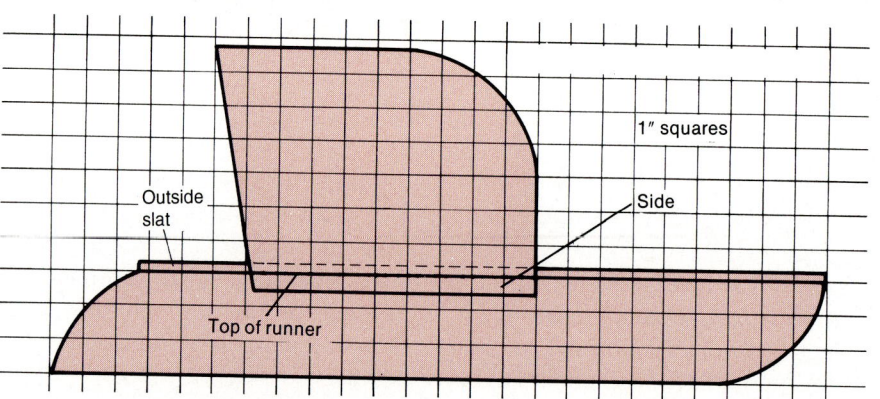

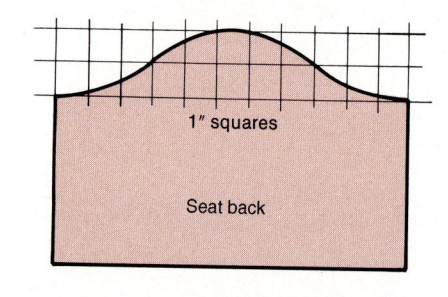

The use of enlarged graph drawings makes cutting the seat back (as well as the other major pieces of the sled) much easier. The pattern can be transferred to the wood with carbon paper, or you can glue the pattern to stiff paper and cut it out with a sharp scissors or mat knife. This will produce a durable template that can be used over and over.

60

*projects for riding toys*

# THREE-WHEEL SEAT SCOOTER

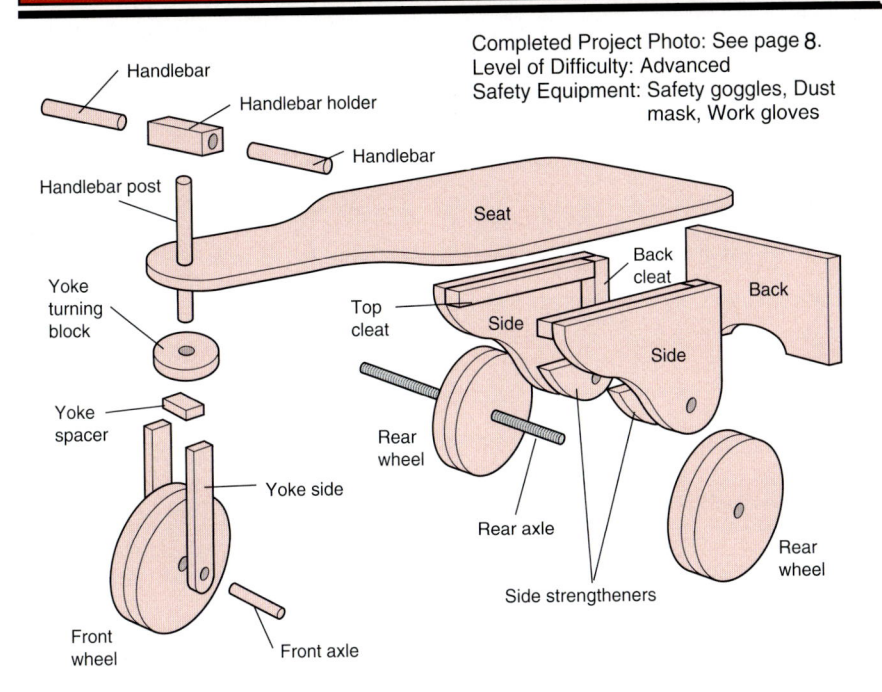

Completed Project Photo: See page 8.
Level of Difficulty: Advanced
Safety Equipment: Safety goggles, Dust mask, Work gloves

This attractive little scooter is patterned on the traditional riding toys that have been popular with children for generations. It's specially designed for those youngsters who haven't yet graduated to a tricycle. This project requires a surprisingly small amount of wood; if you wish, solid stock can be used in place of exterior grade plywood for the seat, sides, side strengtheners, and back.

## 1 CUTTING THE PIECES

Enlarge the graph drawings for the sides, side strengtheners, and seat. Cut out two sides (the whole pattern) and two side strengtheners (lower portion of the pattern). Sand all the edges with a drum sander, then sand by hand until the pieces are perfectly smooth. After sanding the seat, bore a 1-inch-diameter hole through the front end, 2 1/2 inches from the edge of the center line.

### CUTTING THE PIECES

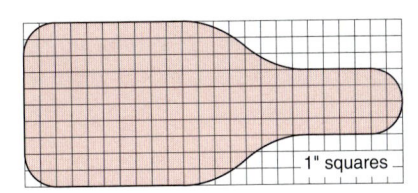

Using this pattern, the seat can be easily cut out with a saber saw.

## 2 ASSEMBLING THE SIDES

Glue the side strengtheners to the bottom of the sides (edges flush) and clamp; allow to dry overnight. Cut the top and back cleats to the dimensions given and glue them to the inside of the sides, flush with the top and back edges, respectively. Clamp and let dry overnight. Then, drill 1/2-inch-diameter holes through the bottoms of the sides for the axle as shown in the Side View.

## 3 MAKING THE WHEELS

Glue enough stock to make three 7 1/4-inch-diameter wheels from two pieces of 3/4-inch lumber. Position the grain of the wood in the two pieces at opposite angles to provide more strength and prevent the wood from splitting apart. Clamp solidly and allow the glue to dry overnight. Then mark the circumference of the wheels with a compass and cut them to shape. Sand the edges thoroughly and round the outside edges with a scraper. Bore 1/2-inch-diameter holes for the axles in the exact centers of the wheels and paint the wheels as desired.

### MATERIALS, PARTS, AND CUTTING LIST

| Material/Part Name | Qty. | Size |
|---|---|---|
| Pressure-treated #2 select white pine | 1 | 1 x 2 x 4' |
|     Top cleats | 2 | 3/4" x 1" x 8" |
|     Back cleats | 2 | 3/4" x 1" x 5" |
|     Yoke sides | 2 | 3/4" x 1 1/2" x 5 3/4" |
|     Yoke spacer | 1 | 3/4" x 7/8" x 1 1/2" |
|     Handlebar holder | 1 | 3/4" x 1 1/2" x 4" |
| Pressure-treated #2 select white pine | 1 | 1 x 4 x 1' |
|     Yoke turning block | 1 | 3/4" x 3"-dia. |
| Pressure-treated #2 select white pine | 2 | 1 x 12 x 1' |
|     Wheels | 3 | 7 1/4" x 3/4"-dia. |
| A-C exterior grade plywood | 1 | 3/4 x 4' x 8' |
|     Seat | 1 | 3/4" x 10" x 24" |
|     Sides | 2 | 3/4" x 8" x 9" |
|     Side strengtheners | 2 | 3/4" x 3" x 5" |
|     Back | 1 | 3/4" x 6" x 8" |
| Hardwood dowel | 1 | 1/2"-dia. x 1' |
|     Front axle | 1 | 1/2"-dia. x 2 1/2" |
| Hardwood dowel | 1 | 1"-dia. x 2' |
|     Handlebar post | 1 | 1"-dia. x 8 1/2" |
|     Handlebars | 2 | 1"-dia. x 3 3/4" |
| Threaded stainless steel rod, washers, and nuts | 1 | 1/2"-dia. x 14" |
| Galvanized finishing nails | 2 | 6d |
| Galvanized flat head wood screws | 16 | #8 x 1" |
| Galvanized flat head wood screws | 2 | #8 x 1 1/4" |
| Galvanized flat head wood screws | 8 | #8 x 1 1/2" |
| Waterproof urea resin or resorcinol glue | 1 | can or bottle |

*projects for riding toys*

## ASSEMBLING THE SIDES

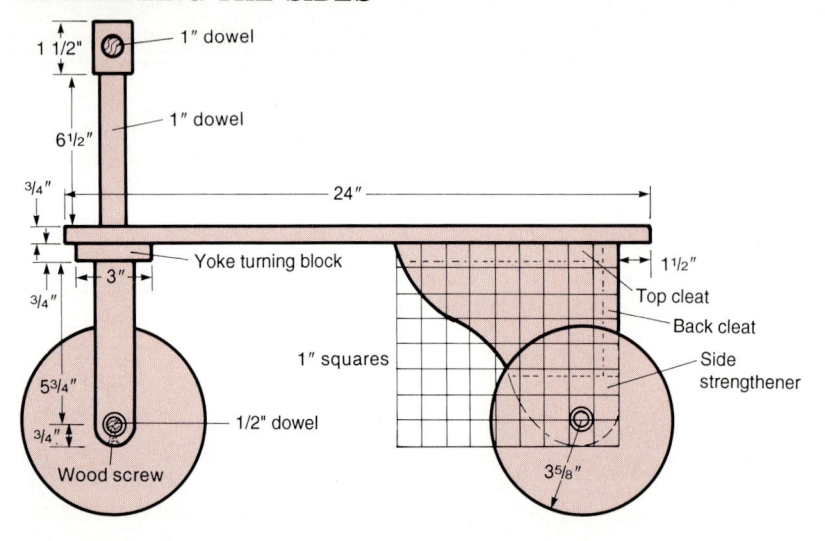

Assemble the scooter by following the construction details in this Side View.

## ASSEMBLING THE BODY

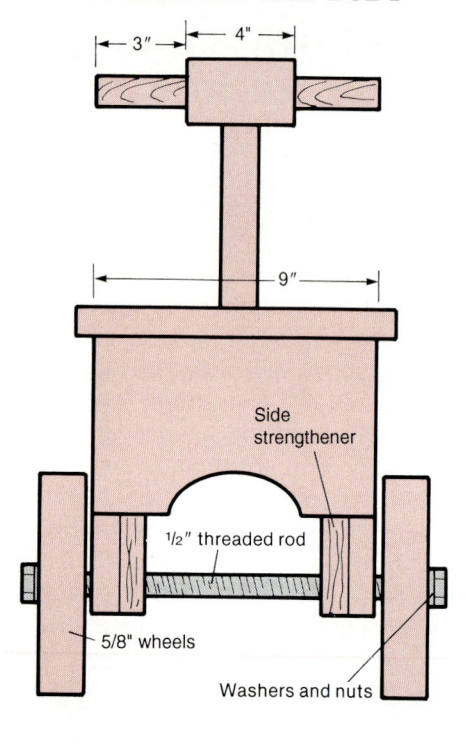

This Back View of the scooter provides a good look at the rear axle setup.

## 4 ASSEMBLING THE BODY

Mark the bottom of the seat for the location of the sides as shown in the Side and Back Views. The sides should be set in 1 inch from either edge, and 1 1/2 inches from the back of the seat. Turn the seat over and drill counterbored holes for screws to attach the sides. Install the sides with glue and #8 x 1 1/2-inch flat head wood screws.

Cut the back to the given dimensions, then cut out the semicircular shape (as shown in the Back View). Install the back flush against the bottom of the seat and flush with the edges of the sides, using countersunk #8 x 1-inch flat head wood screws. Paint or finish the seat and sides as desired.

## 5 MAKING THE WHEEL YOKE

Cut the pieces for the front wheel yoke (sides, turning block, and spacer) to the given dimensions. Use 6d finishing nails and glue to attach the spacer between the yoke sides, flush with the top. Bore a 1-inch-diameter hole in the center of the turning block and use glue and countersunk #8 x 1 1/4-inch flat head wood screws to attach it, centered, on top of the yoke. Finally, bore 1/2-inch-diameter holes through the ends of the yoke sides, at the point indicated in the Side View.

## 6 INSTALLING THE WHEELS

Put the front wheel in the yoke and drive the front axle through the axle holes in the yoke sides and the wheel. Make sure the axle is flush with the side of the yoke, then pin it in place with a countersunk #8 x 1-inch flat head wood screw driven in from the bottom of one of the yoke sides. Slip the rear axle through the holes in the sides and fit a wheel on either end. Secure each wheel with three washers and two nuts.

## 7 MAKING AND ATTACHING THE HANDLEBAR

Cut the handlebar holder to the given dimensions, sand it, and bore stopped 1-inch-diameter holes 1-inch deep in the center of either end and in the center of the bottom. Glue a handlebar into each end and allow it to dry. Cut the handlebar post to the given dimension and glue it into the bottom of the handlebar holder. When the glue is dry, paint the assembly and the yoke.

When the paint has dried, insert the handlebar post through the hole in the seat and glue it into the hole in the yoke turning block. As a safeguard against getting glue on the top of the yoke, put a piece of wax paper over it (with a hole in the paper to let the handlebar post pass through). Allow the glue to dry overnight, and the scooter is ready to ride.

## projects for riding toys
# FULL-SIZED SLED

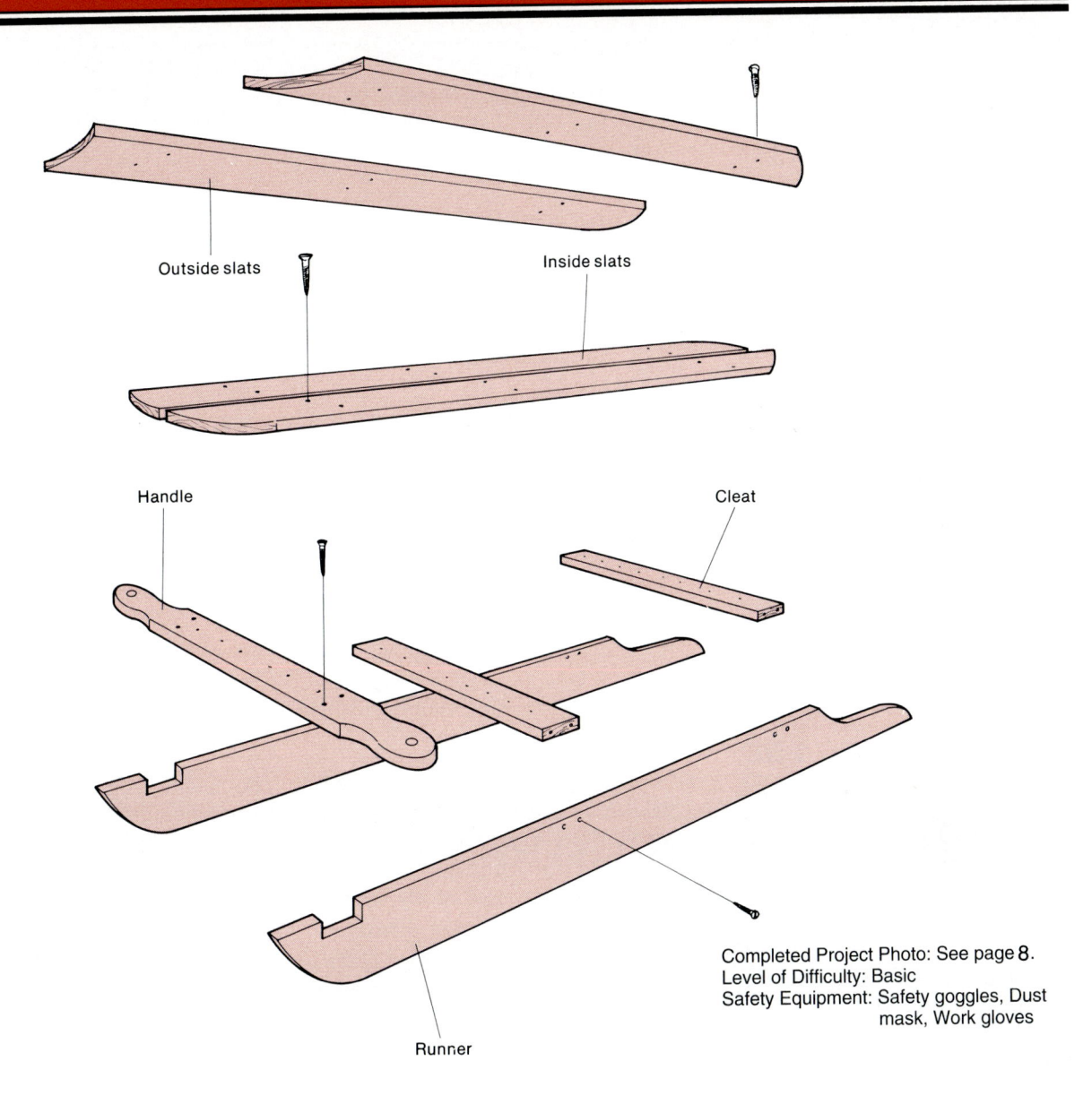

Labels on diagram: Outside slats, Inside slats, Handle, Cleat, Runner

Completed Project Photo: See page 8.
Level of Difficulty: Basic
Safety Equipment: Safety goggles, Dust mask, Work gloves

This is a sled for kids too big for the toddler size. It can carry one teenager or several smaller riders together. It naturally gets rougher use than the toddler sled, but if it is solidly constructed and well painted, it should last a long time. The project is simple, and a power screwdriver makes the job go

### MATERIALS, PARTS, AND CUTTING LIST

| Material/Part Name | Qty. | Size |
|---|---|---|
| #1 select oak | 1 | 1 x 2 x 2' |
| Cleats | 2 | 3/4" x 1 3/4" x 11 1/2" |
| #1 select oak | 1 | 1 x 3 x 3' |
| Handle | 1 | 3/4" x 2 1/2" x 25" |
| #1 select oak | 3 | 1 x 4 x 8' |
| Runners | 2 | 3/4" x 4" x 44" |

| Material/Part Name | Qty. | Size |
|---|---|---|
| Inside slats | 2 | 1/2" x 3 1/4" x 46" |
| Outside slats | 2 | 1/2" x 3 1/4" x 43" |
| Galvanized round head wood screws | 8 | #8 x 1 1/2" |
| Galvanized flat head wood screws | 4 | #8 x 1 1/2" |
| Galvanized flat head wood screws | 24 | #8 x 1" |
| Pull rope | 1 | 2' long |

63

## projects for riding toys

much faster. The sled shown here was built of oak for greatest strength and resilience, but any hardwood will do. The runners are cut from 3/4-inch stock and the slats from 1/2-inch stock.

### 1 CUTTING THE PIECES

Enlarge the graph drawings for the runners, slats, and handle. Make full-size patterns for both ends. Cut the stock for the runners to the given dimensions; then lay out the patterns on either end and cut to shape.

Cut a notch in the front of each runner to accommodate the handle, as shown in the Side View. Cut the slats to the given dimensions, separate the patterns for the ends, transfer them to the stock, and cut them out. Follow the same procedure for cutting out the handle. Cut the cleats to the given dimensions; no pattern is required.

### 2 ASSEMBLING THE SLED FRAME

Use #8 x 1 1/2-inch round head wood screws to attach the cleats between the runners, as shown in the Side View. Drive the screws into the ends of the cleats from the outsides of the runners. Sand the entire assembly smooth and paint it with several coats of exterior paint.

### 3 ATTACHING THE HANDLE

Bore 1/2-inch rope holes in the ends of the handle with a paddle or spur bit, stopping just when the point of the bit starts to come through the other side. Then turn the handle over and finish the hole

**CUTTING THE PIECES**

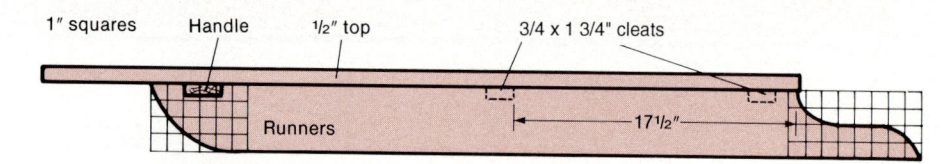

*Attach the cleats between the runners, as shown in this Side View.*

**FINISHING THE SLED**

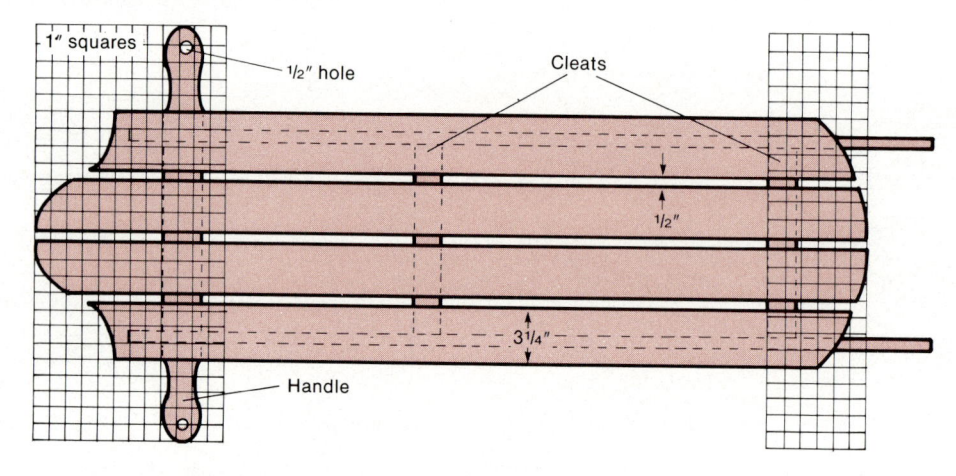

*This Top View doubles as a pattern for the slats and handle.*

from the opposite side—this prevents the drill bit from splintering the stock as it goes through. When sanding the handle, sand the edges of the rope holes with a piece of sandpaper wrapped around a dowel. Attach the handle, centered, in the notches at the front of the runners using #8 x 1 1/2-inch flat head wood screws counterbored flush with the handle.

### 4 FINISHING THE SLED

Sand the slats thoroughly. Mark the exact center of the sled on the handle and the back cleat; then position the two inside slats 1/4 inch from either side of the center, as shown in the Top View. Using a countersink drill bit, bore each slat to accommodate two small wood screws at the handle and each cleat. Fasten the inside slats by driving in #8 x 1-inch flat head wood screws from the top. The screw heads should be just slightly below the surface of the wood. Check to make sure that there are no burrs sticking up from the screw heads—they can tear clothes and give nasty scratches.

Position the outside slats 1/2 inch away from the inside slats and attach them in the same manner, driving screws down into the tops of the runners. Finish the unpainted parts with several coats of exterior varnish, allow them to dry completely, then attach a pull rope to the handle.

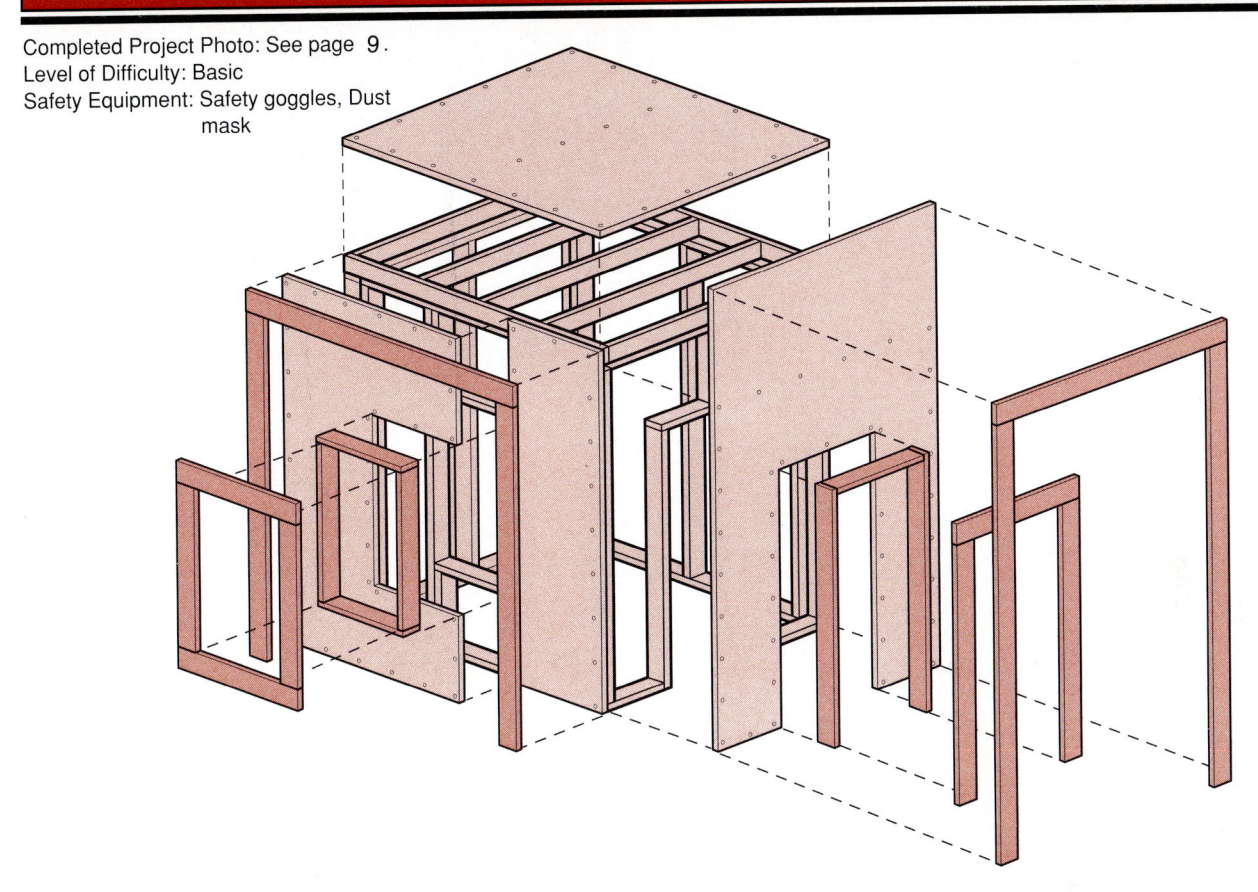

## projects for playhouses
# Frontier General Store

Completed Project Photo: See page 9.
Level of Difficulty: Basic
Safety Equipment: Safety goggles, Dust mask

A child's imagination will run wild in this playhouse. It can become any frontier style building by simply changing the sign. The false front extends 2 feet above the ceiling, allowing room for a good-sized sign. Make it a general store, as shown in the photo on page 11, a hotel, a saloon, the county jail, or any other remnant of the Old West. Platform construction is used, with the wall sections built on the ground and then lifted into place. Spruce and Douglas fir are common choices for framing lumber; whatever wood is used, be sure it is pressure treated. While a floor was not included in this particular design, you can add one by nailing plywood over a 2 x 4 frame.

With the "use zone" figured in, the frontier general store requires an area at least 8 feet long and 8 feet wide for optimum safety.

### MATERIALS, PARTS, AND CUTTING LIST

| Material/Part Name | Qty. | Size |
|---|---|---|
| Pressure-treated common spruce or Douglas fir | 5 | 1 x 4 x 10' |
| (A) Studs | 12 | 1 1/2" x 3 1/2" x 69" |
| (B) Window top trimmer studs | 2 | 1 1/2" x 3 1/2" x 15 1/2" |
| (C) Window bottom trimmer studs | 2 | 1 1/2" x 3 1/2" x 15" |
| (D) Door cripple stud | 1 | 1 1/2" x 3 1/2" x 15 1/2" |
| (E) Door trimmer studs | 2 | 1 1/2" x 3 1/2" x 53 1/2" |
| (F) Window header | 1 | 1 1/2" x 3 1/2" x 18" |
| (G) Windowsill | 1 | 1 1/2" x 3 1/2" x 18" |
| (H) Door header | 1 | 1 1/2" x 3 1/2" x 24" |
| (I) Top plates | 4 | 1 1/2" x 3 1/2" x 48" |
| (J) Sole plates | 3 | 1 1/2" x 3 1/2" x 48" |
| (K) Front sole plates | 2 | 1 1/2" x 3 1/2" x 12" |
| (L) Rafters | 5 | 1 1/2" x 3 1/2" x 45 1/2" |
| (M) Rafter plates | 2 | 1 1/2" x 3 1/2" x 55 1/2" |
| Pressure-treated common spruce or Douglas fir | 15 | 2 x 4 x 10' |
| (N) Door trim | 2 | 3/4" x 3 1/2" x 52" |

| Material/Part Name | Qty. | Size |
|---|---|---|
| (O) Door trim | 1 | 3/4" x 3 1/2" x 24" |
| (P) Window trim | 4 | 3/4" x 3 1/2" x 18" |
| (Q) Front trim | 2 | 3/4" x 3 1/2" x 96" |
| (R) Top trim | 4 | 3/4" x 3 1/2" x 48" |
| A-B or A-C exterior grade plywood | 7 | 1/2" x 48" x 96" |
| (S) Front | 1 | 1/2" x 48" x 96" |
| (T) Back | 1 | 1/2" x 48" x 75 1/2" |
| (U) Sides | 2 | 1/2" x 55" x 75 1/2" |
| (V) Roof | 1 | 1/2" x 48" x 55" |
| Roofing felt | 1 bundle | 15 or 30 lb. |
| Roofing sealer | 1 | gallon can |
| Galvanized finishing nails | 1/4 lb. | 4d |
| Galvanized common nails | 1/2 lb. | 8d |
| Galvanized common nails | 1 lb. | 12d |
| Galvanized common nails | 1 lb. | 16d |
| Staples | 1/2 lb. | 3/8" |

65

## projects for playhouses

**ASSEMBLING THE FRAME**

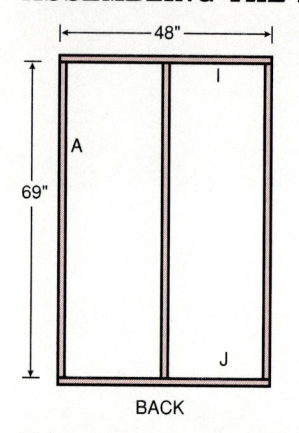

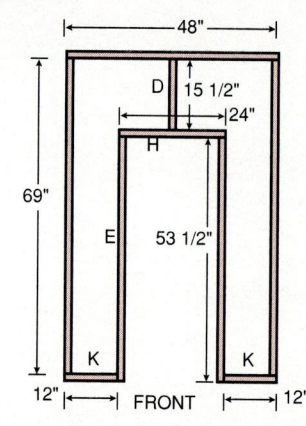

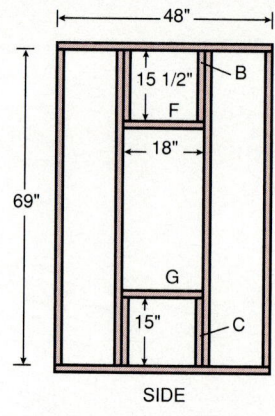

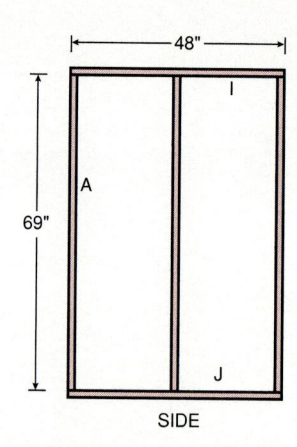

Make sure each of the four wall framing sections are square before proceeding with the installation.

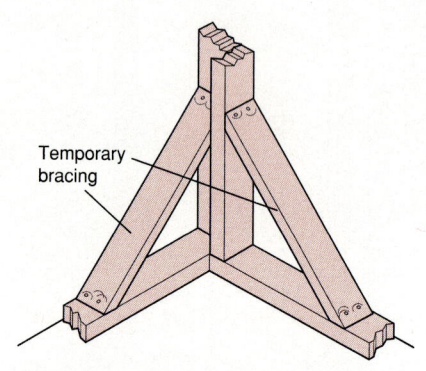

Temporary diagonal bracing can be used during the erection of the walls.

These are the three best methods to choose from when constructing corners.

**ADDING THE ROOF AND SHEATHING**

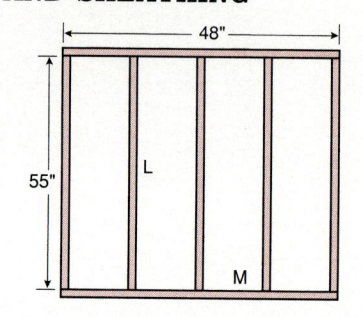

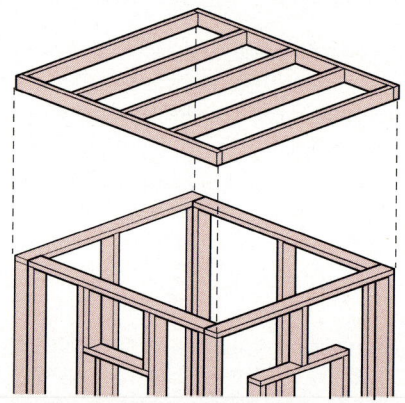

Be sure to have help when hoisting and installing the rafter assembly.

## 1 ASSEMBLING THE FRAME

Cut all of the framing pieces to the sizes shown. Place the sole plates (J and K) and top plates (I) on edge, far enough apart so that the studs (A) can be installed. Nail the sole plates and top plates to the full-length studs using 16d nails. Nail the door trimmer studs (E) in place, and install the door header (H), door cripple stud (D), window header (F), window trimmer studs (B and C), and windowsill (G). The door cripple stud and window trimmer studs must be toe-nailed with 8d nails where they meet the headers and windowsill.

When all of the members have been installed, check each wall section for squareness. To keep the assembly square while erecting, add temporary diagonal bracing made for 1 x 4 stock. Tilt the sections up into position with the help of two other people. There are several methods of tying wall sections together at corners. When building corners, it is very important that the lumber used is perfectly straight and free of defects. Depending on your choice of corner construction, some of the playhouse dimensions may have to be increased slightly to accommodate the corners.

## 2 ADDING THE ROOF AND SHEATHING

Cut the rafters (L) and rafter plates (M) to the dimensions provided. Fasten them together with 12d nails. Use 16d nails to toe-nail the rafter assembly to the top plates. Each of the two sides is bigger than the standard 4- x 8-foot plywood sheet. For this reason, they must be made from two separate pieces of plywood (S). See the

## projects for playhouses

### ADDING THE ROOF AND SHEATHING (CONTINUED)

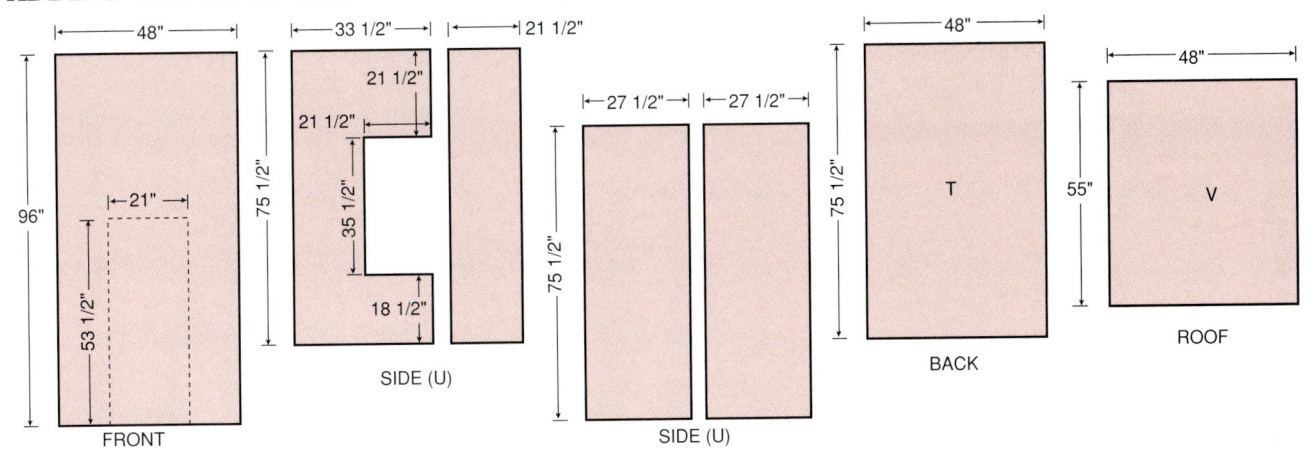

Cut the front, sides, back, and roof to size following these cutting diagrams.

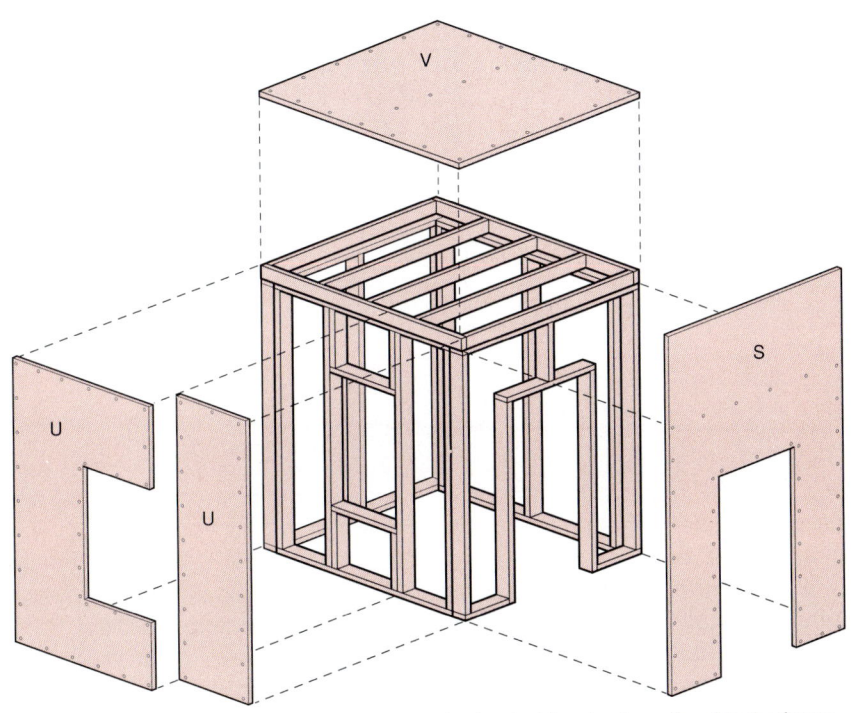

Use 8d finishing nails every 8 inches to secure the front, sides, back, and roof to the frame.

### FINISHING TOUCHES

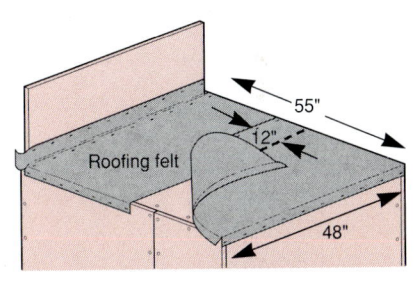

Make sure each row of roofing felt overlaps the previous one by 12 inches.

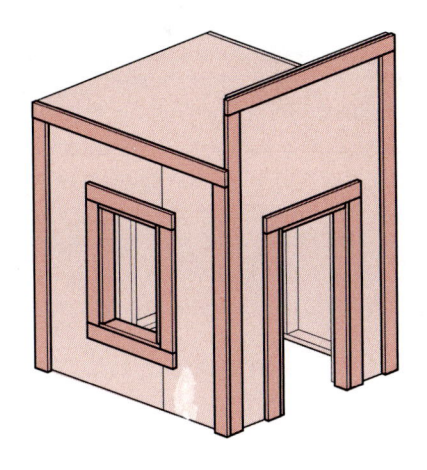

Use 4d finishing nails to install the trim pieces, then paint as desired.

cutting diagrams for details. The front and back sheathing require only one sheet of plywood each. Measure carefully for the door and window openings, cut them out, and attach the front, sides, and back to the frame using 8d nails every 8 inches. Be sure to remove the temporary diagonal bracing before adding the front (S), back (T), and sides (U). When attaching the roof (V), drive all nails squarely into the rafters. Again, use 8d nails every 8 inches.

### 3 FINISHING TOUCHES

Staple roofing felt to cover the entire roof. Each row should overlap the previous one 12 inches. Then coat the roof with a good roofing sealer. Cut all of the trim pieces to size, and install using 4d finishing nails. After covering any nail holes and rough plywood edges with wood putty, paint the playhouse as desired. For a nice effect, you may wish to keep the trim unfinished, while painting the front, sides, and sign.

67

## projects for playhouses
# FRAMED PLAYHOUSE

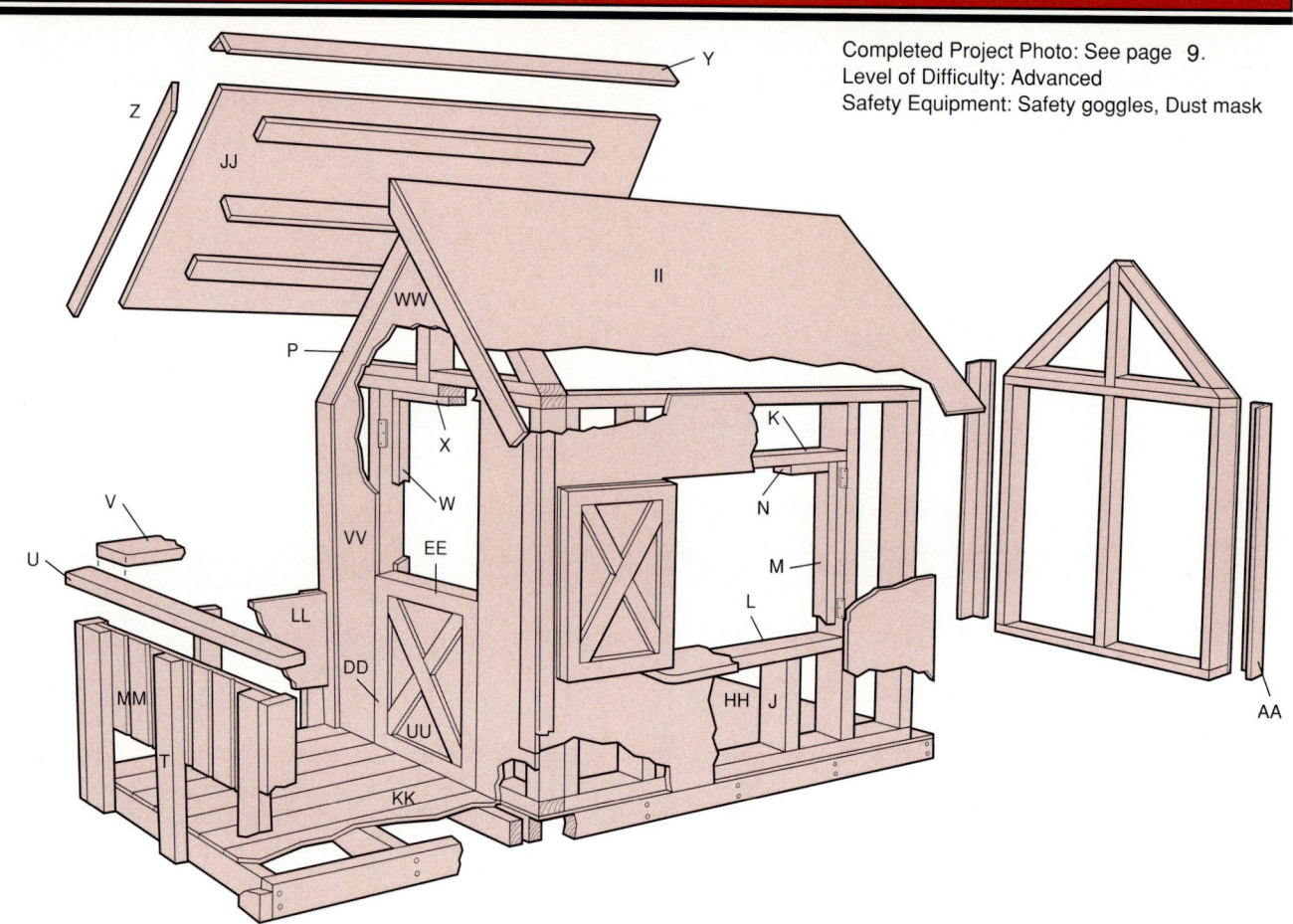

Completed Project Photo: See page 9.
Level of Difficulty: Advanced
Safety Equipment: Safety goggles, Dust mask

This charming playhouse is framed using 2 x 3 lumber. It rests on a foundation of 2 x 4 lumber covered with exterior grade plywood. The wall sheathing and roof are made of Texture 1-11 plywood that gives the structure a handsome, finished look. A small railed deck extends the playhouse front, creating an attractive entrance.

Review the framing and construction details before beginning. Do not precut lumber and sheathing too far ahead into the project. Instead check measurements and dimensions as you progress and make any slight sizing adjustments as needed. This is particularly true when constructing the roof framing, window and door openings, and shutters and doors.

**MATERIALS, PARTS, AND CUTTING LIST**

| Material/Part Name | Qty. | Size |
|---|---|---|
| Texture 1-11 plywood | 5 | 5/8" x 4' x 8' |
| (II) Roof panel* | 1 | 5/8" x 39 5/8" x 84" |
| (JJ) Roof panel* | 1 | 5/8" x 39" x 84" |
| (KK) Deck boards* | 8 | 5/8" x 4" x 36" |
| (LL) Deck side* | 1 | 5/8" x 12" x 36" |
| (MM) Deck side* | 1 | 5/8" x 12" x 48" |
| (NN) Back side (long)* | 1 | 5/8" x 48" x 48" |
| (OO) Back side (short)* | 1 | 5/8" x 48" x 24" |
| (PP) Back end* | 1 | 5/8" x 48" x 48" |
| (QQ) Front side (long)* | 1 | 5/8" x 48" x 24" |
| (RR) Front side (short)* | 1 | 5/8" x 48" x 24" |
| (SS) Shutters* | 2 | 5/8" x 17 1/2" x 23 5/8" |
| (TT) Top door* | 1 | 5/8" x 23 1/2" x 22" |
| (UU) Bottom door* | 1 | 5/8" x 23 1/2" x 23 3/4" |
| (VV) Front end* | 1 | 5/8" x 48" x 72" |
| (WW) Gable ends* | 2 | 5/8" x triangle sides 25 1/2", triangle base 36" |
| Exterior grade plywood | 1 | 1/2" x 4' x 8' |
| (HH) Floor panel | 1 | 1/2" x 48" x 72" |

| Material/Part Name | Qty. | Size |
|---|---|---|
| Pressure-treated common pine or fir | 2 | 2 x 4 x 10' |
| (A) Foundation side members | 2 | 1 1/2" x 3 1/2" x 108" |
| Pressure-treated common pine or fir | 4 | 2 x 4 x 8' |
| (B) Foundation cross-members | 8 | 1 1/2" x 3 1/2" x 45" |
| Pressure-treated common pine or fir | 24 | 2 x 3 x 8' |
| (C) Sole plates | 2 | 1 1/2" x 2 1/2" x 67" |
| (D) Sole plate | 1 | 1 1/2" x 2 1/2" x 48" |
| (E) Sole plates | 2 | 1 1/2" x 2 1/2" x 12" |
| (F) Top plates | 2 | 1 1/2" x 2 1/2" x 67" |
| (G) Top plates | 2 | 1 1/2" x 2 1/2" x 48" |
| (H) Vertical wall studs | 17 | 1 1/2" x 2 1/2" x 45" |
| (I) Cripple studs | 2 | 1 1/2" x 2 1/2" x 6" |
| (J) Cripple studs | 2 | 1 1/2" x 2 1/2" x 12" |
| (K) Window header | 1 | 1 1/2" x 2 1/2" x 36" |
| (L) Window rough sill | 1 | 1 1/2" x 2 1/2" x 36" |
| (P) Roof plates | 4 | 1 1/2" x 2 1/2" x 23 1/2" |
| (Q) Rafters | 4 | 1 1/2" x 2 1/2" x 31 1/4" |
| (R) Truss center supports | 2 | 1 1/2" x 2 1/2" x 24" |

68

*projects for playhouses*

With the "use zone" figured in, the framed playhouse requires an area at least 13 feet long and 8 feet wide for optimum safety.

## 1 CONSTRUCTING THE BASE

The overall foundation of the playhouse and deck measures 9 feet x 4 feet with the deck extension measuring 3 feet x 4 feet. The foundation is made of 2 x 4 pressure-treated common pine or fir that resists ground moisture and rot.

All frame pieces are laid on edge. There are two 9-foot foundation side members (A) and eight 45-inch long foundation cross-members (B) positioned as shown. Attach the cross-members to the foundation side members using 12d galvanized nails.

Attach the 1/2-inch x 6-foot x 4-foot floor panel (HH) to the foundation using 6d galvanized nails spaced at 6-inch intervals around the outside edges and 12-inch intervals on the cross-members.

The deck boards (KK) are cut from texture 1-11 plywood and installed perpendicular to the cross-members. Attach each board using two 6d finishing nails at each stud. Space the boards the width of a nail apart to provide drainage between the boards. Lay out the boards before nailing to test spacing. You may have to rip the outside boards slightly thinner than the 4-inch width to account for board spacing.

## 2 POSITIONING THE BASE

Position the base on six concrete blocks set in a bed of sand slightly below the ground surface. Make certain the blocks are level with one another and aligned.

## 3 FRAMING THE SIDE AND END PANELS

Framing for the side and end walls of the playhouse is made of 2 x 3 stock. Framing can be constructed on site, or in a garage or basement and then carried to the site. Follow the sizing and layout drawings shown for all walls. Note that full length vertical wall studs (H) are 45 inches in length. Front and back walls are covered with single sheets of texture 1-11 plywood. Both side walls require two separate sheets butted together over a stud. Lay out the side wall frames carefully to ensure that this panel joint falls over a stud location that provides a good nailing base.

The side wall frames fit inside the end frames. This means that the sole plates (C) and top plates (F) of the side walls are 5 inches shorter (67 inches) than the overall 72-inch length. End wall sole plates (D) and top plates (G) measure the full 48-inch width, except the door wall which uses two 12-inch sole plates (E) and a 24-inch sole plate opening. The window is framed 36 inches wide and 24 inches high.

End-nail all framing members together using 12d galvanized nails. Attach the sole plate of each wall to the foundation frame using 5/16-inch x 3-inch long lag screws

**CONSTRUCTING THE BASE**

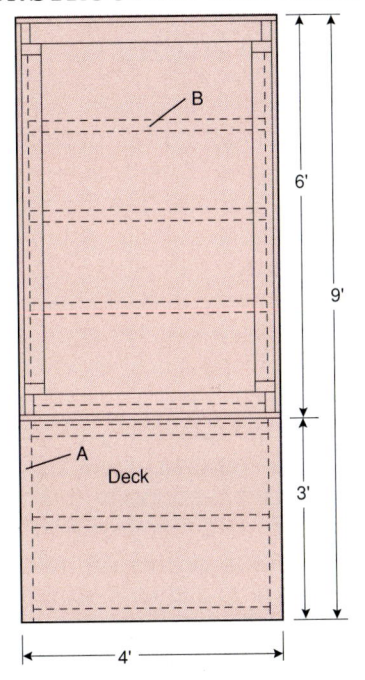

This foundation detail clearly illustrates the 3 foot x 4 foot deck extension.

### MATERIALS, PARTS, AND CUTTING LIST (CONTINUED)

| Material/Part Name | Qty. | Size |
|---|---|---|
| (S) Horizontal roof supports | 4 | 1 1/2" x 2 1/2" x 67" |
| (T) Deck rails | 7 | 1 1/2" x 2 1/2" x 22" |
| (U) Rail cap | 1 | 1 1/2" x 2 1/2" x 48" |
| (V) Rail cap | 1 | 1 1/2" x 2 1/2" x 36" |
| Common pine | 11 | 1 x 3 x 10' |
| (Y) Roof ridge trim | 2 | 3/4" x 2 1/2" x 84" |
| (Z) Gable trim | 4 | 3/4" x 2 1/2" x 34" |
| (AA) Outside corner trim | 4 | 3/4" x 2 1/2" x 45" |
| (BB) Shutter frame vertical pieces | 8 | 3/4" x 2 1/2" x 23 5/8" |
| (CC) Shutter frame horizontal pieces | 8 | 3/4" x 2 1/2" x 17 1/2" |
| (DD) Door section bottom vertical pieces | 4 | 3/4" x 2 1/2" x 23 3/4" |
| (EE) Door section bottom horizontal pieces | 4 | 3/4" x 2 1/2" x 23 1/2" |
| (FF) Door section top vertical pieces | 4 | 3/4" x 2 1/2" x 22" |
| (GG) Door section top horizontal pieces | 4 | 3/4" x 2 1/2" x 23 1/2" |

| Material/Part Name | Qty. | Size |
|---|---|---|
| Common pine | 1 | 1 x 8 x 3' |
| (O) Windowsill | 1 | 3/4" x 7 1/4" x 36" |
| Common fir | 2 | 3/4" x 1" x 8' |
| (M) Vertical window trimmers | 2 | 3/4" x 1" x 24" |
| (N) Horizontal window trimmer | 1 | 3/4" x 1" x 34 1/2" |
| (W) Vertical door trimmers | 2 | 3/4" x 1" x 45 3/4" |
| (X) Horizontal door trimmer | 1 | 3/4" x 1" x 24" |
| Concrete blocks | 6 | standard |
| Hinge sets with screws | 4 | 2" |
| Magnetic cabinet catch with catch plates | 1 | 2" |
| Barrel bolt with mounting screws | 1 | 3" |
| Galvanized finishing nails | 1/2 lb. | 4d |
| Galvanized finishing nails | 2 lb. | 6d |
| Galvanized finishing nails | 1/4 lb. | 10d |
| Galvanized common nails | 3 lb. | 12d |
| Galvanized lag screws with washers | 48 | 5/16" x 3" |

\* Follow plywood panel cutting patterns.

## projects for playhouses

### FRAMING THE SIDE AND END PANELS

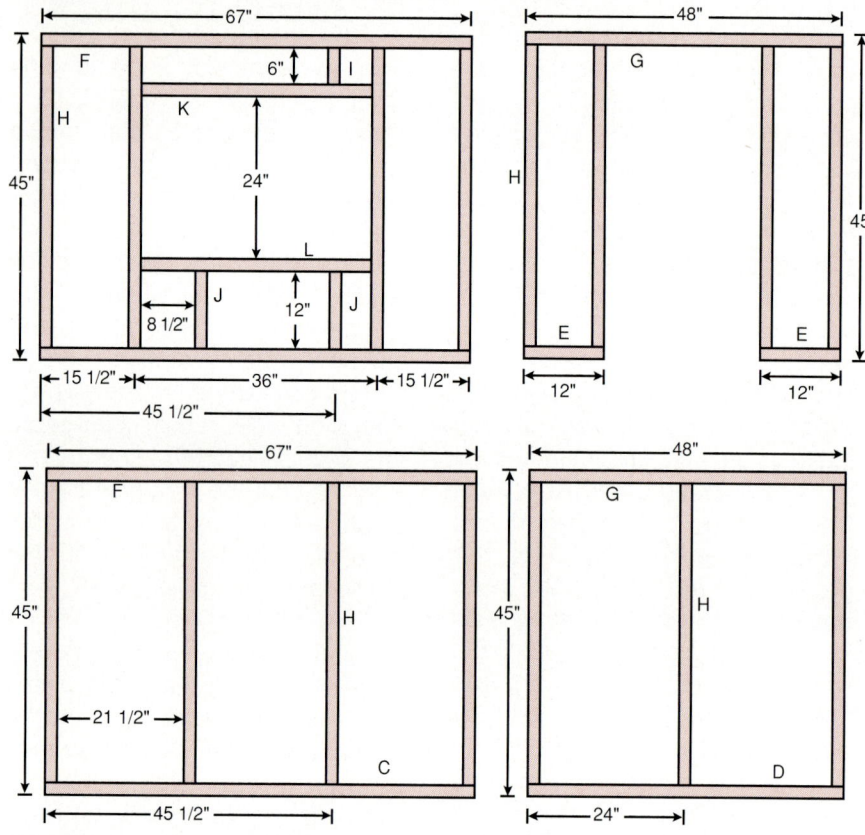

Follow these measurements to cut the framing for the walls.

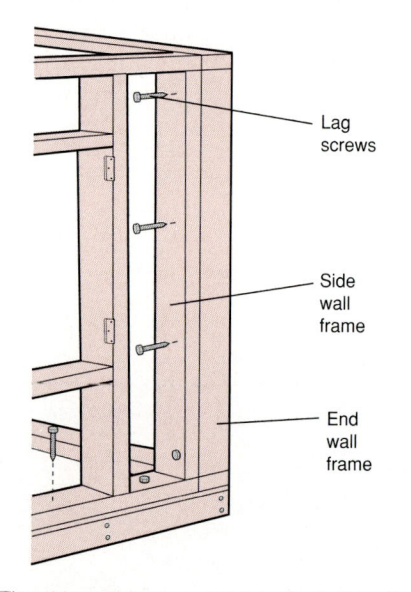

The side wall frames attach to the inside of the end frames.

with washers. Use five lag screws in each side frame sole plate and four screws in the front and back sole plates.

Tie the side and end wall frames together at the corners using four lag screws at each corner joint.

### 4 FRAMING THE ROOF

Construct the two end trusses to the dimensions given. All bevel and miter cuts on the trusses are 45°. Nail all pieces together using 12d nails. Nail the trusses to the top plate of the end frames using 12d nails. After both trusses are in position, measure the span between them and individually cut the four horizontal roof supports (S). These should measure 67 inches, but there may be slight variations. Do not undercut these pieces. They must fit tightly between the trusses. Toe-nail them to the rafters using 12d nails.

### 5 ADDING SHEATHING AND ROOFING

Cut out all wall panels and roof panels based on the cutting diagrams given. Check dimensions against the final framing dimensions before cutting. Attach the side panels (NN, OO, QQ, and RR), front and back (PP and VV) end panels, and gable ends (WW) to the framing studs using 6d finishing nails.

The two roof panels (II and JJ) are installed to the rafters and horizontal roof supports in the same manner. The 39 5/8-inch roof panel overlaps the 39-inch roof panel to form a smooth joint at the ridge. If you do not plan to shingle the roof, cap the ridge with the two 1 x 3 x 84-inch trim pieces attached with 4d finishing nails.

Add the two pieces of gable trim (Z) to the front and back wall. Each 1 x 3 trim piece measures 34

### FRAMING THE ROOF

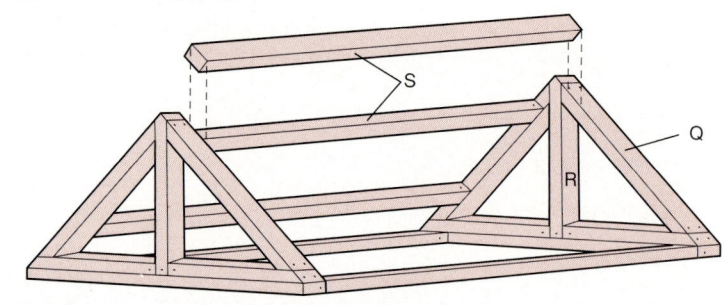

The roof framing is assembled using 12d common nails.

## projects for playhouses

**ADDING SHEATHING AND ROOFING**

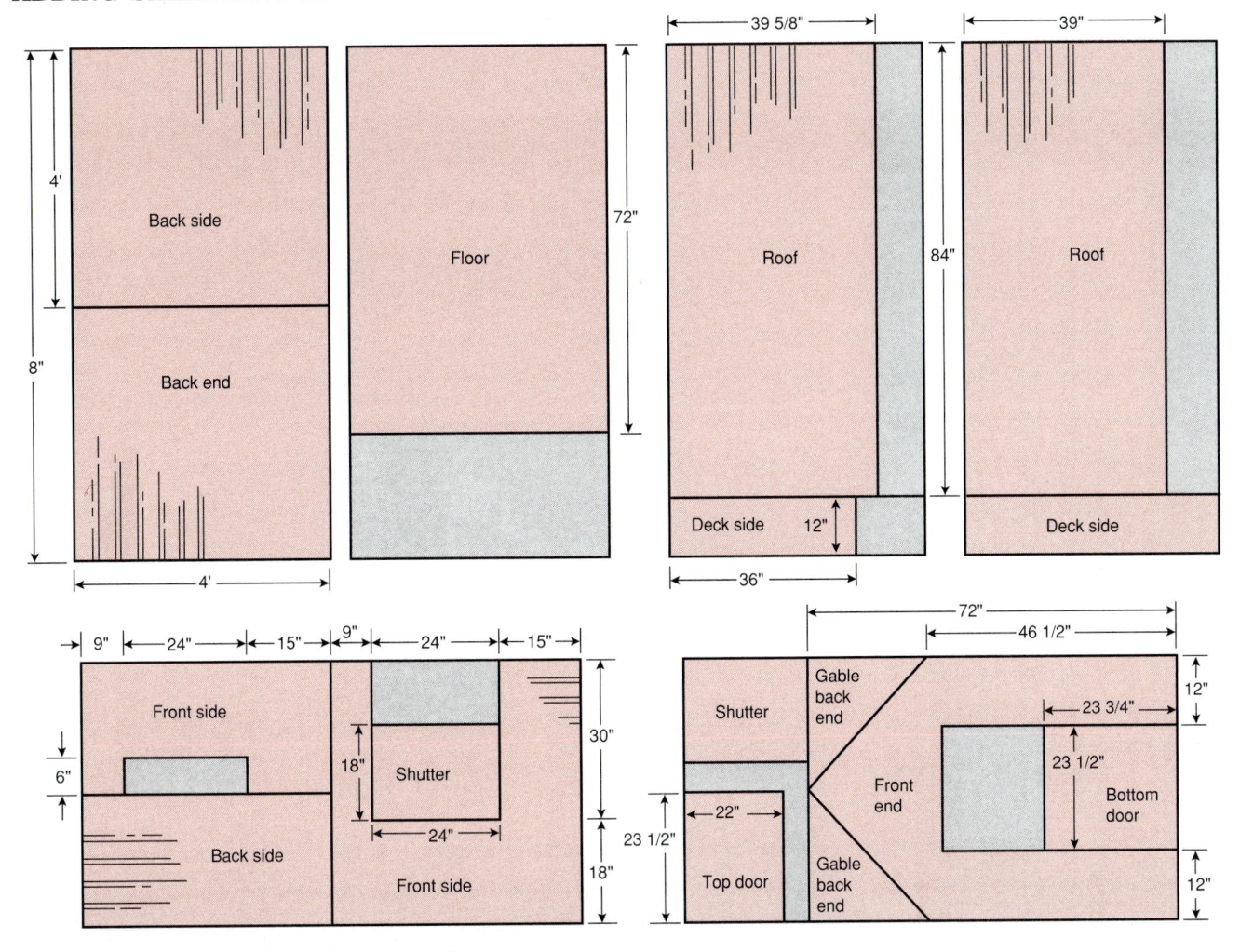

Follow these measurements to cut all wall and roof panels.

inches in length with both ends miter-cut at a 45° angle. Attach with 4d finishing nails.

### 6 FRAMING THE DOOR AND WINDOW OPENINGS

Window and door openings are further framed out using 3/4- x 1-inch trimmers to form stops for the door sections and window shutters. Attach the 3/4- x 1-inch pieces along the inside edge of the 2 x 3 door and window frame using 4d finishing nails. Add the 1 x 8 x 3-foot common pine windowsill (O) to the base of the window opening, centering it on the frame. Attach with 4d nails.

### 7 CONSTRUCTING THE DECK RAIL

Attach the six 22-inch long 2 x 3 deck rails (T) the foundation using two 5/16- x 3-inch lag screws in each rail. Attach the deck boards (KK) using 6d finishing nails and add the rail caps (U and V), using 10d finishing nails.

### 8 CONSTRUCTING THE SHUTTERS

The shutter dimensions shown are 23 5/8 x 17 1/2 inches. This provides a 1/4-inch clearance around the window frame and between the closed shutters. These dimensions are based on a 24- x 36-inch opening. You should measure the final dimensions of the window opening on your project and make any slight adjustments to size as needed.

Each shutter is made of a piece of textured plywood (SS) sandwiched between two frames made of 1 x 3 framing pieces (BB and CC). All stock is mitered 45° at the corners to produce a clean, neat look. Mount the shutters on hinges screwed into the window frame. Recess the mounting area with a wood chisel so the hinges lie flush with the frame. Use the mounting screws supplied with the hinge set.

Mount the magnetic catch at the midpoint of the window's top

## projects for playhouses

### ADDING SHEATHING AND ROOFING (CONTINUED)

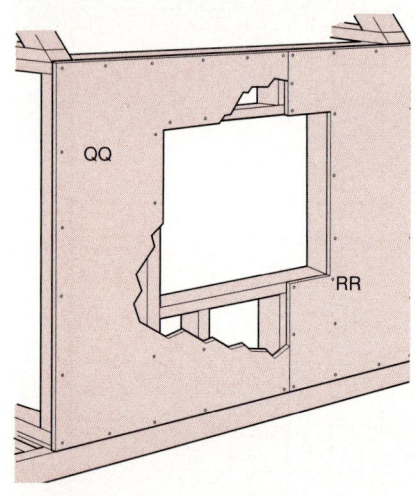

Be sure to use finishing nails to attach the sheathing.

### FRAMING THE DOOR AND WINDOW OPENINGS

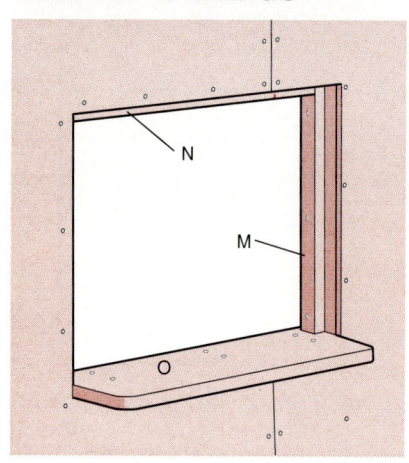

Secure the windowsill to the base of the window opening, centering it on the frame.

frame. Screw the metal catch plate to the inside corner of the shutter.

### 9 CONSTRUCTING THE DOOR

The door design is similar to the shutter. The door is made in two separate sections. The door frame width is 24 inches, so the door width should be 23 1/2 inches to provide a slight clearance on both sides. The bottom door section (UU, DD, and EE) should measure

### CONSTRUCTING THE SHUTTERS

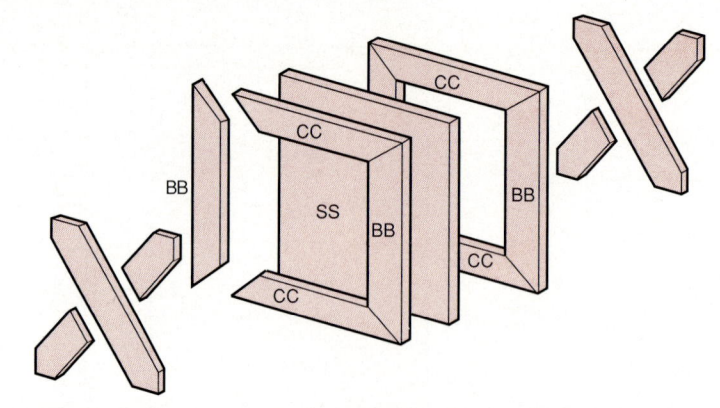

All shutter stock is mitered 45° at the corners. Cross pieces are optional ornamental trim.

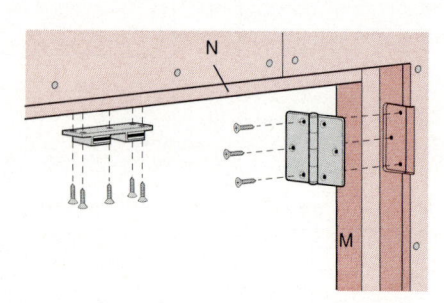

Mount the hinges and magnetic catch using the hardware provided.

### CONSTRUCTING THE DOOR

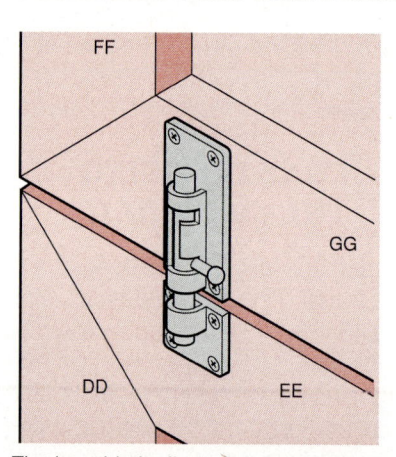

The barrel bolt allows the door sections to be opened individually or as a unit.

23 3/4 inches and the top section (TT, FF, and GG), 22 inches in height. This allows 1/4 inch at the top and bottom of the frame and 1/4 inch between sections. As previously done with the window, check all dimensions before sizing the lumber. If you plan to alter the door section sizes, keep in mind that the top section should clear the deck rail when it is swung open.

Each door section mounts on its own set of hinges. A barrel bolt is also mounted across the joint between the top and bottom sections. This allows the sections to be opened independently or bolted together and swung open as a unit.

### 10 FINAL FINISHING

The playhouse pictured at the beginning of the project offers a good basic design. The roof can be left as is or shingled. Basic shingling techniques are covered in the "Log Cabin" project.

The outside corner trim (AA) consists of two 45-inch lengths of 1 x 3 stock at each corner. It is nailed in place using 6d finishing nails. This gives the wall corners a clean, finished appearance.

Other types of ornamental trim can be added. These include cross pieces for the door sections and window shutters, roof edge trim, and scroll sawn designs mounted to the roof eaves. The textured plywood can be left natural or painted. Unpainted wood should be given a coat of clear waterproofing sealant.

## projects for playhouses
# Log Cabin

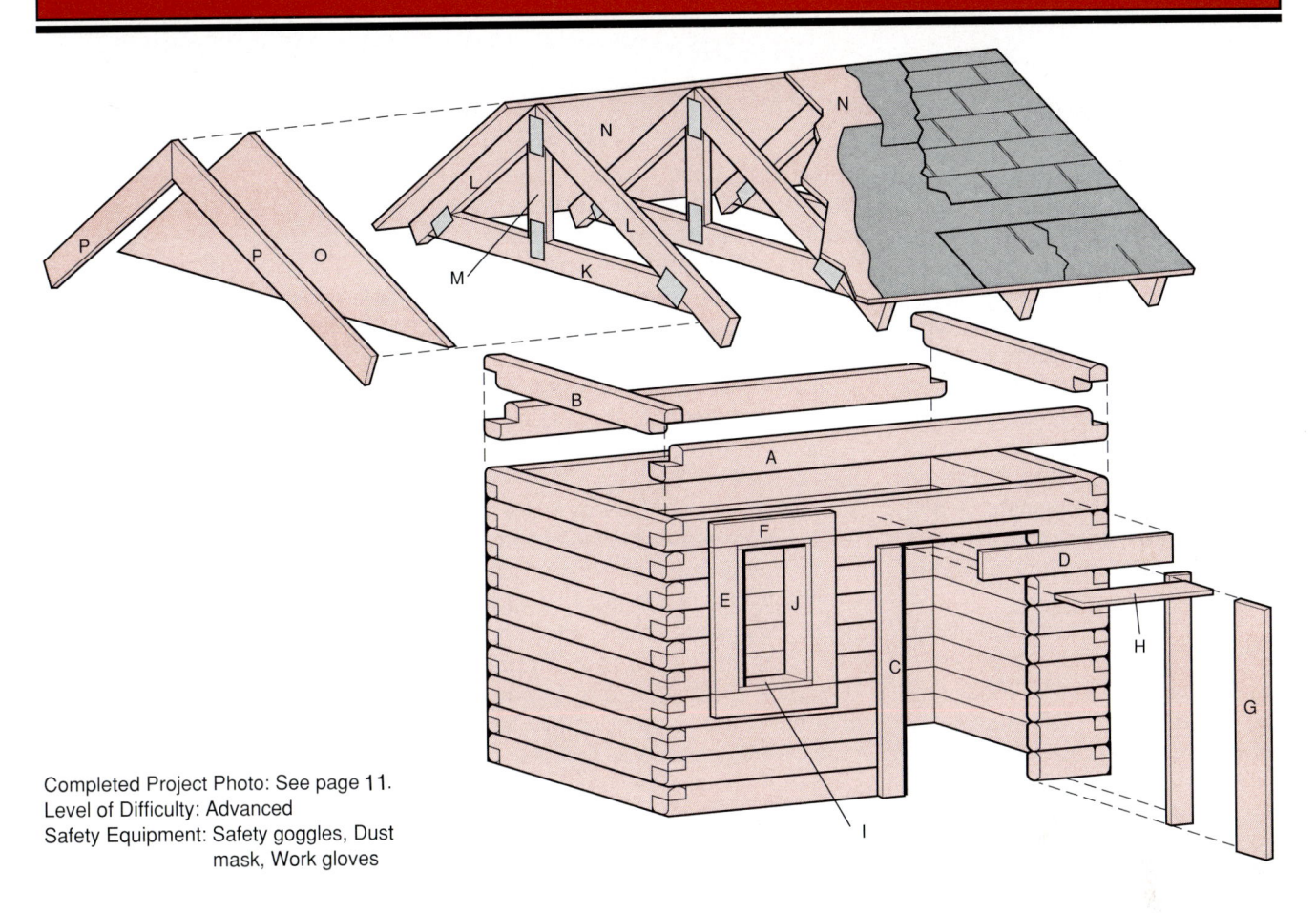

Completed Project Photo: See page 11.
Level of Difficulty: Advanced
Safety Equipment: Safety goggles, Dust mask, Work gloves

A log cabin will transport your child's imagination back to frontier days, to Daniel Boone, Abe Lincoln, and the adventurous families that first settled the west.

This cabin uses simple notched landscape timbers that are tied together at the corners using nails and construction adhesive. The main structure is a rectangle, eleven timbers high. The end wall eaves are made of exterior grade plywood. Four trusses form the framework for the roof, which is plywood covered with shingles.

### MATERIALS, PARTS, AND CUTTING LIST

| Material/Part Name | Qty. | Size |
|---|---|---|
| Landscape timbers | 22 | 8' long |
| (A) Long wall timbers | 22 | 3" x 4 1/2" x 72" |
| Landscape timbers | 22 | 4' long |
| (B) Short wall timbers | 22 | 3" x 4 1/2" x 48" |
| Exterior grade plywood | 3 | 5/8" x 4' x 8' |
| (N) Roof panels | 2 | 5/8" x 48" x 84" |
| (O) Eave caps | 2 | 5/8" triangle (Base 86 1/2"; Sides 48"; Height 20 3/4") |
| Pressure-treated common pine or fir | 4 | 1 x 4 x 8' |
| (C) Outside door frame sides | 2 | 3/4" x 3 1/2" x 36" |
| (D) Outside door frame top | 1 | 3/4" x 3 1/2" x 31" |
| (E) Outside window frame sides | 2 | 3/4" x 3 1/2" x 22" |
| (F) Outside window frame top and bottom | 2 | 3/4" x 3 1/2" x 19" |
| (P) Eave cap trim | 4 | 3/4" x 3 1/2" x 48" |
| Pressure-treated common pine or fir | 2 | 1 x 6 x 8' |
| (G) Inside door frame sides | 2 | 3/4" x 5 1/2" x 35 1/4" |
| (H) Inside door frame top | 1 | 3/4" x 5 1/2" x 24" |

| Material/Part Name | Qty. | Size |
|---|---|---|
| (I) Inside window frame top and bottom | 2 | 3/4" x 5 1/2" x 12" |
| (J) Inside window frame sides | 2 | 3/4" x 5 1/2" x 20 1/2" |
| Pressure-treated common pine | 8 | 2 x 4 x 8' |
| (K) Truss cross braces | 4 | 1 1/2" x 3 1/2" x 72" |
| (L) Rafters | 8 | 1 1/2" x 3 1/2" x 48" |
| (M) Center supports | 4 | 1 1/2" x 3 1/2" x 13 1/2" |
| Roofing felt | 1 | 15-lb. roll |
| Roofing shingles | 2 | bundles |
| Galvanized roofing nails | 1 lb. | 3/4" |
| Galvanized common nails | 1 lb. | 6d |
| Galvanized common nails | 1 lb. | 10d |
| Galvanized common nails | 1 lb. | 16d |
| Galvanized decking nails | 5 lb. | 20d |
| Construction adhesive | 6 | tubes |
| Truss clips | 16 | |
| Storm clips | 8 | |

\* All window/door framing dimensions based on 4 1/2" high landscape timbers.

73

## projects for playhouses

With the "use zone" figured in, the log cabin requires an area at least 10 feet long and 8 feet wide for optimum safety.

### 1 SIZING THE TIMBERS

Begin by assembling the needed materials. The final room dimension of the cabin will be 6 x 4 foot. You may be able to purchase 4-foot-long timbers or have the lumberyard cut 8-foot timbers to 4- and 6-foot lengths for you. If you must size the timbers yourself, you will need a circular saw with an 8 1/4-inch cutting blade to handle the thickness of the timbers (A and B) in one pass. You can also use a log saw or two-man saw to cut the timbers.

There will be minor variations in height and thickness between the landscape timbers. Final timber dimensions may also vary between suppliers and geographical regions. The timbers shown in this project measure 3 inches thick x 4 1/2 inches wide. The timbers are set on edge when stacked so the cabin walls are 3 inches thick with the 4 1/2-inch flat sides forming the inside and outside wall surfaces.

In this design, the timbers will be notched and the walls constructed to the top of the door and window levels before the door and window openings are cut.

### 2 NOTCHING THE TIMBERS

Once the timbers are cut to size, notch both ends of each timber. Set each timber on edge, and mark out the area to be cut away. On this size timber, the notch is 3 inches long x 2 1/4 inches deep. Mark out the 3-inch dimension using a combination square.

Set the circular saw to a 2 1/4-inch cutting depth. Make a test-cut in some scrap timber to confirm this 2 1/4-inch setting. Once the cutting depth is confirmed, make at least six passes in the notch area to cut away most of the stock. Complete the notch using a wide wood chisel and hammer to cut out the remaining wood chips. Recheck the notch dimensions and test-fit the lap joint on two timbers before notching all timbers.

**NOTCHING THE TIMBERS**

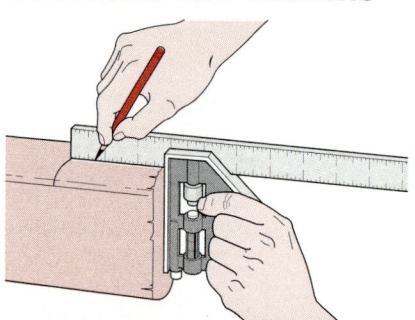

Mark out the area to be notched using a combination square.

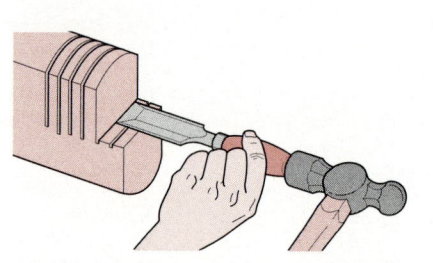

Kerf the notched area with a circular saw then clear the waste using a hammer and wood chisel.

### PREPARING THE BASE

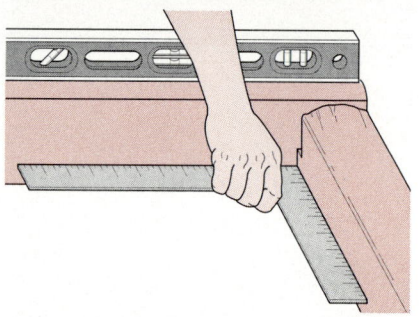

As seen in this first course joint detail, it is very important that the logs are level before proceeding with the construction.

### 3 PREPARING THE BASE

If the cabin site is level, the first course of timbers can rest directly on the ground. If there are slight irregularities in the site, dig a 3-inch deep trench for the first course. Level the base of the trench and lay the timbers in this bed. Small flat rocks or cedar shakes can be used to shim the logs, but try to avoid excessive shimming by selecting a level site.

Position the two 4-foot timbers first. Place a dollop of construction adhesive on each notch and place a 6-foot notched timber in position to form the lap joint at each corner. Complete the joint by driving a 20d galvanized decking nail down through the notches to tie them together.

### 4 BUILDING THE WALLS

Once the first course of logs is in position, check all timbers for levelness before positioning the second course. Form the second course of logs by placing a dollop of adhesive at the corner positions on the first course. Position the two 4-foot timbers in place and nail down through the notches, tieing the notch of the second course 4-

**SIZING THE TIMBERS**

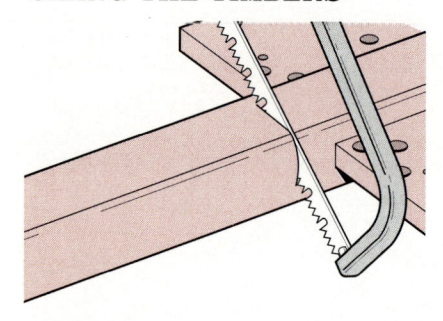

A large tooth log saw is an easy way to cut landscaping timbers.

74

projects for playhouses

## BUILDING THE WALLS

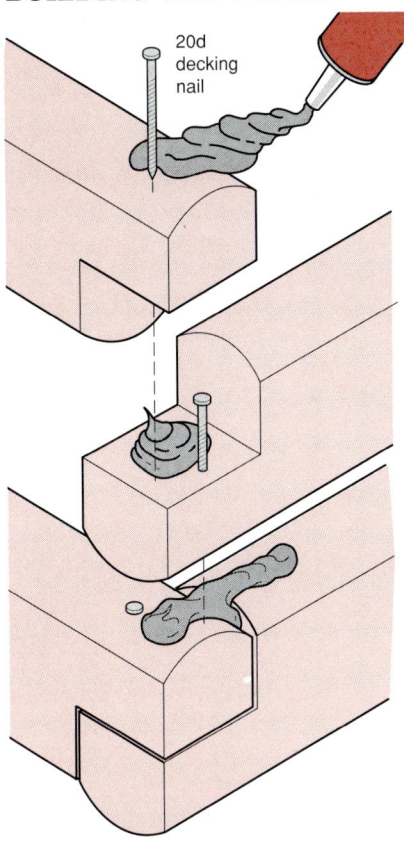

## CUTTING THE DOOR OPENINGS

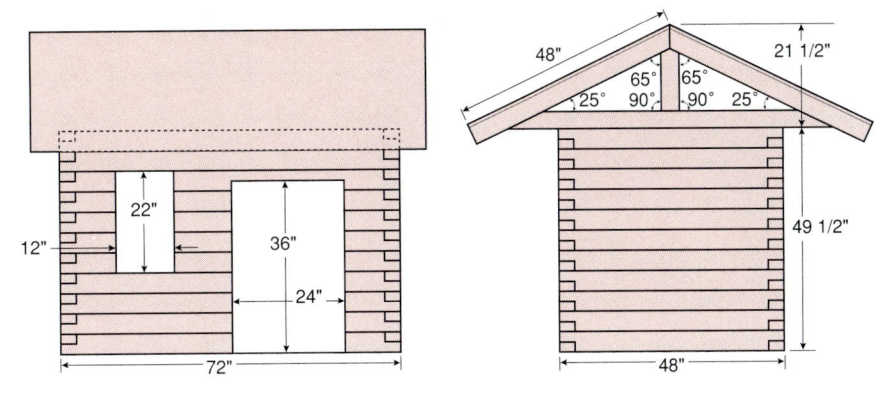

These Front and Side Views can be used for reference when cutting the door and window openings and when constructing the roof.

Cut the door opening using the door frame as a guide.

Construction of the second and subsequent courses utilizes nails and adhesive.

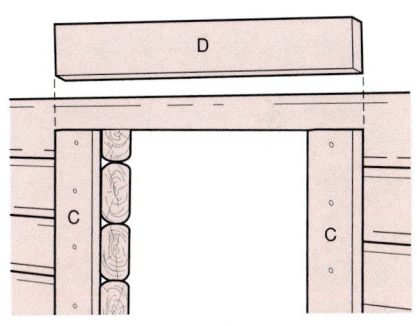

Nail the top outside door frame in place to complete the ninth course.

foot timbers into the notch of the first course 6-foot timbers. Place a dollop of adhesive on the second course 4-inch timber notches, position the two 6-foot timbers, and nail as before.

Check that each course is level and that the wall is being constructed plumb. Continue construction in this way until eight courses of logs are in place.

### 5 CUTTING THE DOOR OPENINGS

The outside sides (C) of the door opening are framed using 1 x 4 lumber and the opening is cut using the frame pieces as a guide. Cut two 36-inch lengths of 1 x 4 lumber. Position these outside frames as shown in the illustration and nail them to the outside cabin walls using 10d common nails. With a log saw or two-man saw, cut down through the timbers, using the inside edge of the door frame as a guide.

Temporarily position the ninth course of logs, and mark out the notch for the top of the door opening on the log spanning the doorway. Remove this log and cut the notch using repeated passes with the circular saw and clearing with the 2-inch wood chisel.

Now glue and nail the ninth course in position. Nail the top of the door frame sides to the ninth course of timbers to tie all pieces together.

### 6 CUTTING THE WINDOW OPENING

The window opening spans from the fifth to the ninth courses of timbers. Cut two 22-inch lengths of 1 x 4 and nail them to the wall in the window position as shown. As with the door opening, cut down through the timbers using a log saw or two-man saw. Again, use the inside of the window frame as a guide.

### 7 FINISHING THE WALLS

Construct the tenth and eleventh log courses to complete the basic box structure.

75

## projects for playhouses

**CUTTING THE WINDOW OPENING**

Cut down through the timbers to make the window opening.

### 8 FRAMING THE DOOR AND WINDOW

Complete the outside door frame top (D), and top and bottom (F) and sides (E) of the outside window frames by cutting 1 x 4 stock to size and nailing in place with 10d common nails.

Cut inside frame pieces (G, H, I, and J) for the sides, bottom, and tops of the door and window openings, using 1 x 6 stock. Position the slight overhang of the 1 x 6 to the inside of the cabin. Nail these pieces to the timbers using 10d common nails.

### 9 CONSTRUCTING THE ROOF TRUSSES

The roof is supported by four trusses equally spaced 24 inches, on center. Trusses are constructed of 2 x 4 lumber. Each truss consists of a 6-foot cross brace (K), two 4-foot rafters (L), and a 13 1/2-inch center support (M). Pieces are joined using metal truss clips that are nailed over adjoining pieces.

Each end of the cross brace is mitered at a 25° angle. Lay out this angle using a T-bevel or combination set, or by measuring in along the top edge of the piece 7 1/2 inches and drawing a line between this point and the bottom edge of the piece.

The top edges of the 4-foot rafters must be cut with a matching 65° miter to form the joint at the ridge of the roof. You can lay out this angle by measuring down along the bottom edge of the rafter 1 1/2 inches and drawing a line between this point and the top edge of the rafter.

Create the pointed tip at the top of the center support by measuring down from the top edges of the piece 7/8 inch and connecting these two points to the center point of the top, as shown.

Cut the pieces for one truss and test-fit before cutting the others. Join the pieces using four truss clips as shown. Secure the clips with 20d decking nails.

The assembled trusses rest on the top course of timbers and are jointed to the timbers using storm clips and 20d decking nails. Storm clips are structural wood connectors. They are used to eliminate wind uplift problems by anchoring trusses and rafters

**FRAMING THE DOOR AND WINDOW**

Secure the door and window inside framing with 10d nails.

*projects for playhouses*

securely to plates and studs. Center the overhang on each side of the cabin and position each truss 24 inches, on center.

## 10 INSTALLING THE ROOF

Cut the 5/8-inch x 4-foot x 7-foot plywood roof panels (N) to size. Remember that the top edge of the panels must be beveled 65° to match the rafter miter at the ridge. Center the panel so there is a 6-inch overhang on each end of the cabin. Fasten the panels into the rafters using 6d common nails, 6 inches on center.

Cut out the triangular eave caps (O) and attach to the eave framing using 6d nails. Decorative 1 x 4 trim pieces (P) can also be nailed to the eave caps. These trim pieces are the same size as the truss rafters that were cut earlier—4 foot long with a 65° miter at the ridge.

## 11 SHINGLING

Cover the roof with overlapping layers of 15-pound roofing felt, tacking it in place with several 3/4-inch roofing nails. Shingles are installed from the bottom up. The very first row is installed upside down and covered with the second row. This fills in all exposed areas at the cutouts and creates two layers of shingles along the bottom edge of the roof.

End shingles are also trimmed to create a staggered pattern as shown. Install each full shingle with three roofing nails positioned above the coverage line for the next row of shingles.

For the ridge, cut shingles in thirds and nail them over the ridge, overlapping the previous shingle to cover its nail heads.

**CONSTRUCTING THE ROOF TRUSSES**

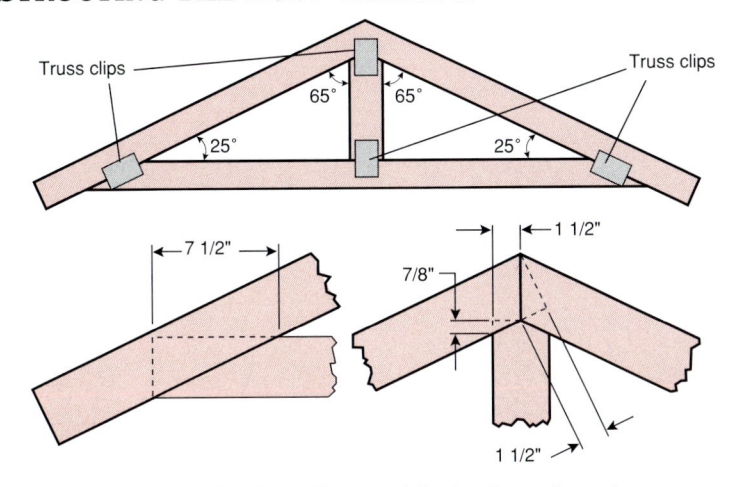

Use metal truss clips to assemble the roof trusses following these dimensions.

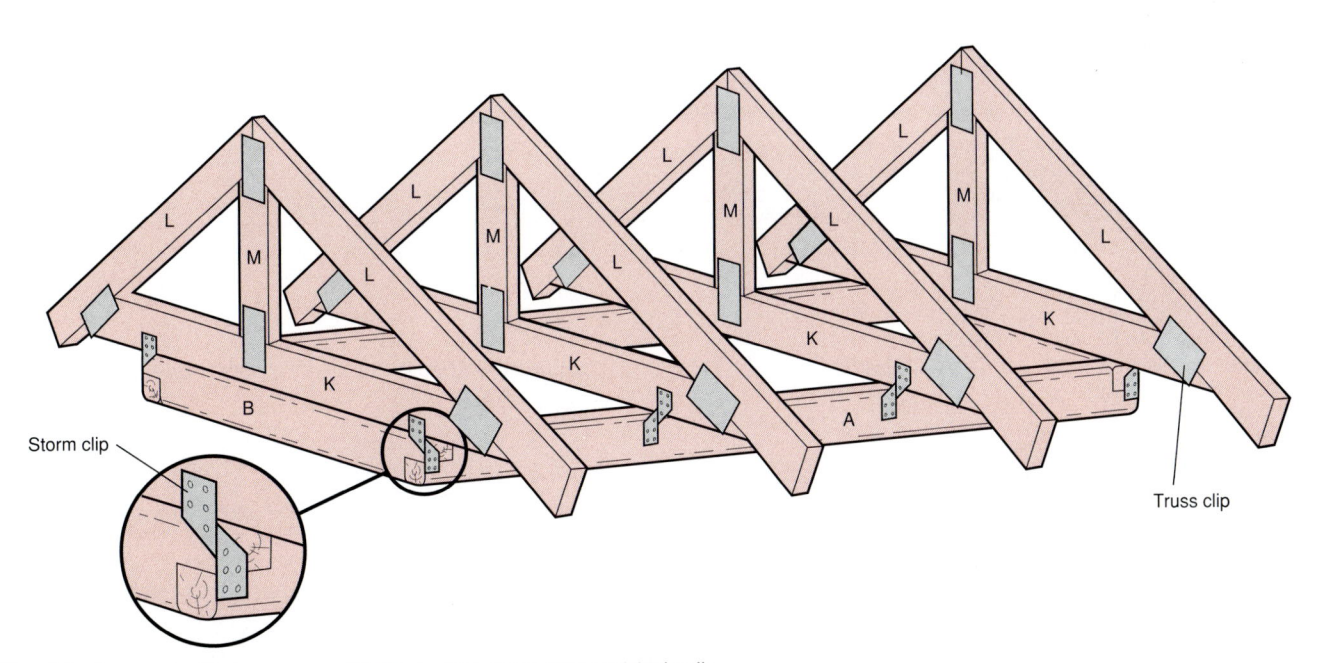

Mount the trusses on the top course of timbers using storm clips and 20d nails.

77

*projects for playhouses*

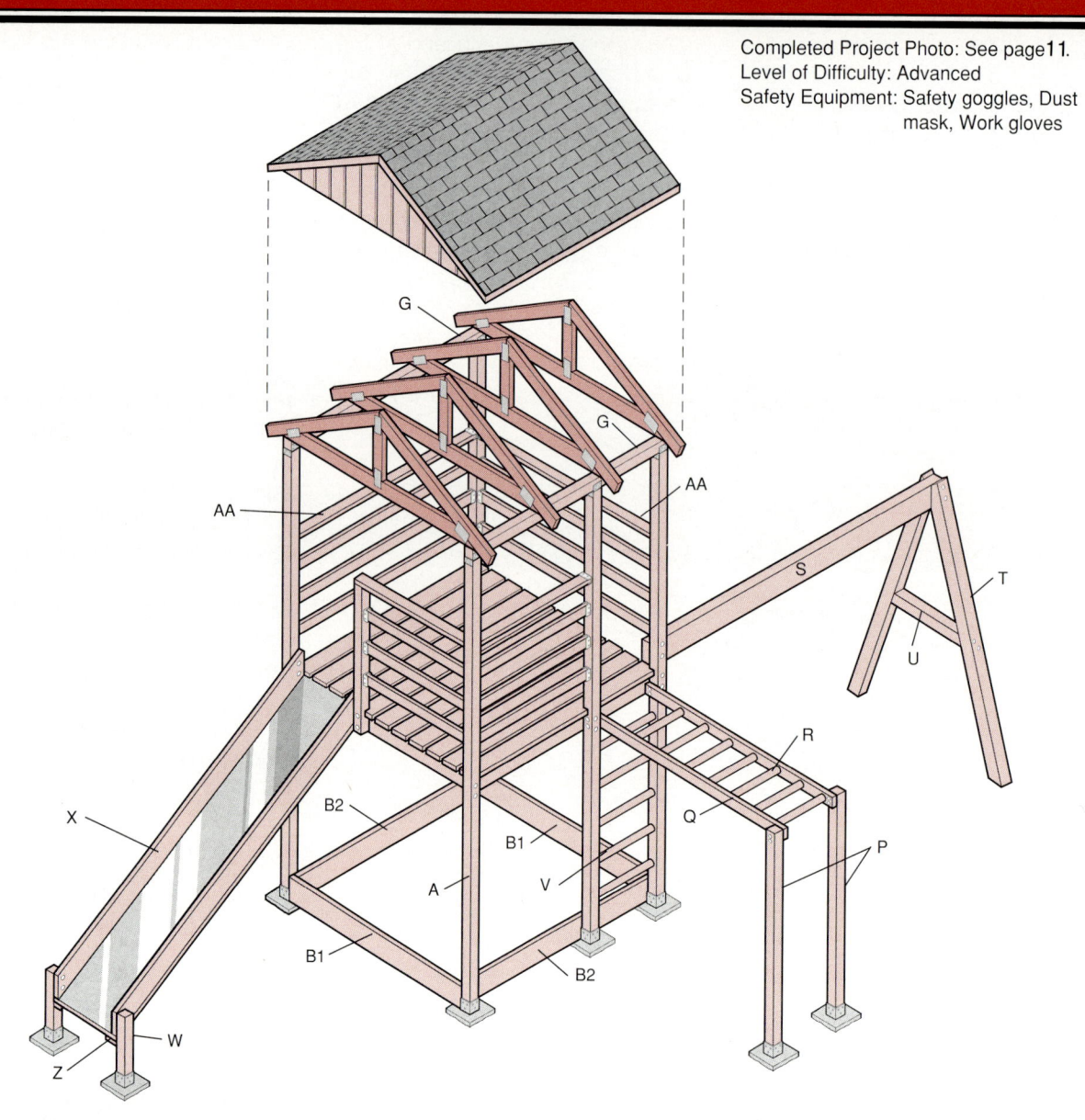

# Elevated Playhouse

Completed Project Photo: See page 11.
Level of Difficulty: Advanced
Safety Equipment: Safety goggles, Dust mask, Work gloves

## MATERIALS, PARTS, AND CUTTING LIST

| Material/Part Name | Qty. | Size |
|---|---|---|
| Pressure-treated #2 select pine | 5 | 4 x 4 x 12' |
| (A) Tower posts | 5 | 3 1/2" x 3 1/2" x 144" |
| Pressure-treated #2 select pine | 5 | 4 x 4 x 8' |
| (E) Deck rail post | 1 | 3 1/2" x 3 1/2" x 48" |
| (P) Overhead rung side rails | 2 | 1 1/2" x 3 1/2" x 70" |
| (T) A-frame legs | 2 | 3 1/2" x 3 1/2" x 93" |
| (U) A-frame cross brace | 1 | 3 1/2" x 3 1/2" x 36" |
| (W) Lower slide support posts | 2 | 3 1/2" x 3 1/2" x 20" |
| Pressure-treated #2 select pine | 2 | 4 x 4 x 6' |
| (G) Roof beams | 2 | 3 1/2" x 3 1/2" x 72" |
| Pressure-treated select pine | 4 | 2 x 8 x 6' |
| (B1) Long sandbox sides | 2 | 1 1/2" x 7 1/4" x 65" |
| (B2) Short sandbox sides | 2 | 1 1/2" x 7 1/4" x 62" |
| Pressure-treated #2 select pine | 2 | 2 x 8 x 10' |
| (X) Slide sides | 2 | 1 1/2" x 7 1/4" x 120" |
| Pressure-treated #2 select pine | 17 | 2 x 6 x 6' |
| (C) Deck beams | 2 | 1 1/2" x 5 1/2" x 72" |
| (D) Deck joists | 4 | 1 1/2" x 5 1/2" x 62" |

| Material/Part Name | Qty. | Size |
|---|---|---|
| (F) Deck boards | 11 | 1 1/2" x 5 1/2" x 72" |
| Pressure-treated #2 select pine | 1 | 4 x 6 x 10' |
| (S) Overhead swing beam | 1 | 3 1/2" x 5 1/2" x 120" |
| Pressure-treated #2 select pine | 15 | 2 x 4 x 6' |
| (H) Truss cross brace | 4 | 1 1/2" x 3 1/2" x 72" |
| (J) Center supports | 4 | 1 1/2" x 3 1/2" x 13 1/2" |
| (Q) Overhead rung side rails | 2 | 1 1/2" x 3 1/2" x 72" |
| (AA) Full side rails | 8 | 1 1/2" x 3 1/2" x 65" |
| Pressure-treated #2 select pine | 8 | 2 x 4 x 8' |
| (I) Rafters | 8 | 1 1/2" x 3 1/2" x 48" |
| (BB) Medium side rails | 4 | 1 1/2" x 3 1/2" x 41 1/2" |
| (CC) Short side rails | 4 | 1 1/2" x 3 1/2" x 49 1/2" |
| Pressure-treated #2 select pine | 4 | 1 x 4 x 6' |
| (N) Eave base trim | 2 | 3/4" x 3 1/2" x 72" |
| (O) Rafter edging side rails | 2 | 3/4" x 3 1/2" x 72" |
| Pressure-treated #2 select pine | 4 | 1 x 4 x 4' |
| (M) Eave rafter trim | 4 | 3/4" x 3 1/2" x 48" |

# projects for playhouses

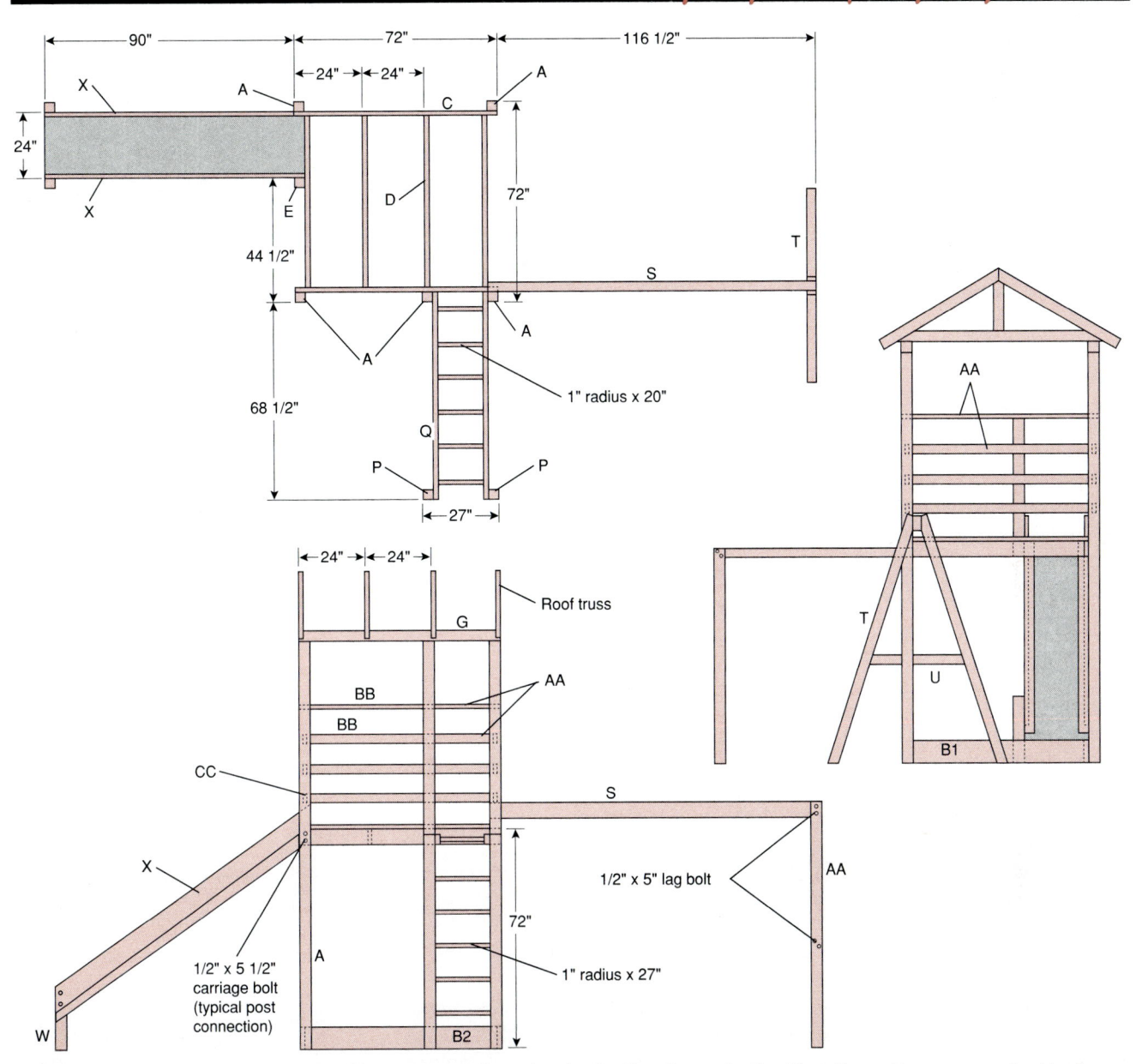

These overall views of the completed unit show important dimension details. Note that on the Top View, the roof trusses are not yet in place.

## MATERIALS, PARTS, AND CUTTING LIST (CONTINUED)

| Material/Part Name | Qty. | Size |
|---|---|---|
| Texture 1-11 plywood | 2 | 5/8" x 4' x 8' |
| (K) Roof panels | 2 | 5/8" x 48" x 84" |
| Texture 1-11 plywood | 3 | 3/4" x 4' x 8' |
| (L) Eave caps | 2 | 3/4" triangle (Base 86 1/2"; sides 48"; height 21 3/4") |
| (Y) Slide bottom | 1 | 3/4" x 24" x 120" |
| (Z) Slide cleats | 1 | 1 1/2" x 3 1/2" x 120" |
| Hardwood dowels | 5 | 1"-dia. x 3' |
| (V) Ladder rungs | 5 | 1"-dia. x 27" |
| Hardwood dowels | 6 | 1"-dia. x 2' |
| (R) Overhead rungs | 6 | 1"-dia. x 20" |
| Metal roof flashing | 1 | 2' x 10' |
| Roofing felt | 1 | 15-lb. roll |
| Shingles | 2 | bundles |
| Joist hangers | 8 | |
| Rafter ties | 8 | |
| Post base ties | 9 | |

| Material/Part Name | Qty. | Size |
|---|---|---|
| Beam clips | 5 | |
| Fence brackets | 31 | |
| Truss clips | 32 | |
| Galvanized roofing nails | 1 lb. | 3/4" |
| Galvanized barbed nails | 2 lb. | 1 1/2" |
| Galvanized decking nails | 1 lb. | 10d |
| Galvanized common nails | 1 lb. | 10d |
| Galvanized finishing nails | 1 lb. | 6d |
| Galvanized lag bolts | 8 | 1/2" x 5" |
| Galvanized carriage bolts | 24 | 1/2" x 5 1/2" |
| Galvanized carriage bolts | 2 | 1/2" x 8" |
| Galvanized flat washers | 34 | 1/2" |
| Nuts | 26 | 1/2" |
| Premixed concrete | | 50-lb. bags |
| Sand | | 50-lb. bags |
| Wood lattice | | |

79

## projects for playhouses

This playhouse combines a slide, an overhead set of bars, swings, and a tire swing to provide as many opportunities for imagination and exercise as possible. Pressure-treated pine is used to provide weather resistance, and various types of structural wood connectors are used to simplify construction and provide maximum strength at joints.

Round or bevel all wood edges and deburr all metal parts with a metal file before beginning construction.

With the "use zone" figured in, the elevated playhouse requires an area at least 27 feet long and 16 feet wide for optimum safety.

### 1 SETTING THE ELEVATED PLAYHOUSE POSTS

Layout the locations of the five playhouse tower posts. Be sure the post locations form a true square by using the rule of right triangles or by measuring the diagonals of the square formed.

The posts will be set on top of concrete footers using metal post base ties set in the concrete. Each footer should extend down at least 18 inches (depending on the local frost line levels in your area, the footers may have to be set deeper in the ground). Use a hard cardboard tube form to place the footers. Dig each hole to the required depth, position the form and temporary bracing, and place the concrete.

After allowing the concrete to cure overnight, attach the five 4 x 4 x 12-foot tower posts to the post base ties using 1 1/2-inch barbed nails. Before attaching the ladder upright posts, measure and drill the 1-inch-diameter holes for the ladder rungs. Hole depth should be 1 inch. Install the 2-foot 3-inch rungs into the ladder posts before securing the second ladder upright to its anchor by nailing.

### SETTING THE ELEVATED PLAYHOUSE POSTS

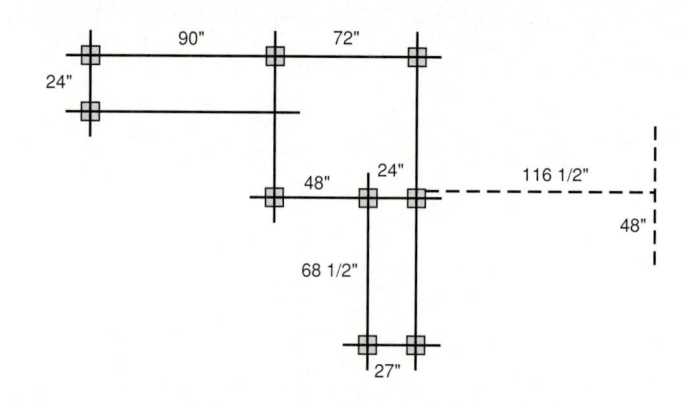

Layout the locations of the postholes according to this diagram. Dashed lines are used to represent the swing A-frame, since no posts are sunk for this portion of the playhouse.

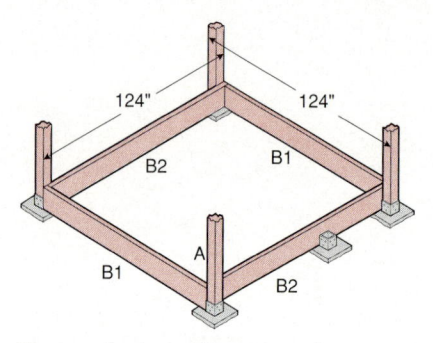

Be sure the layout is square when setting the tower post locations.

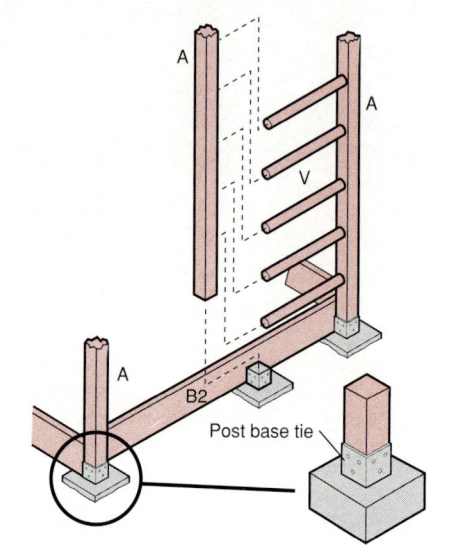

After the concrete footers have cured, proceed with the tower post mounting and ladder rung installation.

### 2 INSTALLING THE SANDBOX

Attach the four 2 x 8 x 6-foot sandbox sides (B) to the outside of the tower posts using 10d galvanized nails.

### 3 CONSTRUCTING THE ELEVATED DECK

Measure up 6 feet on the five tower posts (A). This will be the location of the top edge of the deck beams (C). Use a string or level to make certain you are working at the same height on all five posts.

Mark out and drill holes through the posts for the two 1/2- x 5-inch carriage bolts that are used to attach the two 2 x 6 x 6-foot beams (G) to the posts. Drill matching holes in the beams and bolt them to the posts.

Install the four 2 x 6 x 5-foot 2-inch deck joists (D) between these beams using metal joist hangers at each end. Position and attach the 4 x 4 x 4-foot slide support/rail post (E) to the outer joist using two 1/2- x 5 1/2-inch carriage bolts, washers, and nuts.

Install the 2 x 6 x 6-foot deck boards (F) perpendicular to the joists using 10d decking nails with three nails at each joist location. Install the deck boards bark side up to minimize cupping.

## projects for playhouses

### CONSTRUCTING THE ELEVATED DECK

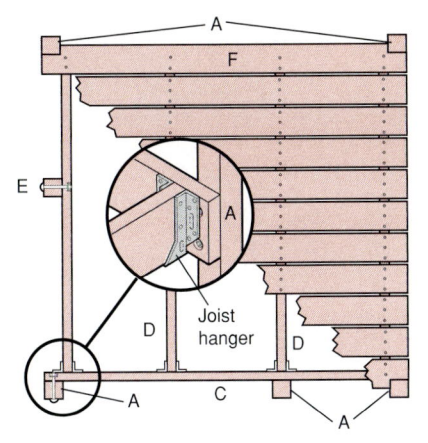

Space the decking 1/4-inch apart to allow rainwater drainage.

### 4 INSTALLING THE PLAYHOUSE RAILING

Install the 2 x 4 railing pieces (AA, BB, and CC) between the tower posts. There are three equally spaced rungs of railing between the posts, plus a rail cap piece. The railing can be toe-nailed to the posts, using 10d common nails, but metal fence brackets and 1 1/2-inch barbed nails make installation easier as shown.

### 5 ROOF BEAM INSTALLATION

Recheck the level of the top of the tower posts before installing the two

### INSTALLING THE PLAYHOUSE RAILING

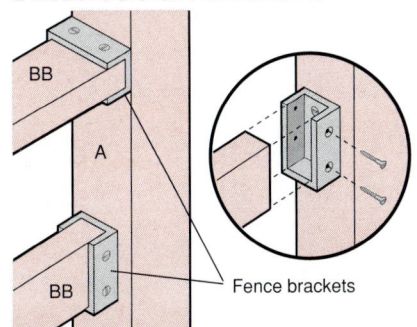

Fence brackets make installing railing easy.

### ROOF BEAM INSTALLATION

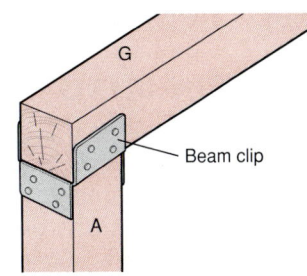

The roof beams are installed using beam clips and barbed nails.

4 x 4 x 6-foot roof beams with beam clips using 1 1/2-inch barbed nails.

### 6 CONSTRUCTING THE ROOF TRUSSES

The roof is supported by four trusses equally spaced 24 inches, on center. Trusses are constructed of 2 x 4 lumber. Each truss consists of a 6-foot truss cross brace (H), two 4-foot rafters (I), and a 13 1/2-inch center support (J). Pieces are joined using metal truss clips that are nailed over adjoining pieces.

As shown, each end of the cross braces is mitered at a 25° angle. This angle can be laid out using a T-bevel or combination set, or by measuring in along the top edge of the piece 7 1/2 inches and drawing a line between this point and the bottom edge of the piece.

The top edges of the 4-foot rafters must be cut with a matching 65° miter to form the joint at the ridge of the roof. You can lay out this angle by measuring down along the bottom edge of the rafter 1 5/8 inches and drawing a line

### CONSTRUCTING THE ROOF TRUSSES

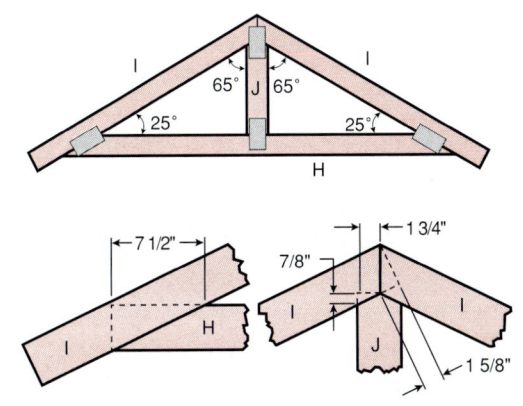

Test-fit the first truss before cutting parts for other trusses.

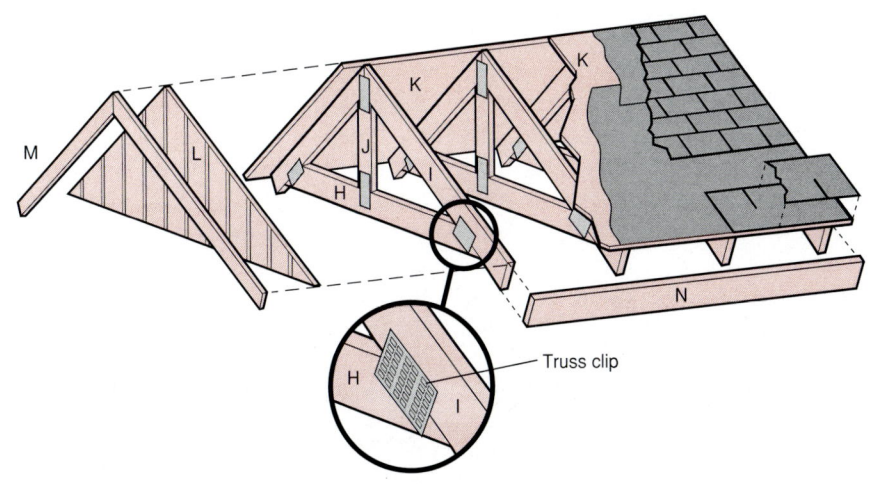

Use this illustration as a guide for truss, roof, eave, shingling, and trim details.

## projects for playhouses

between this point and the top edge of the rafter.

Create the pointed tip at the top of the center support by measuring down from the top edges of the piece 7/8 inch and connecting these two points to the center point of the top as shown.

Cut the pieces for one truss and test-fit before cutting the others. Join the pieces using four truss clips positioned as shown. Secure the clips with 1 1/2-inch barbed nails.

The assembled trusses rest on the 4 x 4 roof beams and are joined to them using storm clips and 1 1/2-inch barbed nails. Center the overhang on each side of the cabin and position each truss 24 inches, on center.

### 7 INSTALLING THE ROOF

Cut the two 5/8-inch x 4-foot x 7-foot plywood roof panels (K) to size. Keep in mind that the top edge of the panels must be beveled 65° to match the rafter miter at the ridge. Center the panels so there is a 6-inch overhang on each end of the playhouse. Fasten the panels into the rafters using 1 1/2-inch barbed nails 6 inches, on center.

Eave caps (L) can be constructed of plywood. This project uses texture 1-11 plywood with 3/8-inch wide, 1/4-inch deep grooves. Cut out the triangular caps and install to the end trusses. Decorative 1 x 4 trim pieces (M, N, O) can also be installed to the eave caps. These trim pieces are the same size as the rafters and truss cross braces cut earlier. They also use the same mitered angles. A 1 x 4 x 6-foot trim piece can also be nailed to the ends of the roof rafters to give this edge a finished look. Use 6d finishing nails.

### 8 SHINGLING

Cover the roof with overlapping layers of 15-pound roofing felt, tacking it in place with several 3/4-inch roofing nails. Shingles are installed from the bottom up. The very first row is installed upside down and covered with the second row. This fills in all exposed areas at the cutouts and creates two layers of shingles along the bottom edge of the roof.

End shingles are also trimmed to create a staggered pattern as shown. Install each full shingle with three roofing nails positioned above the coverage line for the next row of shingles.

For the ridge, cut shingles in thirds and nail them over the ridge, overlapping the previous shingle to cover its nail heads.

### 9 CONSTRUCTING THE OVERHEAD RUNGS

Lay out the two post positions for the overhead rungs (R). Dig and place the footer as with the tower posts. The post measures 5-feet 10-inches. The overhead rung side rails (Q) are made of 2 x 4 x 6-foot lumber. As with the tower ladder, lay out and drill mounting holes for the 1-inch-diameter dowel rungs in the side rails. Hole depth should be 1 inch.

Insert each of the six 1-foot 8-inch dowels into the side rails during final side-rail mounting. The side rails are mounted to their two overhead rung support posts (P) using 1/2- x 5-inch lag bolts at the tower posts and 1/2- x 5 1/2-inch carriage bolts at the outer posts.

### CONSTRUCTING THE SWING A-FRAME

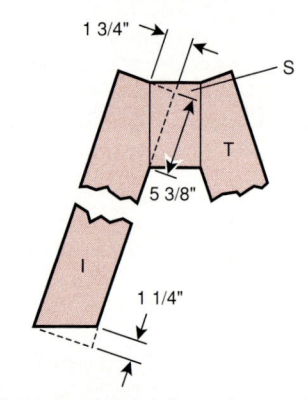

Cut the tops of the A-frame legs to these dimensions to ensure proper mounting on the 4 x 6 beam.

### 10 CONSTRUCTING THE SWING A-FRAME

Assemble the A-frame for the 4 x 6 x 10-foot overhead swing beam (S) using two 4 x 4 x 7-foot 9-inch A-frame legs (T) braced with a 4 x 4 x 36-inch cross brace (U). Fit and cut the angle on the cross brace after the overhead beam and A-frame have been installed.

Cut the top ends of the A-frame legs as shown to create an angle that will accept the 4 x 6 beam. The legs of the A-frame are fastened to the 4 x 6 beam using two 1/2- x 5-inch lag bolts and washers installed from each side. The opposite end of the beam is bolted to the corner tower post of the playhouse using two 1/2- x 8-inch carriage bolts, washers, and nuts. Check that the swing beam is level before marking out and drilling the holes for these bolts.

### 11 CONSTRUCTING THE SLIDE

Measure out 7 feet 6 inches from the side of the left rear corner post

## projects for playhouses

**CONSTRUCTING THE SLIDE**

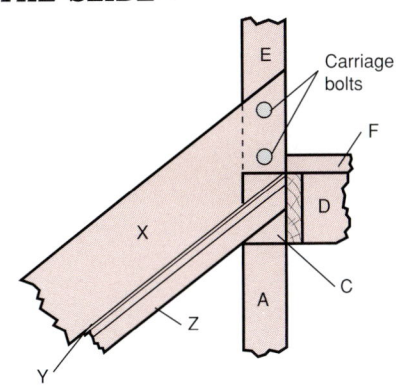

Carriage bolts are used to secure the slide to the lower slide support posts.

and spot the site for the lower slide support post (W). The second post is located 2 feet away at a right angle to this point. Place concrete footers at these points and attach the 1-foot 8-inch lower slide support posts to these footers using post base ties set in the concrete.

The slide itself is 10 feet long and 2 feet wide. The sides are constructed of 2 x 8s. The bottom (Y) is constructed of 3/4-inch plywood. Two plywood sections, one 2 feet x 8 feet and another 2 feet x 2 feet, are needed. The deburred metal roof flashing is positioned on the plywood surface before it is nailed to the bottom on the slide sides (X). Use 10d common nails for construction.

Once the flashing is sandwiched between the bottom and side pieces, the entire slide is further braced with two 2 x 4 x 10-feet cleats (Z) nailed to the bottom edges of the slide body.

The assembled slide is attached to the lower slide support posts at the top and bottom using two 1/2-inch x 5 1/2-inch carriage bolts, washers, and nuts through each post. Keep the rounded heads of the carriage bolts to the inside of the slide.

## 12 FINAL ASSEMBLY AND TRIM

Swings, tire swings, etc., should be mounted to the overhead swing beam using hardware recommended by the swing manufacturer. Any eyebolts or screw eyes used should be squeezed closed to prevent chain links from slipping off.

As shown in the photo on page 4, the open railing and underside of the playhouse roof can be covered with wood lattice. In addition to closing off the openings between the rails, the lattice gives the playhouse a finished appearance. Check that all metal flashing is deburred and any wood splinters have been removed. The pressure-treated pine can be sealed with a clear protective coating or allowed to weather. It can also be painted or stained, although it is advisable to allow the wood to weather naturally for at least two seasons before applying paint or stain.

*projects for playhouses*

# PLAY CASTLE

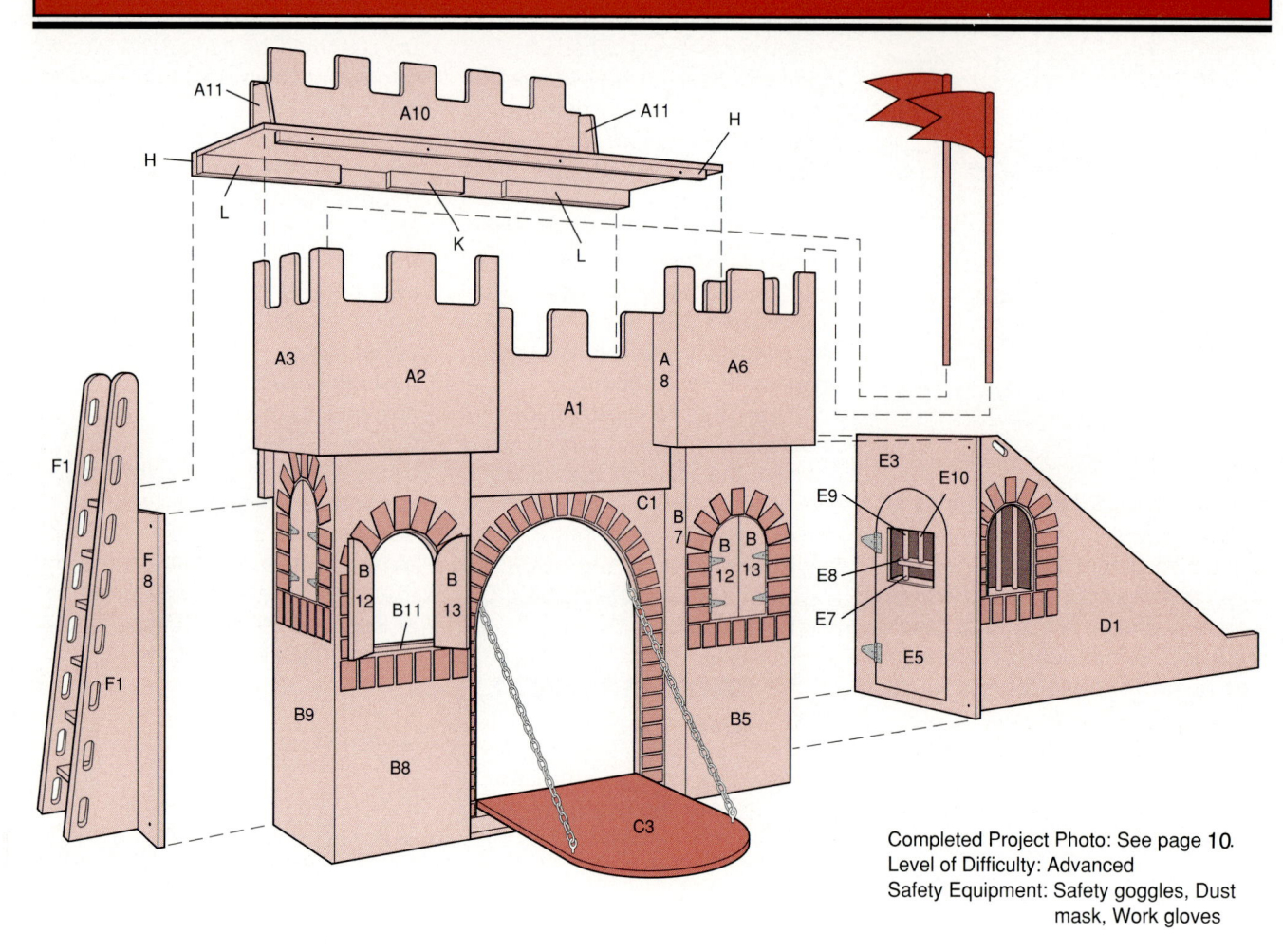

Completed Project Photo: See page 10.
Level of Difficulty: Advanced
Safety Equipment: Safety goggles, Dust mask, Work gloves

## MATERIALS, PARTS, AND CUTTING LIST

| Material/Part Name | Qty. | Size |
|---|---|---|
| Medium-density overlay plywood, or A-B or A-C grade exterior plywood, or waferboard or oriented strand board | 5 | 3/4" x 4' x 8' |
| (A1) Front turret | 1 | 3/4" x 24" x 34 1/2" |
| (A2) Left front turret | 1 | 3/4" x 24" x 24 1/4" |
| (A3) Left side turret | 1 | 3/4" x 24" x 23 1/2" |
| (A4) Left inside turret | 1 | 3/4" x 5 1/4" x 24" |
| (A5) Left turret back piece | 1 | 3/4" x 6" x 30" |
| (A6) Right front turret | 1 | 3/4" x 24" x 24 1/4" |
| (A7) Right side turret | 1 | 3/4" x 23 1/2" x 24" |
| (A8) Right inside turret piece | 1 | 3/4" x 5 1/4" x 24" |
| (A9) Right turret back piece | 1 | 3/4" x 6" x 30" |
| (A10) Back turret | 1 | 3/4" x 21" x 60" |
| (A11) Back turret supports | 2 | 3/4" x 3 1/2" x 11" |
| (A12) Back turret extensions | 2 | 3/4" x 4" x 7 1/4" |
| (B1) Right tower floor | 1 | 3/4" x 22 1/2" x 22 3/4" |
| (B2) Left tower floor | 1 | 3/4" x 22 3/4" x 22 3/4" |
| (B3) Right tower riser | 1 | 3/4" x 6" x 24 3/8" |
| (B4) Left tower riser | 1 | 3/4" x 6" x 24 3/8" |
| (B5) Right tower front | 1 | 3/4" x 18 1/4" x 48" |
| (B6) Right tower side | 1 | 3/4" x 20 5/8" x 48" |
| (B7) Right tower inside wall | 1 | 3/4" x 6" x 48" |

| Material/Part Name | Qty. | Size |
|---|---|---|
| (B8) Left tower front | 1 | 3/4" x 18 1/4" x 48" |
| (B9) Left tower side | 1 | 3/4" x 20 5/8" x 48" |
| (B10) Left tower inside wall | 1 | 3/4" x 6" x 48" |
| (B11) Tower shelves | 2 | 3/4" x 5" x 16 3/4" |
| (B12) Left-hand tower shutters | 4 | 3/4" x 5" x 14" |
| (B13) Right-hand tower shutters | 4 | 3/4" x 5" x 14" |
| (B14) Shutter stops | 4 | 3/4" x 1" x 10" |
| (C1) Front drawbridge wall | 1 | 3/4" x 34 1/2" x 42" |
| (C2) Entryway sill | 1 | 3/4" x 6" x 34 1/2" |
| (C3) Drawbridge | 1 | 3/4" x 26 1/2" x 36 1/4" |
| (C4) Drawbridge stops | 2 | 3/4" x 1 1/2" x 6" |
| (D1) Slide front side | 1 | 3/4" x 41 3/4" x 61 3/8" |
| (D2) Slide back side | 1 | 3/4" x 41 3/4" x 61 3/8" |
| (D3) Slide landing | 1 | 3/4" x 12" x 18 3/4" |
| (D4) Slide | 1 | 3/4" x 18 3/4" x 52 3/8" |
| (D5) Lower slide landing | 1 | 3/4" x 8" x 18 3/4" |
| (D6) Slide front | 1 | 3/4" x 3 1/2" x 18 3/4" |
| (E1) Dungeon seat | 1 | 3/4" x 9" x 18 3/4" |
| (E2) Dungeon door stop | 1 | 3/4" x 1 3/4" x 5" |
| (E3) Dungeon wall | 1 | 3/4" x 23" x 41 3/4" |
| (E4) Dungeon back wall | 1 | 3/4" x 18 3/4" x 23 3/4" |
| (E5) Dungeon door | 1 | 3/4" x 10 7/8" x 31 1/2" |

84

## projects for playhouses

This play castle is loaded with details that will bring your children's medieval fantasies to life—towers, barred windows, a real drawbridge, and even a dungeon. Your backyard knights, kings, and queens can lower the drawbridge and cross the "moat" to enter this two-story castle. A ladder leads to the look out towers and walkway, which are complete with flags. A slide makes for a quick escape back to the lower level. The dungeon is located under the slide.

This project is unique in that it is constructed entirely of 3/4-inch thick sheathing. Medium density overlay plywood is the finest wood for this type of work. Other less expensive grades, such as A-B or A-C grade exterior plywood, or nonveneer structural wood panels such as waferboard or oriented strand board can be used. In the castle pictured, waferboard panels were used on the castle front to give it a textured finish. Medium density overlay plywood was used for all other sections.

The plywood is thick enough to eliminate the need for traditional framing and supports in most cases. Castle panels are simply cut to size and assembled using glued butt joints secured with 10d finishing nails spaced 18 inches, on center. Careful pattern layout and cutting is required to attain the smooth, accurately matched butt joints needed for assembly, so measure, mark, and cut very carefully.

The castle is assembled in four main sections: the lower front section, the upper front turret section, the ladder and back turret section, and the slide/dungeon section. When all four sections are complete, the castle can be set up in its final location and all sections bolted together to form a single unit.

With the "use zone" figured in, the play castle requires an area at least 17 feet long and 11 feet wide for optimum safety.

## 1 LAYING OUT THE PATTERNS

A major portion of this project is laying out the cutting patterns on the five pieces of 3/4-inch x 4-foot x 8-foot sheathing. Follow the panel layouts given, drawing all parts on the panels using a straightedge and framing square for accuracy. Use a compass to draw the corner radii. Be sure to check the width of your saw blade kerf and allow for saw kerfs when plotting dimensions. Check all dimensions, measuring twice and cutting once. Check dimensions of pieces in relation to one another to assure, for example, that butted sides are the same length.

## 2 CUTTING

When hand-sawing, support the panel firmly with the best side facing up. Use a 10 to 15 point crosscut saw. Use a fine-toothed coping saw for curves. For inside cuts, start a hole with a drill and use a coping or keyhole saw. When power sawing on a radial or table saw, the best side of the panel should be face up. A plywood blade gives excellent results, but a sharp combination blade may be used. When using a portable power saw, the best side of the

### MATERIALS, PARTS, AND CUTTING LIST (CONTINUED)

| Material/Part Name | Qty. | Size |
|---|---|---|
| (E6) Dungeon door top windowsill | 1 | 3/4" x 3" x 10" |
| (E7) Dungeon door bottom windowsill | 1 | 3/4" x 3" x 10" |
| (E8) Dungeon door bar support | 1 | 3/4" x 1" x 8" |
| (E9) Dungeon door window bars (long) | 2 | 3/4" x 1 1/2" x 9" |
| (E10) Dungeon door window bars (short) | 1 | 3/4" x 1 1/2" x 9" |
| (E11) Dungeon wall windowsills | 2 | 3/4" x 3" x 10" |
| (E12) Dungeon wall window bars | 3 | 3/4" x 1" x 10" |
| (E13) Dungeon door stop | 1 | 3/4" x 1 3/4" x 5" |
| (F1) Ladder rails | 2 | 3/4" x 8 7/8" x 59 3/4" |
| (F2) 1st step | 1 | 3/4" x 7 3/16" x 11 3/4" |
| (F3) 2nd step | 1 | 3/4" x 6 1/2" x 11 3/4" |
| (F4) 3rd step | 1 | 3/4" x 5 13/16" x 11 3/4" |
| (F5) 4th step | 1 | 3/4" x 5 1/8" x 11 3/4" |
| (F6) 5th step | 1 | 3/4" x 4 7/16" x 11 3/4" |
| (F7) 6th step | 1 | 3/4" x 3 3/4" x 11 3/4" |
| (F8) Ladder wall | 1 | 3/4" x 23" x 41 3/4" |
| (G) Front floor section | 1 | 3/4" x 17 1/2" x 63 1/4" |
| (H) Joists | 2 | 3/4" x 1 1/2" x 71" |
| (I) Handle | 1 | 3/4" x 3" x 12" |
| (J) Handle support | 1 | 3/4" x 3" x 12" |
| (K) Rear section floor supports (long) | 2 | 3/4" x 2 3/4" x 24" |

| Material/Part Name | Qty. | Size |
|---|---|---|
| (L) Rear section floor support (short) | 1 | 3/4" x 2 3/4" x 11 7/8" |
| (M) Flag pole holders | 4 | 3/4" x 2 3/4" x 2 3/4" |
| (N) Rear floor section | 1 | 3/4" x 21" x 75 1/2" |
| (O) Top step support | 1 | 3/4" x 1 1/2" x 6 1/2" |
| (P) Tee-nut block piece | 1 | 3/4" x 3" x 3 1/8" |
| Hardwood dowel | 1 | 1" x 8' |
| Galvanized tee-hinges | 11 sets | 3" |
| Galvanized flat head wood screws | 300 | #12 x 1 1/2" |
| Galvanized finishing nails (in place of wood screws) | 3 lb. | 10d |
| Galvanized lag bolts | 8 | 3/8" x 1 1/2" |
| Galvanized lag bolts | 2 | 3/8" x 2 1/2" |
| Washers | 10 | 3/8" |
| Galvanized tee-nuts | 10 | 3/8" |
| Pine or fir lumber strips | 2 | 1 x 3 x 10" |
| Galvanized screw eyes (open) | 2 | |
| Galvanized screw eyes (closed) | 2 | |
| Plastic chain | 1 | 7' length |
| Paste wood filler | | |
| Medium fine sandpaper | | |
| Construction adhesive or resorcinol or urea resin glue | | |
| Decorative brick veneer | | |

* See panel layouts for exact shapes, radii, and dimensions.

# projects for playhouses

## LAYING OUT THE PATTERNS

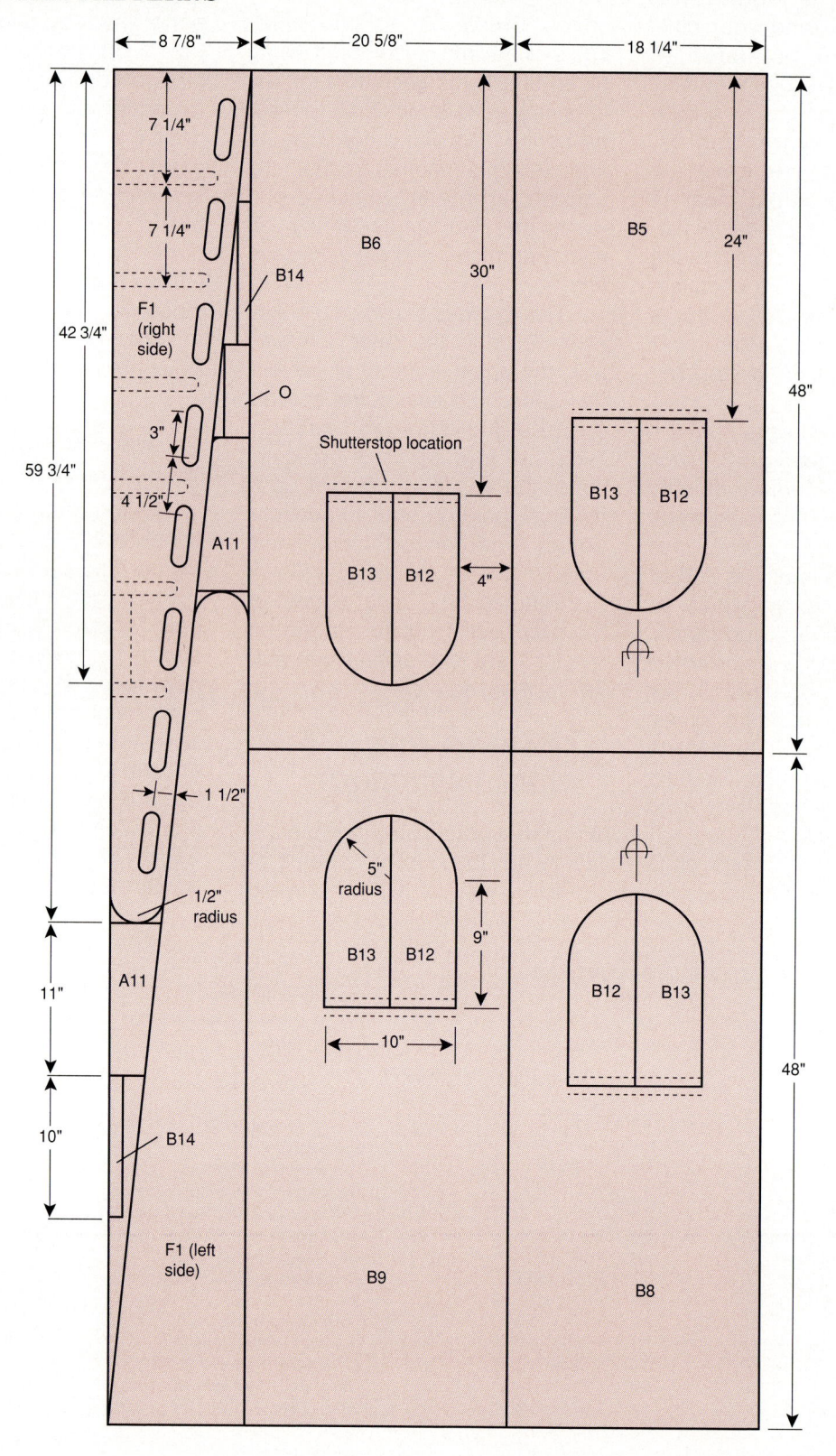

Use these panel layouts to make the five 3/4-inch x 4-foot x 8-foot panels.

**projects for playhouses**

## LAYING OUT THE PATTERNS (CONTINUED)

Panel layouts continued.

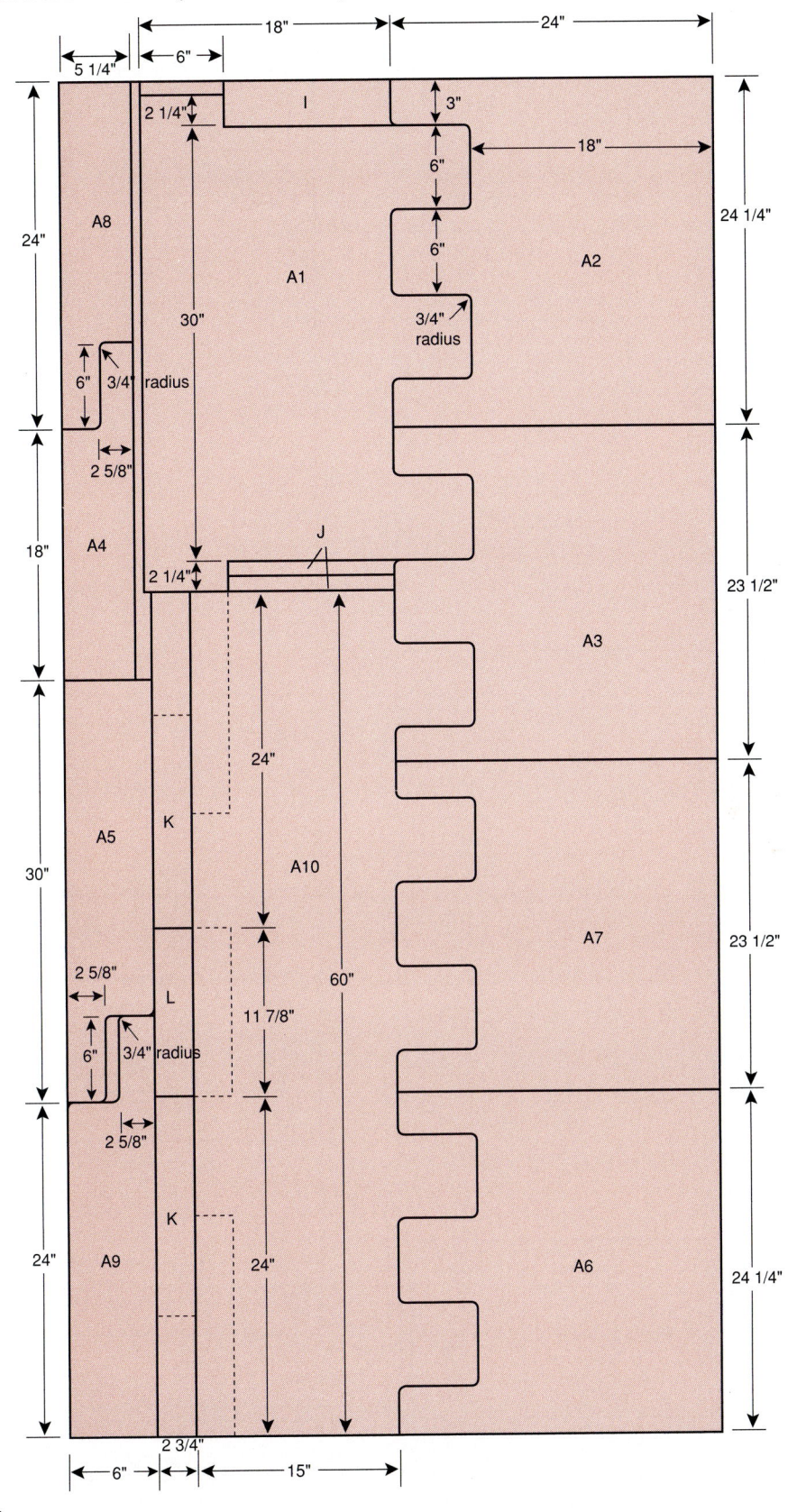

# projects for playhouses

## LAYING OUT THE PATTERNS (CONTINUED)

Panel layouts continued.

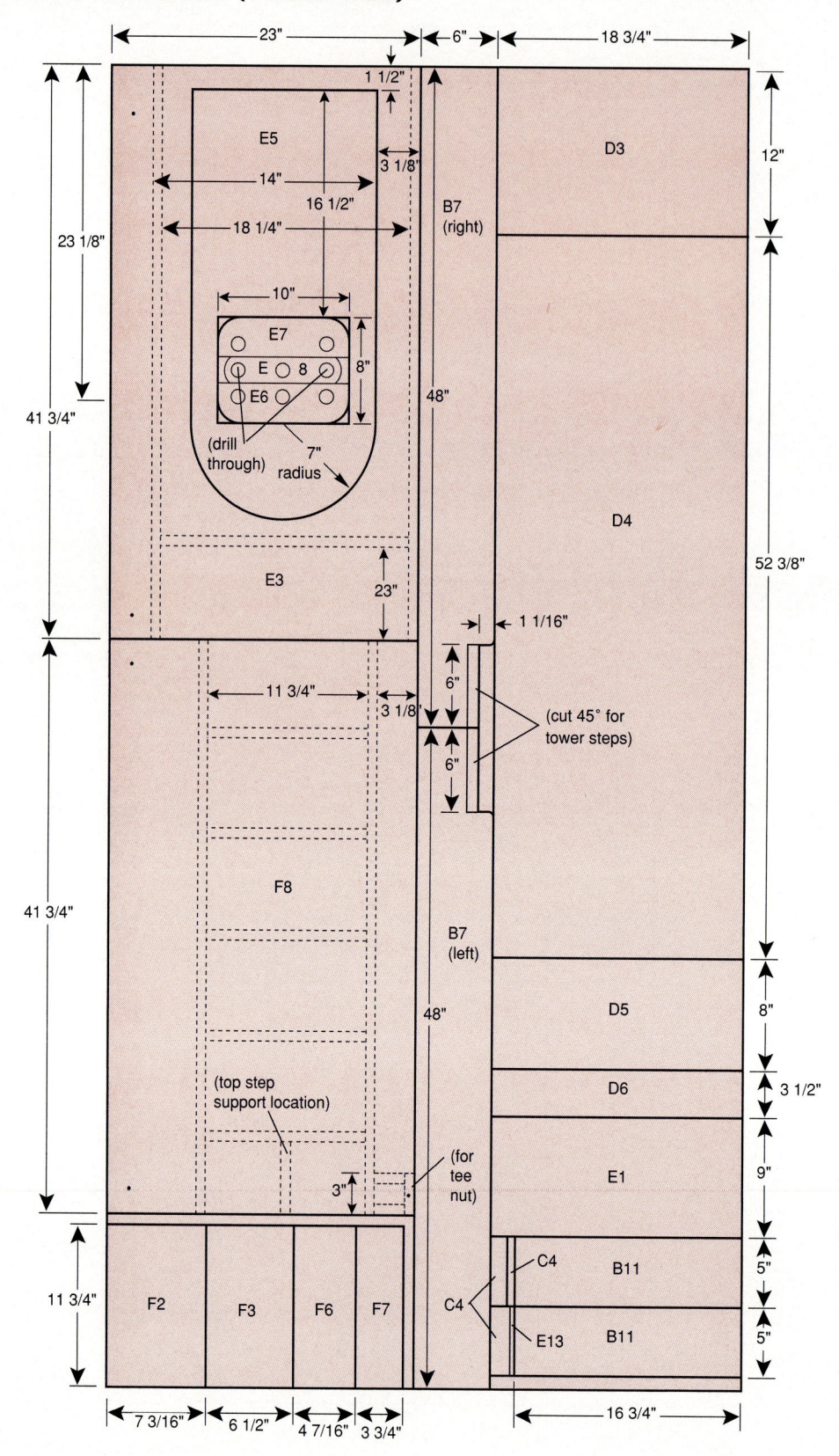

## projects for playhouses

### LAYING OUT THE PATTERNS (CONTINUED)

Panel layouts continued.

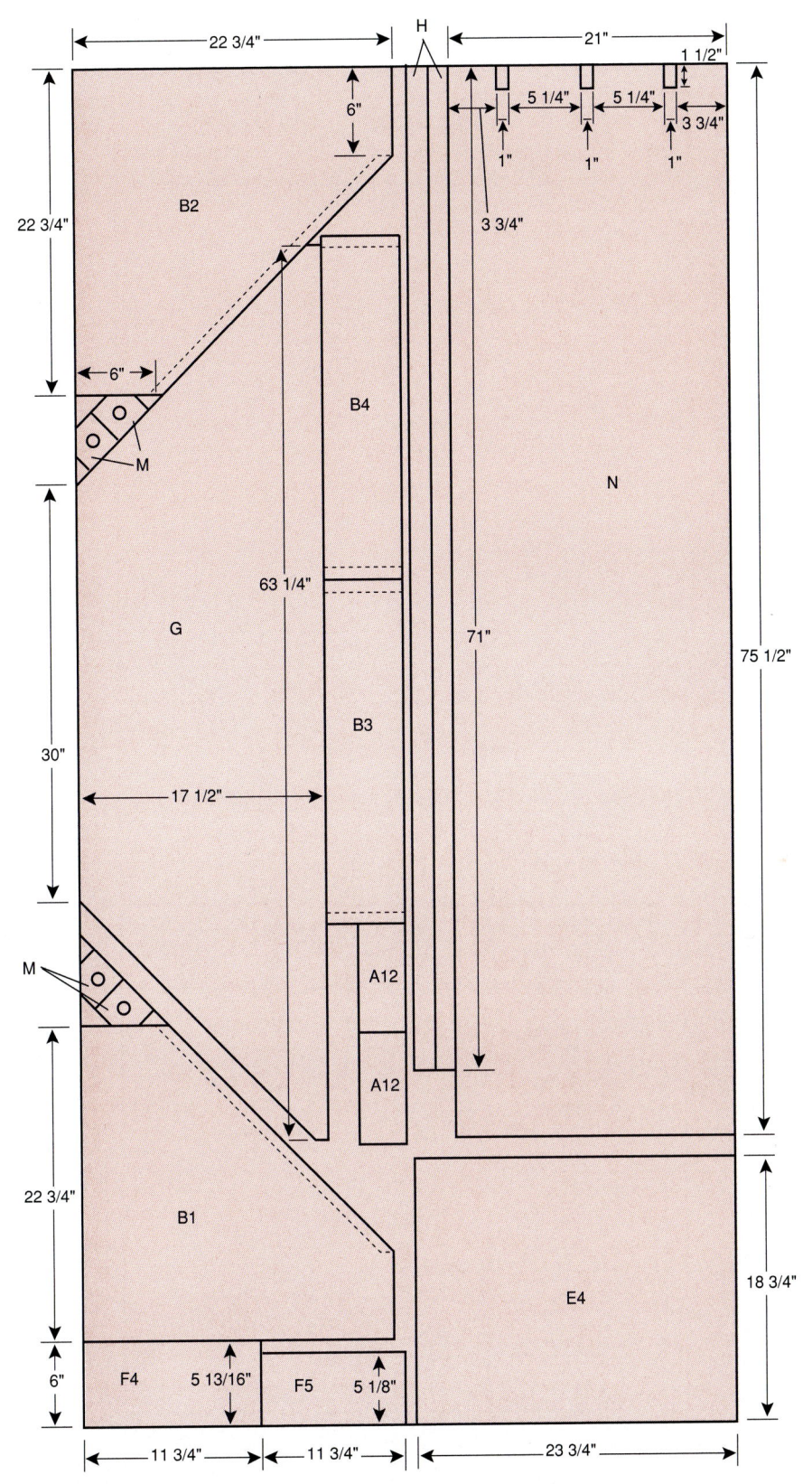

89

## projects for playhouses

**LAYING OUT THE PATTERNS (CONTINUED)**

Panel layouts continued.

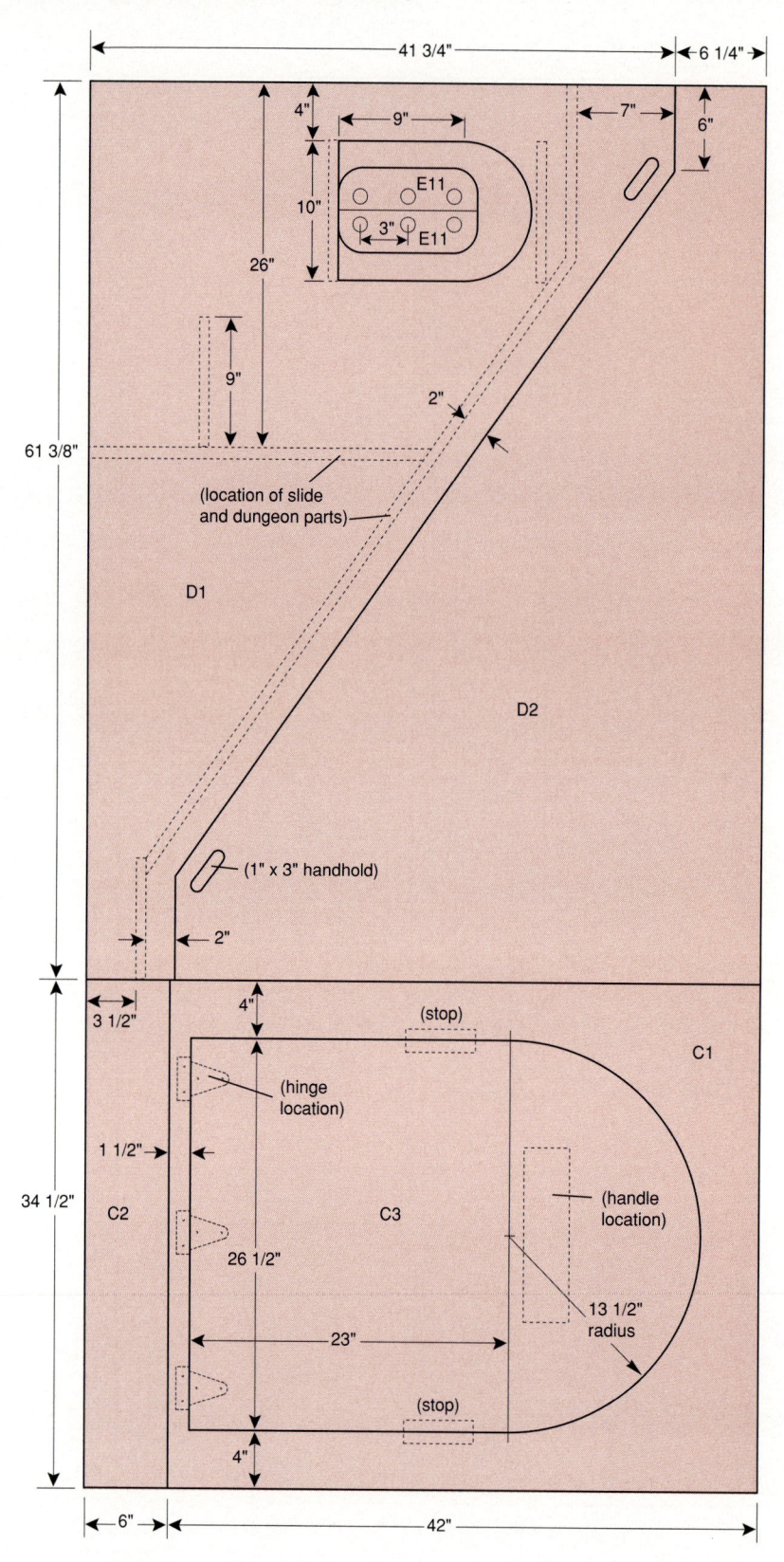

90

*projects for playhouses*

panel should be down. For curved cuts, use a saber saw or scroll saw. Be sure the blade enters the face of the panel. Use the finest tooth possible for a smooth and even cut. For prolonged cutting of nonveneer panels and those containing layers of reconstituted wood, a carbide-tipped blade is best.

Reduce the panel to pieces small enough for easy handling with first cuts. Plan to cut matching parts with the same saw setting. Scrap lumber clamped or tacked securely in place beneath the panel prevents splintering on the back side.

Overlaid panels can be worked in the same manner as regular grades with these exceptions: sawing and drilling should always be done with the cutting edge of the tool entering the panel face. To minimize chipping at the point of tool exit, use a piece of scrap wood as a backup or place tape along the cutting line.

## 3 PLANING, FILLING, AND SANDING

It is very important that the butting edges are level and smooth. Plane any rough edges using a shallow set blade and planer. Remember, the grain of the panel runs in alternate directions, so plane from the ends toward the center and use shallow cuts only.

**PLANING, FILLING, AND SANDING**

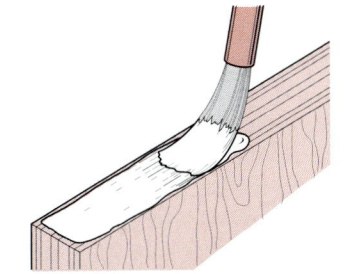

Apply paste filler to fill and seal the end grains of all pieces.

The end grain should also be filled and sealed using paste wood filler. Apply the filler to the end grain as well as any slightly splintered areas. Allow the filler to dry for several hours before sanding.

Wear a dust mask when sanding paste filler. Sand with the grain using medium to fine sandpaper to sand the paste filler smooth and to finish any rough areas on the face of the panels. The need to sand the panel face surfaces should be minimal.

You may find it more helpful to final-sand the panel edges just prior to gluing and fastening them together. In this way you can remove any irregularities that may affect the strength of the glue bond.

## 4 BASIC ASSEMBLY TIPS

Constructing the castle one section at a time makes the final assembly easier. All joints should be made using glue and screws or nails. Check for good fit by holding the pieces together. Plane or sand to attain a clean joint. Contact should be made at all points along the seam for lasting strength.

Mark nail or screw locations. Nails or screws should be placed every 4 inches, on center, to form

**BASIC ASSEMBLY TIPS**

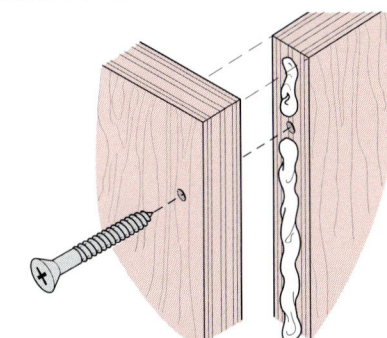

All butt joints must be glued and screwed or nailed. Position pilot holes or nails carefully; a 3/4-inch edge leaves very little room for error.

a strong joint. Screws provide the strongest joints; always predrill pilot holes for the screws. Nail holes can also be predrilled using a bit slightly smaller than the diameter of the nail.

Align holes and screws/nails carefully. Drive the screw or nail straight in. If the fastener is driven in at an angle it may splinter the back piece.

Apply glue to clean surfaces according to the instructions on the glue container. Press the joint together until a slight bead appears at the joint. Check for square and then nail or screw and apply clamps if possible to maintain pressure until the glue sets.

## 5 ASSEMBLING THE LOWER FRONT SECTION

Study the illustration to determine how all panels and pieces butt together and are joined. Begin by joining the two inside walls to the ends of the entry wall. Note how the top of the inside walls are mitered 45° to match the miter on the tower step risers used in the upper front section.

Next, attach the left and right tower fronts to the inside walls, and the left and right side tower walls to the tower fronts as shown. Remember, all joints are butt joints using glue and screws or nails. Complete the lower front section shell by installing the 3/4- x 1 1/2- x 71-inch joist piece between the top back edges of the left and right tower sides.

Attach the entryway door sill to the structure. Attach the drawbridge door using three hinges. The four sets of shutters also attach using two sets of hinges for each set of shutters. Install the shutter and door stops and the shutter shelves as illustrated. Cut the plastic chain into two equal

91

# projects for playhouses

## ASSEMBLING THE LOWER FRONT SECTION

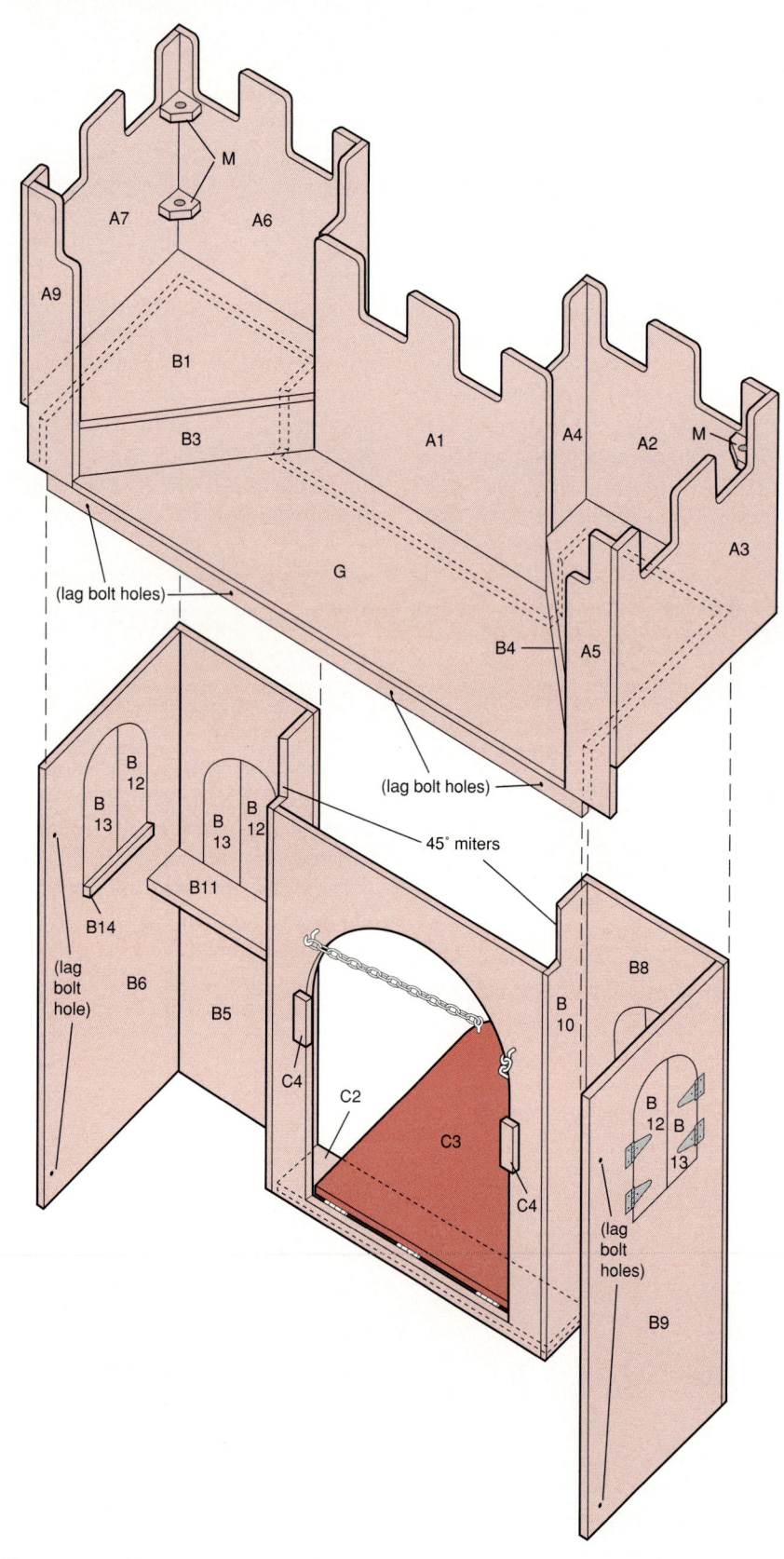

The upper and lower front turret sections are secured with lag bolts, tee-nuts, and washers.

lengths and install the screw eyes attached to the drawbridge door and entry wall. Drill 1/2-inch deep pilot holes when installing the screw eyes and take care not to penetrate through the outside wall.

## 6 ASSEMBLING THE UPPER FRONT TURRET SECTION

The upper front turret section overhangs the lower front section by 3 inches on all sides. Study the position and relationship of the upper front section pieces and how they butt and join together.

The front floor piece rests on and is attached to the joist of the lower front section. The mitered front end of the tower step risers is fastened to the mitered edge of the inside walls of the lower front section.

Assemble the left and right tower floors, and the front, side, and back turret wall pieces as shown. The flagpole holders act as corner blocks for the side and front turret walls.

Fasten the upper front section to the lower front section by screwing or nailing down through the tower floors and front floor sections.

## 7 ASSEMBLING THE LADDER AND BACK TURRET SECTION

The rear floor section is mounted to a 3/4- x 1 1/2- x 71-inch joist piece that matches the joist piece installed in the lower front section assembly. There are also three floor support pieces that help support the rear floor and tie together the floor, back turret wall, and back turret extensions. Back turret supports give rigidity to the back turret wall.

The ladder wall is fastened to the rear floor section, joist, and left floor support. The ladder consists of two rails and six steps 7 1/4 inches apart. Attach the steps to

92

*projects for playhouses*

## ASSEMBLING THE LADDER AND BACK TURRET SECTION

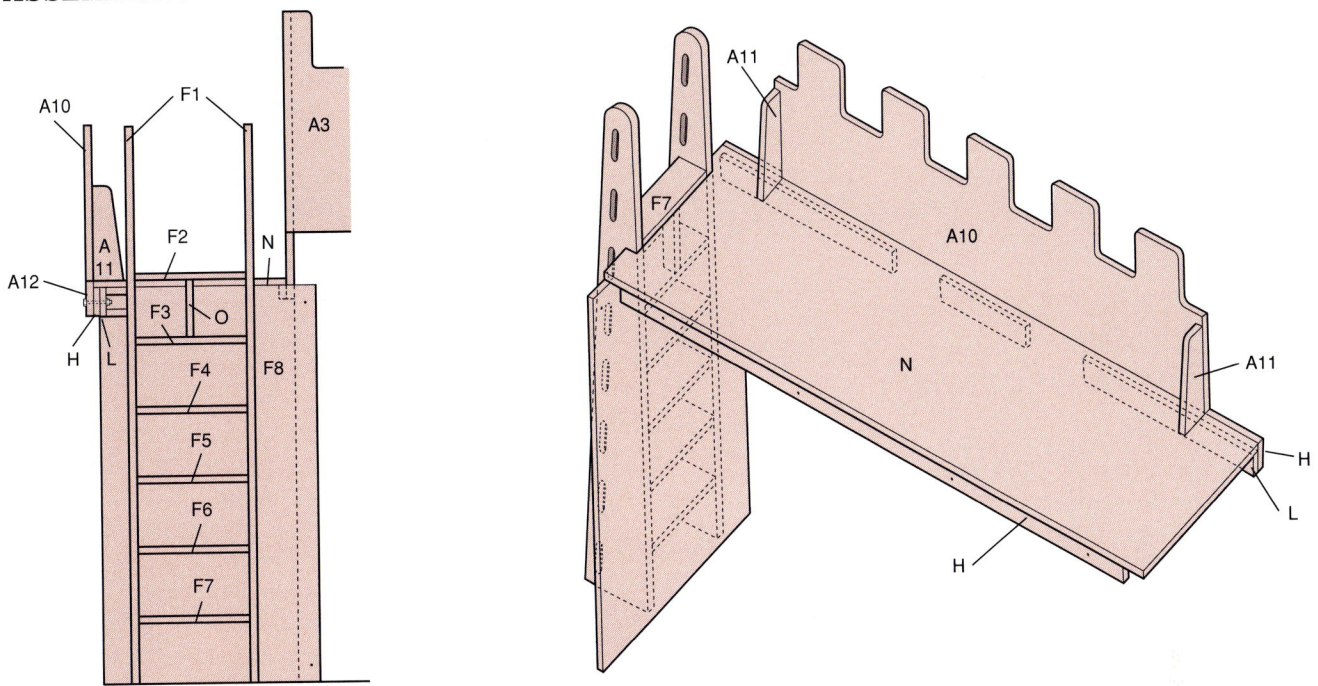

Assemble the ladder and back turret section as shown in these detail drawings.

## ASSEMBLING THE SLIDE AND DUNGEON SECTION

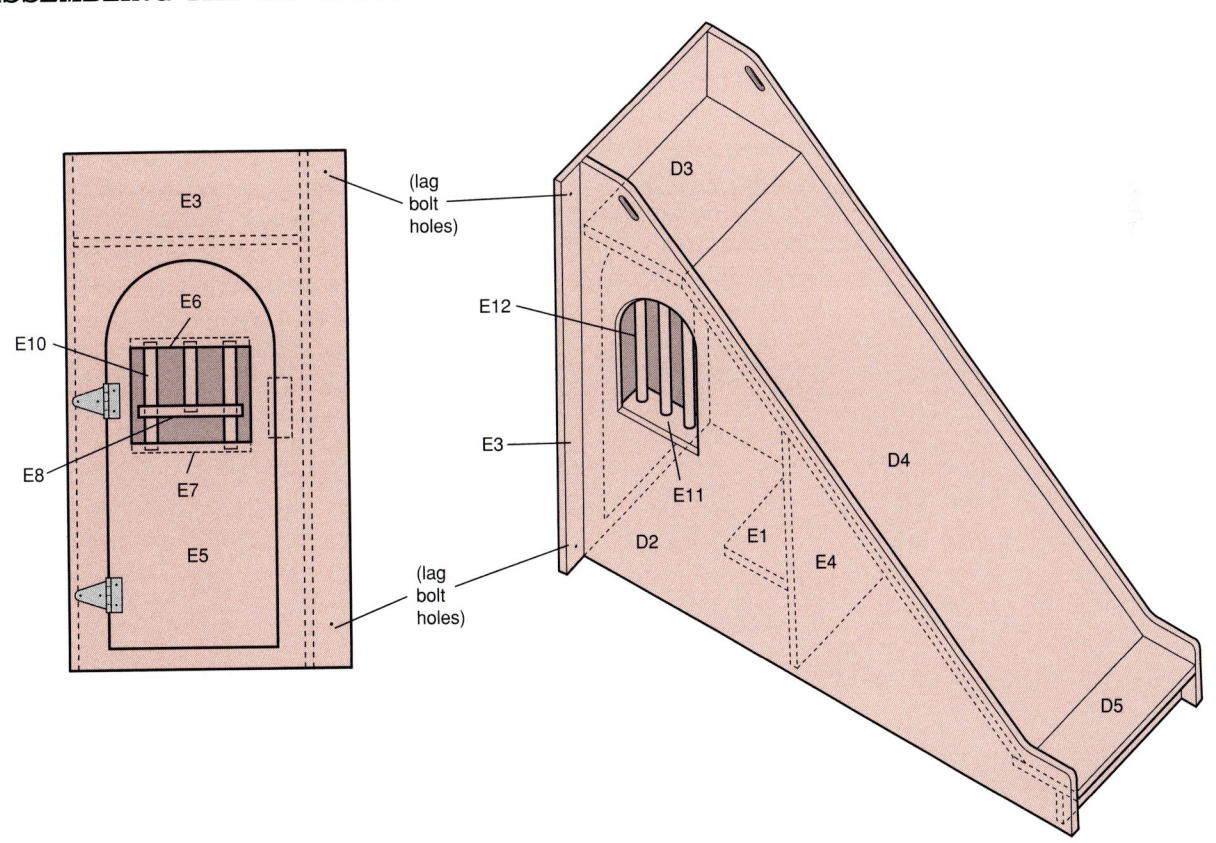

The slide and dungeon section fasten to the right side of the castle.

93

*projects for playhouses*

the rails by fastening through the rail sides. The top step requires an additional support piece. The rear floor section is notched to receive the ladder rails and top step support. The ladder rails and steps are attached to the ladder wall with screws or nails installed from the back side of the ladder wall.

## 8 ASSEMBLING THE SLIDE AND DUNGEON SECTION

The slide and dungeon section is attached to the right side of the main castle structure. It consists of front and back sides, front and back dungeon wall, top and lower landing, plus a small front piece. The dungeon is equipped with a hinged door, barred window, and dungeon seat.

Assembly is straightforward once all pieces have been properly sized and mitered. The panel layout for the front and back sides indicates the proper miter angles for the slide and back dungeon wall, plus the proper position for the landings, slide, front piece, and front dungeon wall.

Dungeon windowsills are drilled to accept the 1-inch dowels.

## 9 BOLTING TOGETHER THE SECTIONS

Once all sections have been constructed, they are bolted together using lag bolts, washers, and tee-nuts. The front and rear sec-

### BOLTING TOGETHER THE SECTIONS

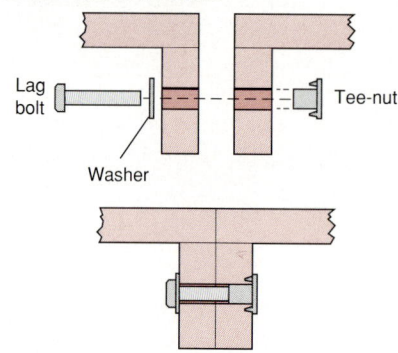

Bolt all castle sections together using lag bolts, tee-nuts, and washers.

tions are fastened together with four lag bolts, washers, and tee-nuts installed through holes drilled in the matching joist support pieces.

The dungeon wall of the slide and dungeon assembly overlaps the back edge of the right tower side wall and bolts to it using two 3/8- x 1 1/2-inch lag bolts, washers, and tee-nuts.

The front side of the ladder wall overlaps the back edge of the left tower side wall and bolts to it using a 3/8- x 1 1/2-inch lag bolt, washer, and tee-nut at the top and bottom corners.

The back side of the slide and the ladder walls are bolted to the floor supports of the rear floor section using 3/8- x 2 1/2-inch lag bolts, washers, and tee-nuts. A small wood block should be nailed or screwed to the inside of the ladder wall to provide a bearing surface for the lag bolts.

## 10 FINISHING

A top quality stain or paint will help maintain the panels' appearance and protect them from weathering. Since end grain absorbs and loses moisture rapidly, panels should be edge-sealed to help minimize possible damage. Use paint primer to seal panels to be painted, or use a paintable water-repellent preservative for panels that are to be stained.

For rough or textured panels, either high quality stain or acrylic house paint is recommended. Use a solvent-thinned, semi-transparent stain for maximum grain showthrough. Use only acrylic latex solid-color stain when it is desirable to hide the grain and color of the wood surface, but not its texture. Maximum protection of the wood is obtained by using a house paint that consists of a stain-resistant primer and one or more acrylic latex topcoats. Finish medium density overlaid panels with solid-color acrylic latex stain or a two-coat paint (primer plus companion topcoat).

It is best to apply the first coat of finish by brushing. If the first coat of finish is sprayed on, it should be back-brushed or back-rolled to work it well into the wood surface. Additional coats may be sprayed without back-brushing.

Whatever finishing method is used—paint or stain—always use top quality materials and follow the manufacturer's instructions.

Lightweight brick veneer can be glued to the castle around windows and the drawbridge opening to create a more authentic look.

*projects for quiet time*

# KIDDIE PICNIC TABLE

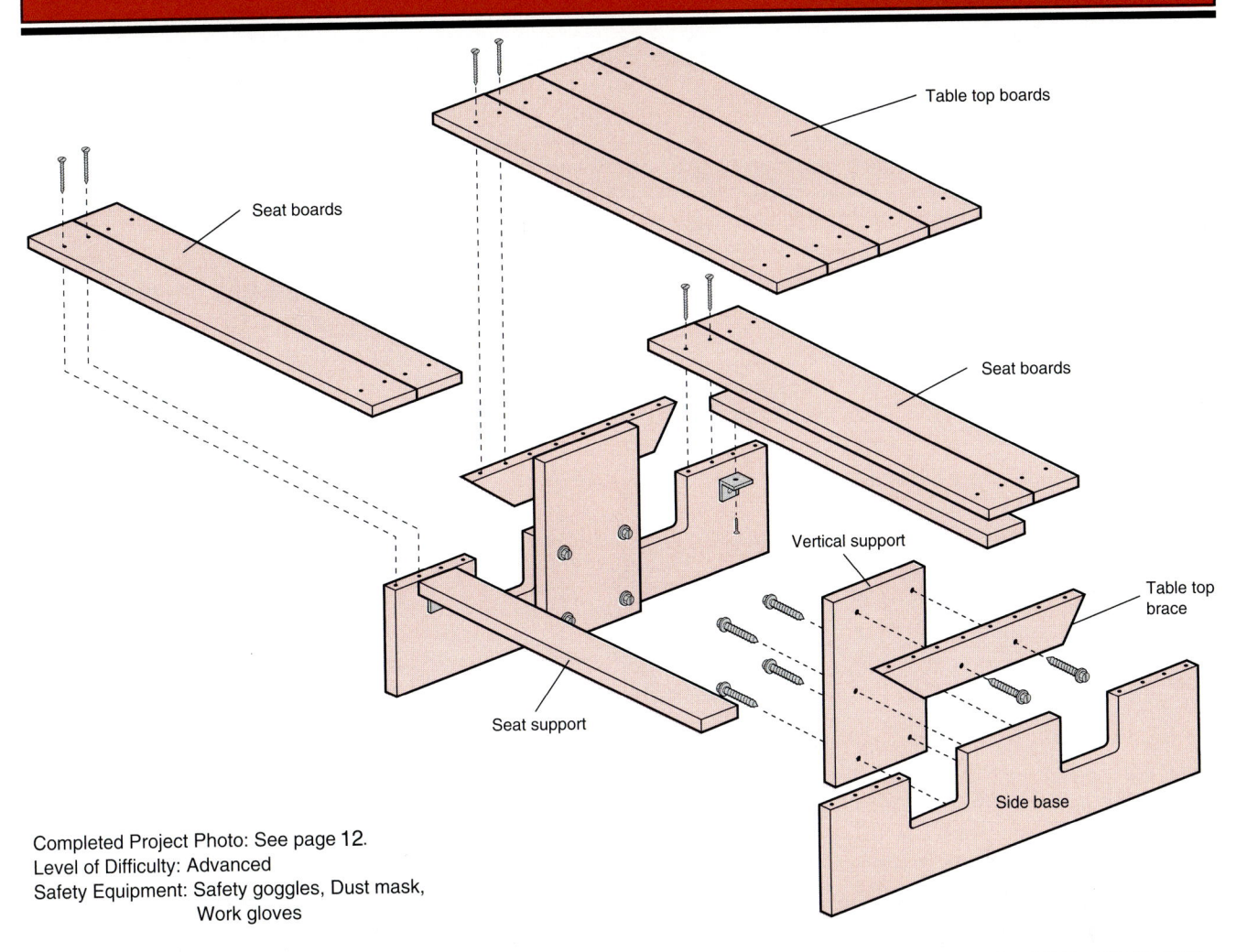

*Labels on exploded diagram:* Table top boards, Seat boards, Seat boards, Vertical support, Table top brace, Side base, Seat support

Completed Project Photo: See page 12.
Level of Difficulty: Advanced
Safety Equipment: Safety goggles, Dust mask, Work gloves

The picnic table has been a part of American yard decor for generations. Reproducing such a table in a size and style easily used by children will provide youngsters with a special place of their own for sit-down outdoor activities. A child-size picnic table is also a great space reliever at family picnics, where the crowd and food can often overflow a single adult size table.

The table shown in this project was constructed of pressure-treated southern pine; redwood is also a popular choice for picnic tables. Once the lumber is accurately cut to size, assembly is very straightforward and basic.

With the "use zone" figured in, the kiddie picnic table requires an area at least 7 feet long and 8 feet wide for optimum safety.

## 1 SIZING ALL STOCK

Mark out and cut two 46-inch long pieces of 2 x 12 stock to use as side bases. Use a framing square and tape measure to carefully mark out the pattern shown here on each side base. Cut the two notches in each side base using a saber saw or bench top scroll saw. Clearing the inside corners will be

### MATERIALS, PARTS, AND CUTTING LIST

| Material/Part Name | Qty. | Size |
|---|---|---|
| Pressure-treated #1 select southern pine | 1 | 2 x 4 x 10' |
|     Seat supports | 2 | 1 1/2" x 11 1/4" x 21" |
|     Table top braces | 2 | 1 1/2" x 3 1/2" x 28" |
| Pressure-treated #1 select southern pine | 1 | 2 x 12 x 12' |
|     Side bases | 2 | 1 1/2" x 11 1/4" x 46" |
|     Vertical supports | 2 | 1 1/2" x 11 1/4" x 21" |
| Pressure-treated #1 select radius edge southern pine decking | 2 | 5/4 x 6" x 12' |
|     Seats and table top boards | 8 | 5/4 x 6" x 36" |

| Material/Part Name | Qty. | Size |
|---|---|---|
| Galvanized lag screws | 10 | 1/4" x 2 1/2" |
| Galvanized flat head wood screws | 32 | 2 1/2" |
| Galvanized flat head wood screws | 8 | 1" |
| Galvanized "L" braces | 4 | |
| Water repellent sealer | 1 | quart |
| Construction adhesive | 1 | caulking tube |
| Medium grade sandpaper | 1-2 | sheets |

95

## projects for quiet time

### SIZING ALL STOCK

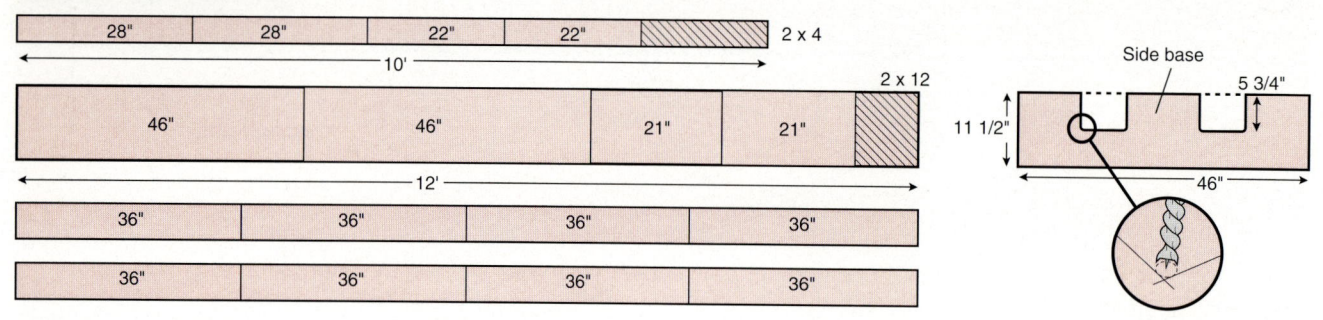

Cutting diagrams help reduce wasted wood. The inside corners of the side bases can be easily cleared by drilling a 1-inch-diameter hole at these points and making clearing cuts with a saber saw.

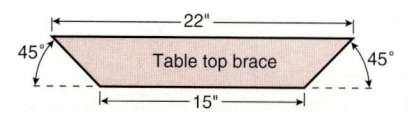

Cut 45° miters on the ends of the table top braces.

### ASSEMBLING THE FRAME

easier if you drill a 1-inch-diameter hole just inside the corner borders. This will give you room to maneuver the cutting blade and also prevent splintering at the corners.

Cut two 21-inch lengths of 2 x 12 stock to serve as vertical supports. Cut two 28-inch lengths of 2 x 4 stock to serve as seat supports and two 22-inch lengths of 2 x 4 stock to use as table top braces. Mark and cut 45° miters on the ends of the 22-inch table top braces as shown.

Slightly round off all exposed edges on the side bases, vertical supports, and table top braces using a medium grade sandpaper. Wrap the paper around a small block of wood to make sanding easier.

Cut the 5/4-inch radius edge decking lumber into eight lengths measuring 36 inches to use as seat and table top surfaces.

### 2 ASSEMBLING THE FRAME

Fasten the vertical supports to the inside of the base supports using four 2 1/2-inch lag screws with washers. Drill a 3/8-inch-diameter pilot hole for each screw. Pilot hole depth should be 2 inches. Be care-

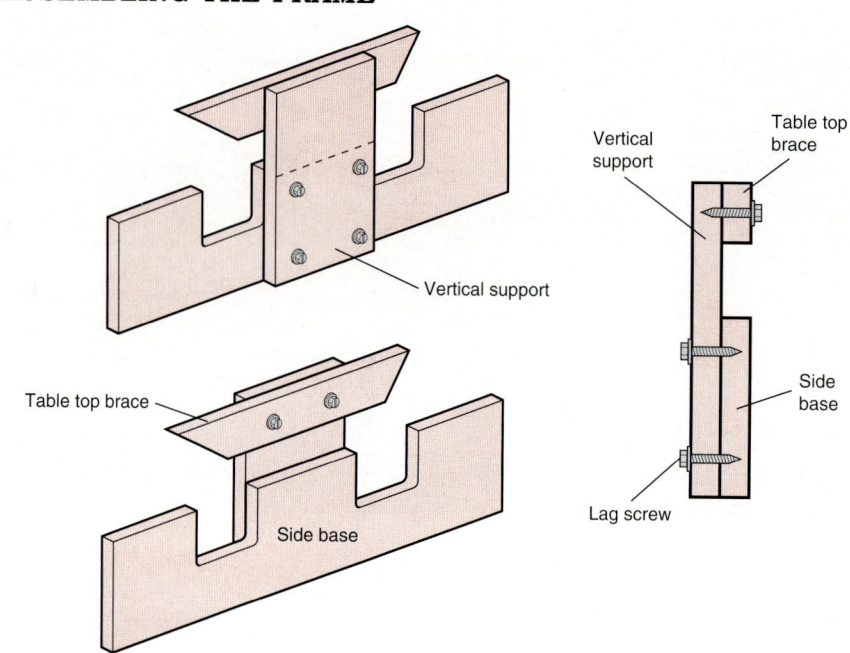

Assemble the end frame using lag screws.

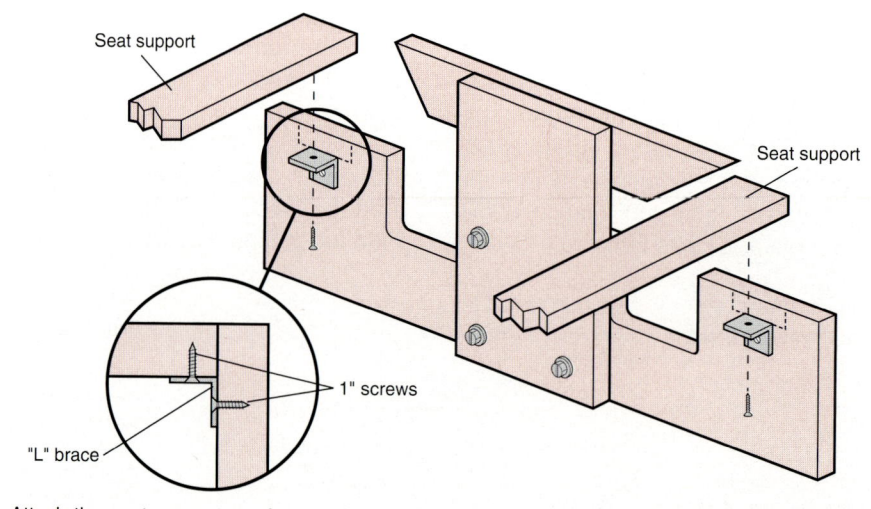

Attach the seat supports to the end frame assemblies using metal "L" braces and 1-inch flat head wood screws.

*projects for quiet time*

ful not to drill all the way through to the other side. A piece of tape wrapped around the drill bit at the correct depth is a good method of preventing this mistake.

Attach the two 22-inch table top braces to the vertical supports using two lag screws with washers in each brace. Again drill pilot holes to the correct depth through the vertical support and into the table top brace.

Complete the frame by attaching the two 28-inch long seat supports between the side bases. Center the seat support under the seating area and attach it to the side bases using metal "L" braces and countersunk 1-inch flat head wood screws. Mark out the screw locations on the seat supports and side bases and drill 3/4-inch deep pilot holes for the screws.

## 3 APPLYING SEAT AND TABLE TOP

Position the 5/4 x 6- x 36-inch decking stock on the seat supports and vertical supports, then predrill pilot holes in all screw locations. The decking should be applied bark side up; this will prevent the lumber from cupping as the wood ages.

Apply a bead of construction adhesive to the table top braces, side base edges and seat supports before securing the decking pieces with 2 1/2-inch flat head wood screws. Use two screws in each board end. Be careful not to apply too much adhesive or it will squeeze out of the joint and smear the face of the wood.

### APPLYING SEAT AND TABLE TOP

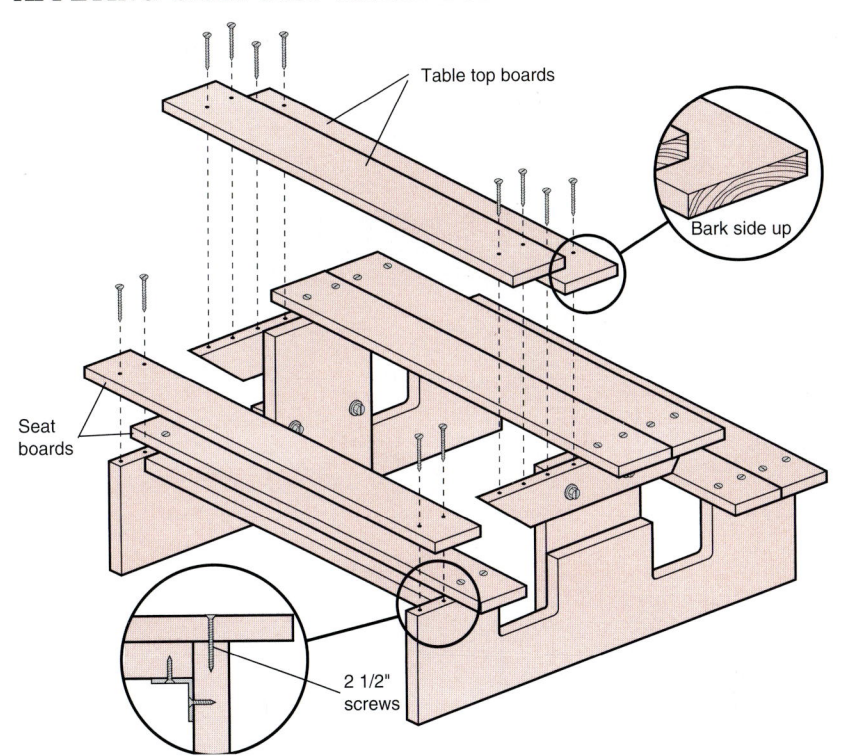

Attach the seat and table top boards with adhesive and 2 1/2-inch flat head wood screws. Position the boards bark side up to prevent cupping as the wood ages.

## 4 FINAL TOUCHES

Round the outside edges of the table top and seat boards using medium grade sandpaper. Apply a coat of water repellent sealer to all wood surfaces to protect against the elements.

97

## projects for quiet time

# Sandbox

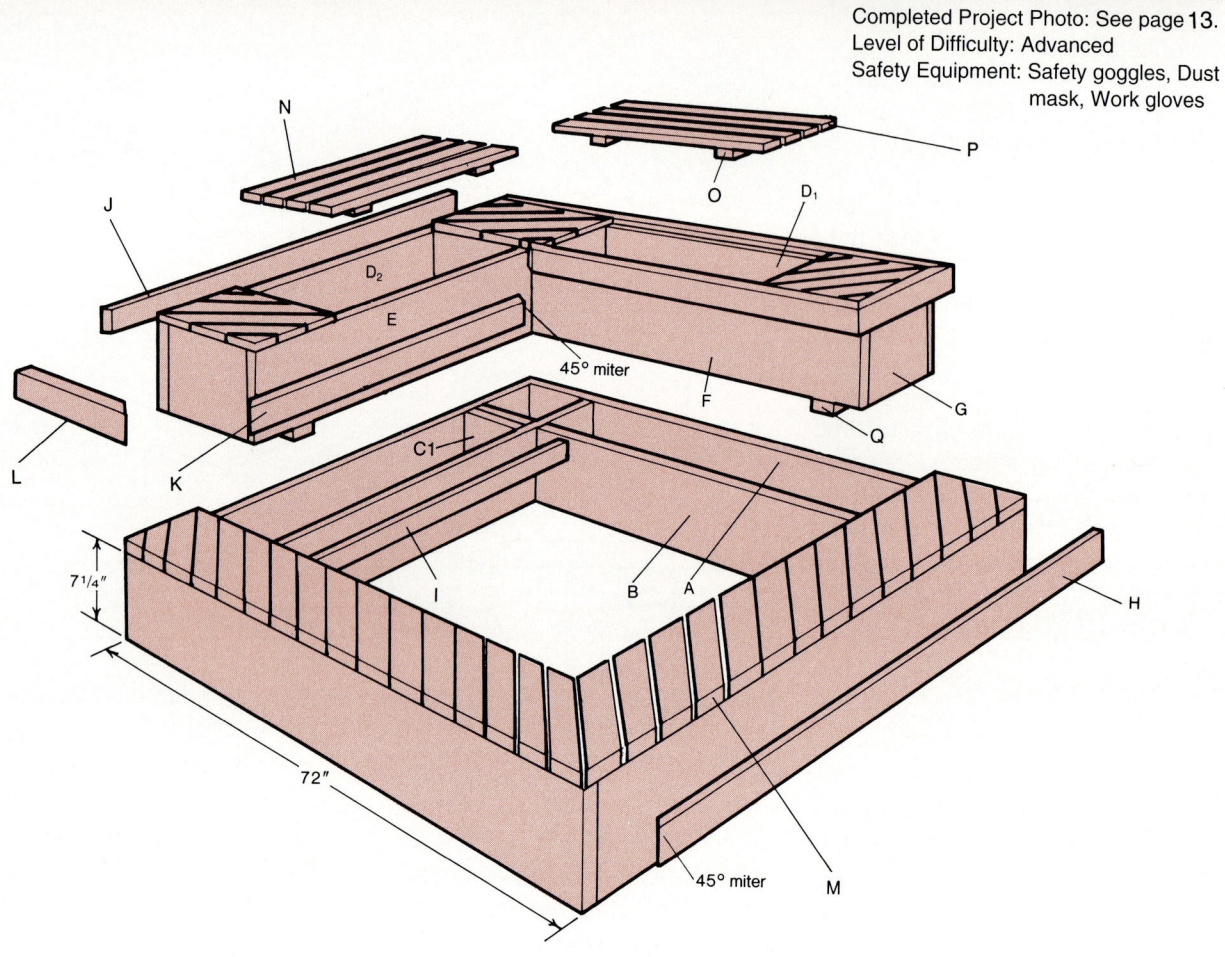

Completed Project Photo: See page 13.
Level of Difficulty: Advanced
Safety Equipment: Safety goggles, Dust mask, Work gloves

What child can resist the lure of a sandbox? This sandbox is a great play area for toddlers, and its usefulness extends even beyond childhood. When the kids have outgrown it, you have an attractive double-decked planter.

The all-redwood construction and stainless steel hardware are as durable as they are beautiful; this sandbox can withstand the playful assaults of the most active child. The top "L" section, which contains two hatch-covered storage areas for shovels, buckets, and other toys, can be removed from the base for easy transportation.

With the "use zone" figured in, the sandbox requires an area at least 10 feet long and 10 feet wide for optimum safety.

### MATERIALS, PARTS, AND CUTTING LIST

| Material/Part Name | Qty. | Size |
|---|---|---|
| Clear heart redwood | 6 | 2 x 8 x 12' |
| (A) Outer bottom sides | 4 | 1 1/2" x 7 1/4" x 70 3/8" |
| (B) Inner bottom sides | 4 | 1 1/2" x 7 1/4" x 56 3/4" |
| (C1) Bridge bottoms | 4 | 1 1/2" x 7 1/4" x 10 3/8" |
| (C2) Blocking | 1 | 1 1/2" x 3 1/2" x 10 3/8" |
| (D1) Long outer top side | 1 | 1 1/2" x 7 1/4" x 58 1/8" |
| (D2) Short outer top side | 1 | 1 1/2" x 7 1/4" x 56 3/4" |
| (E) Short inner top side | 1 | 1 1/2" x 7 1/4" x 44 3/4" |
| (F) Long inner top side | 1 | 1 1/2" x 7 1/4" x 56 3/4" |
| (G) Bridge top ends | 5 | 1 1/2" x 7 1/4" x 10 3/8" |
| Clear heart redwood | 19 | 1 x 4 x 10' |
| (H) Outer bottom trim | 4 | 3/4" x 2 11/16" x 74 1/2" |
| (I) Inner bottom trim | 4 | 3/4" x 2 11/16" x 45 1/2" |
| (J) Outer top trim | 2 | 3/4" x 2 11/16" x 60 1/2" |

| Material/Part Name | Qty. | Size |
|---|---|---|
| (K) Inner top trim | 2 | 3/4" x 2 11/16" x 46" |
| (L) End top trim | 2 | 3/4" x 2 11/16" x 16" |
| (M) Deck boards | 39 | 3/4" x 3 1/2" x 24 1/2" |
| (N) Small hatch cover boards | 4 | 3/4" x 2 11/16" x 27 1/2" |
| (O) Hatch nailers | 4 | 3/4" x 2 11/16" x 10 1/8" |
| (P) Large hatch cover boards | 4 | 3/4" x 2 11/16" x 29 1/2" |
| (Q) Lock dogs | 4 | 3/4" x 2 11/16" x 6" |
| Stainless steel flat head and Phillips head wood screws | 150 | #10 x 3" |
| Stainless steel flat head and Phillips head wood screws | 270 | #8 x 1 1/2" |
| Stainless steel flat head and Phillips head wood screws | 32 | #8 x 1 1/4" |

*projects for quiet time*

# 1 ASSEMBLING THE BOTTOM SECTION

Cut out all structural parts from the 2 x 8s according to the cutting schedule and parts list. Assemble the four inner bottom members (B) with screws, driven into holes predrilled with a combination bit. Then, join the outer bottom members (A) into an open square with each end overlapping the adjacent one.

Next, place the inner bottom assembly inside the outer bottom and draw centerlines representing the ends of the inner members on the faces of the outer members. Drill holes and drive the screws; it is recommended to countersink the holes and drive in the screws slightly below the surface as a safety measure. Add the bridge bottoms (C1) and blocking (C2) to complete the bottom section.

# 2 DECKING THE BOTTOM SECTION

Cut out and miter both ends of 39 deck boards (M) at 45°. Note that only two full sides of the bottom are covered with decking, specifically the area *not* covered by the top "L" section.

Select any convenient area on the bottom and mark off a line on the structure that makes a 45° angle with the sides. Start the first deck piece against this line and place any overhang so that it lies outside the outer member; this will make it easy later to trim away all of the overhang with one pass of a circular saw. Continue to add decking, holding a 1/4-inch spacer between adjacent pieces as a guide. Try to drill the holes and drive the screws in a straight line to create a neat appearance. At the ends and corners, the size of the overhang will increase, but the installation and trimming are done in the same way.

**ASSEMBLING THE BOTTOM SECTION**

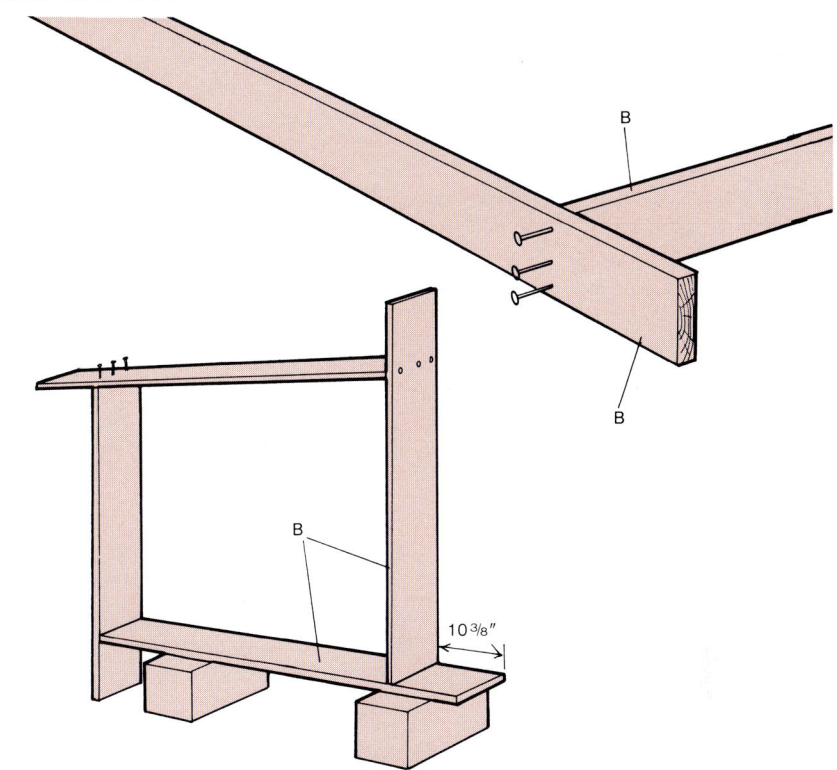

Assemble the inner bottom sides by screwing together two parts of offset "L"s. Be sure to keep the overhang dimensions the same as that of the bridges, blocking, and top ends. Join the two "L"s to form a square with four overhangs.

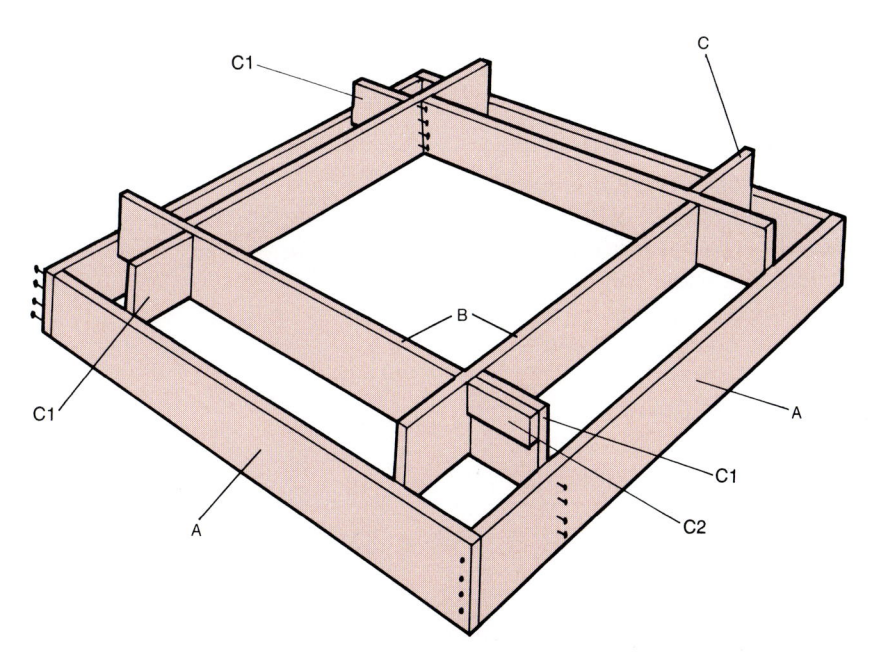

Assemble the outer bottom sides by predrilling the holes and driving the screws. This forms a square, 72 inches on a side, with each end overlapping the adjacent one. Place the inner bottom inside the outer bottom and join the two. Add blocking and bridges.

## projects for quiet time

### DECKING THE BOTTOM SECTION

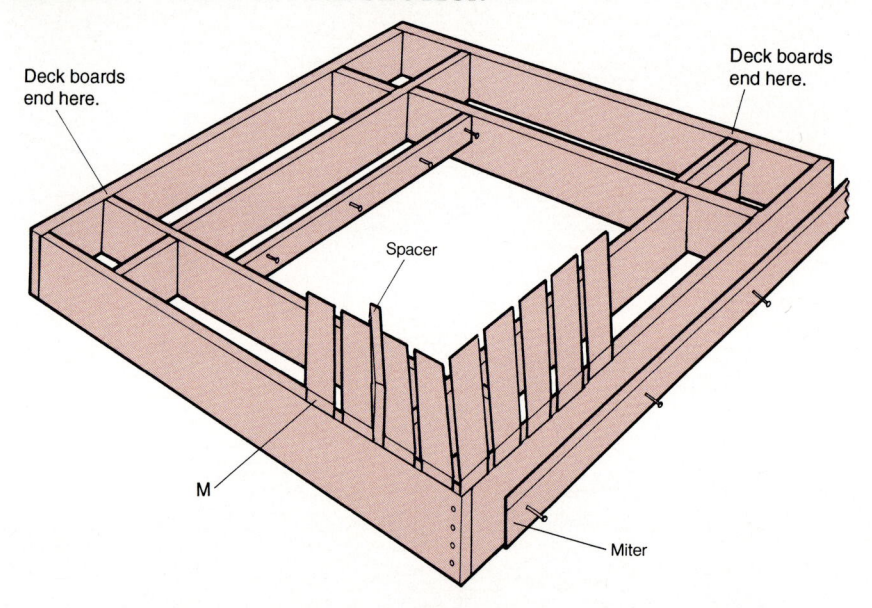

Check for squareness. Then start to attach the deck boards in a corner, orienting them 45° to the square. Try to get the inside miters flush with the inner faces of the inner sides; space the boards 1/4 inch apart. Saw and sand the outer miters flush. Install all bottom trim.

### 3 ASSEMBLING THE TOP "L" SECTION

The top section, though "L"-shaped, is constructed similar to the bottom. Here, the bridges and ends are the same size, and the bridge bottoms help to outline the hatch-covered storage areas.

Before decking the top "L" section, make sure that it fits properly over the bottom. At this time, screw the lock dogs (Q) in place to the inner surfaces of the top "L" section. Then, except for the hatches, complete the corner and end decking on the top "L" section.

The hatch covers (N and P) are made from boards with nailers (O) attached from below and at right angles to them. The hatch cover boards should be evenly spaced and held in place by screws that fasten them to the nailers.

### 4 ADDING THE TRIM

Before fitting any of the trim, block-sand all decking edges. Make sure both the inner and outer faces of the bottom section trim fit flush with the top of the decking. Note that in areas that have no decking, this trim will cover about 3/4 inch of the bottom of the top "L" section for an eye-appealing fit.

The top "L" section trim will require end pieces as well as long pieces, inasmuch as the ends are exposed at the top. As with the bottom, align the trim so it is flush with the top section decking. Note that the trim in areas that have no decking will serve as outer borders for the hatches.

In applying the trim, use butt joints on internal corners and 45° miter joints on external corners. Finally, check the entire project over for any splinters or burrs, and sand these smooth.

### ASSEMBLING THE TOP "L" SECTION

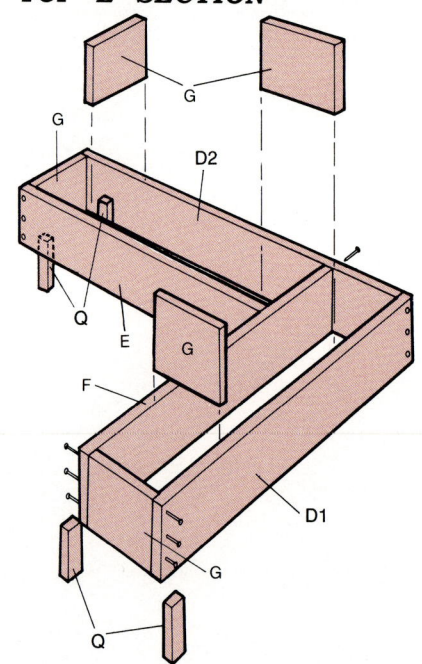

Assemble all major top section inner and outer members, forming an "L." Then add the bridge bottoms and lock dogs.

### ADDING THE TRIM

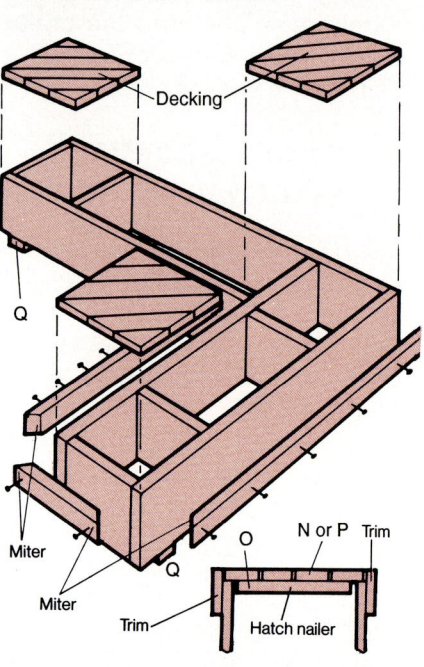

Install decking at the corner and ends. Add the trim on the inside, outside, and ends. Fit and build the hatches.

100

*projects for quiet time*

# Drawing Easel

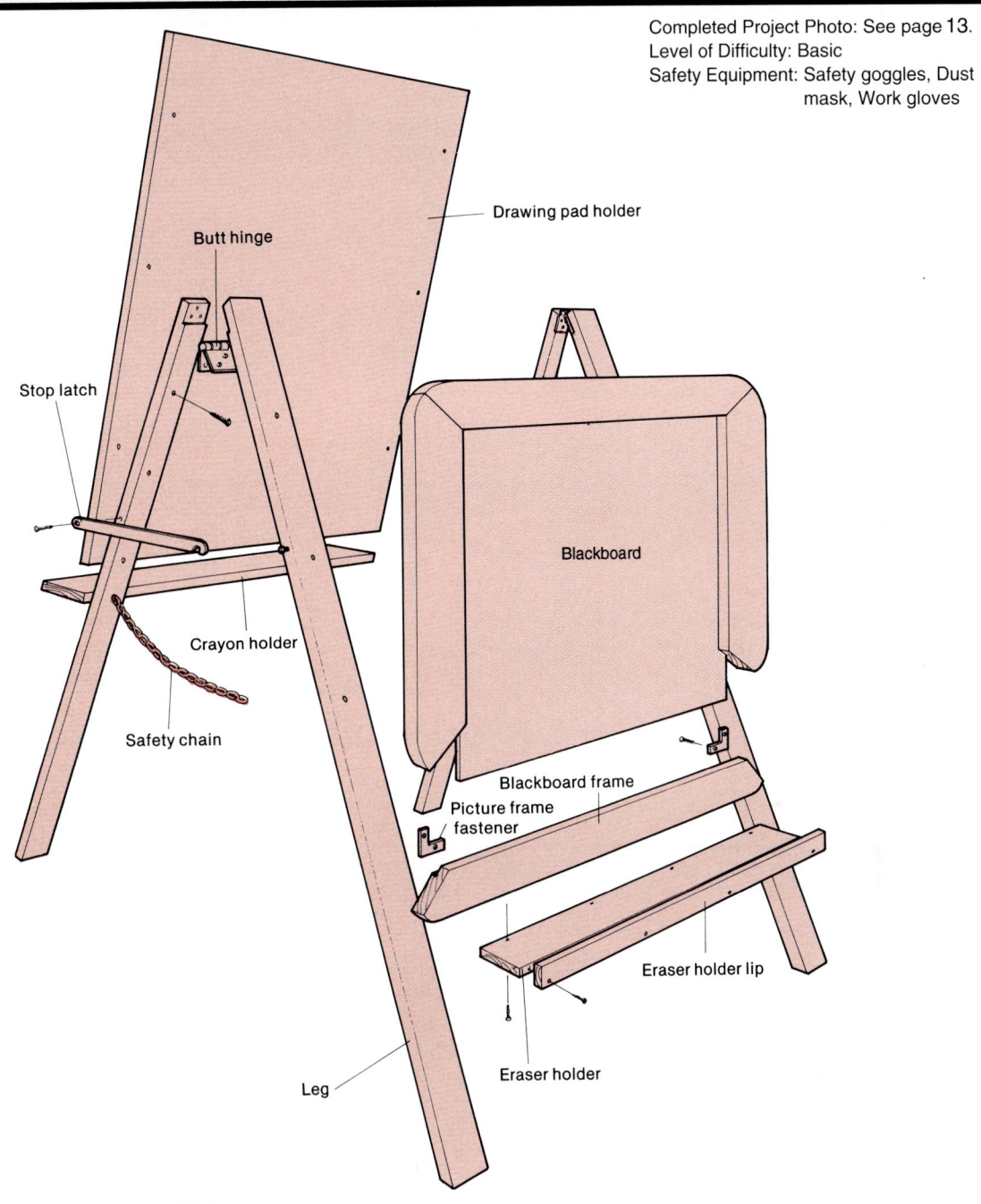

Completed Project Photo: See page 13.
Level of Difficulty: Basic
Safety Equipment: Safety goggles, Dust mask, Work gloves

*(Labeled diagram parts: Drawing pad holder, Butt hinge, Stop latch, Crayon holder, Safety chain, Leg, Blackboard, Blackboard frame, Picture frame fastener, Eraser holder, Eraser holder lip)*

## MATERIALS, PARTS, AND CUTTING LIST

| Material/Part Name | Qty. | Size |
|---|---|---|
| Pressure-treated #3 select white oak | 1 | 1 x 2 x 4' |
|     Eraser holder lip | 1 | 1/2" x 1 1/2" x 17 1/2" |
|     Stop latch | 1 | 1/2" x 3/4" x 9" |
| Pressure-treated #3 select white oak | 3 | 1 x 3 x 3' |
|     Blackboard frame | 4 | 3/4" x 2" x 18" |
|     Eraser holder | 1 | 3/4" x 2 1/2" x 17 1/2" |
|     Crayon holder | 1 | 3/4" x 2" x 18" |
| Pressure-treated #3 select white oak | 4 | 1 x 3 x 4' |
|     Legs | 4 | 3/4" x 2" x 46" |
| Slate | 1 | 1/4" x 14" x 14" |
|     Blackboard | 1 | 1/4" x 14" x 14" |

| Material/Part Name | Qty. | Size |
|---|---|---|
| A-C exterior grade plywood | 1 | 3/4" x 4' x 8' |
|     Drawing pad holder | 1 | 3/4" x 17 1/2" x 24" |
| Brass butt hinges | 2 | 1" |
| Brass chain | 1 | 14" |
| Brass miter-corner picture frame fasteners | 4 | |
| Galvanized round head wood screws | 26 | 1 1/4" |
| Galvanized round head wood screws | 20 | 1/2" |
| Brass round head wood screws | 2 | 1/2" |
| Galvanized finishing nails | 1/2 lb. | 3d |
| Galvanized brads | 1/2 lb. | 1/2" |

## projects for quiet time

This two-sided drawing easel offers double fun for youngsters. One side has a blackboard, and the other has a drawing pad holder. This easel not only provides two separate skill areas, but it allows two children to work at the easel at the same time.

The easel shown on page 11 was constructed of solid white oak and given a natural finish, but almost any hardwood will do. The easel is hinged at the top so that it can be folded up and stored away when not in use. Its legs are held apart at the proper angle by a stop latch and safety chain. The chain provides extra security in case a young artist accidentally knocks the latch out of its locked position.

The steps given here are for constructing the easel one component at a time. Because you will have to wait for the finish on the various pieces to dry during the construction process, move along to the next step and complete the previous steps when the pieces are ready.

With the "use zone" figured in, the drawing easel requires an area at least 6 feet long and 6 feet wide for optimum safety.

## 1 MAKING THE ERASER HOLDER

Cut the eraser holder and its lip, and round the upper corners of the lip with a saber saw. Sand both pieces and finish or stain as desired. The easel shown on page 11 was finished with acrylic varnish.

## 2 FRAMING THE BLACKBOARD

Cut the pieces for the blackboard frame from 3/4-inch stock. Lay the pieces roughly in position (they will be mitered to fit together in a moment) and lightly mark the pieces so you can tell which are

### FRAMING THE BLACKBOARD

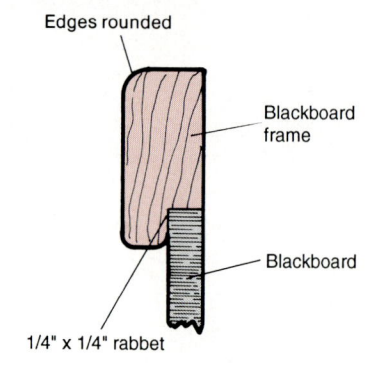

Cut a rabbet in the frame pieces to accommodate the blackboard.

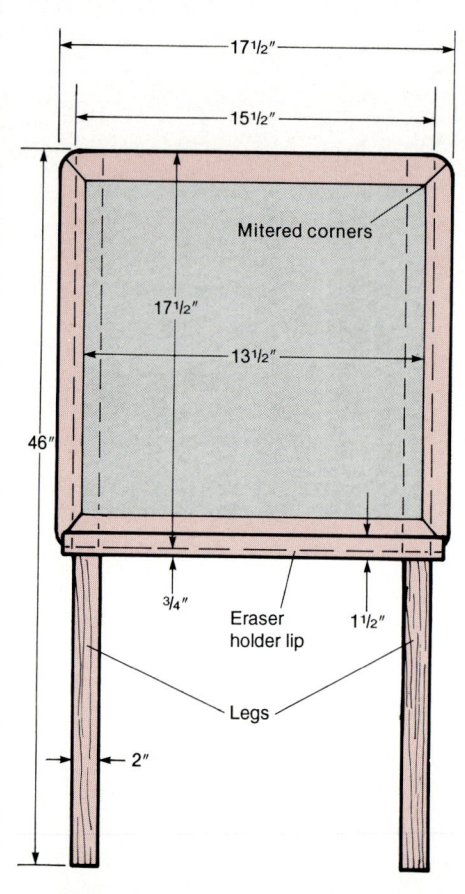

The blackboard frame pieces are mitered for easy assembly.

the front and back sides. Round the inside front edge of the frame pieces with a router, then cut a 1/4- x 1/4-inch rabbet in the inside back edges of the pieces; smooth the inside edge of the rabbet with sandpaper. Finally, miter the pieces at a 45° angle at the ends to the 17 1/2-inch length.

Glue the blackboard frame pieces together and clamp solidly, checking to be sure that the frame is square. Leave overnight to dry. When dry, use miter-corner picture frame fasteners to give the frame extra strength; then round the outside edges, front and back. Use a saber saw to round the corners of the frame; then round the edge of these cuts. Stain or finish the frame, as desired.

## 3 ASSEMBLING THE BLACKBOARD

Glue the slate into the back of the frame and tack in two brads on each side for extra strength. Attach the lip to the eraser holder with glue and 3d finishing nails set below the surface. Attach the assembled eraser holder to the

### ASSEMBLING THE BLACKBOARD

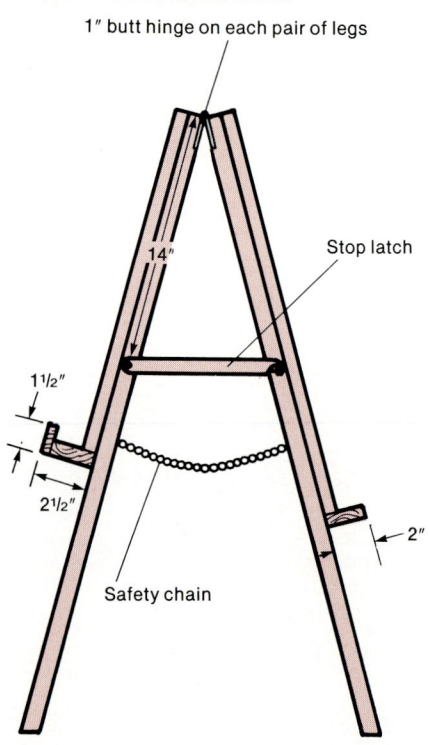

The safety chain and stop latch are important safety features.

102

*projects for quiet time*

bottom of the blackboard frame with glue and four countersunk round head wood screws.

### 4 MAKING THE DRAWING PAD HOLDER

Cut the drawing pad holder from plywood and sand thoroughly. Cut the crayon holder, round the outside corners, and sand thoroughly. Finish both the pad holder and the crayon holder with the same finish used for the blackboard frame. When dry, attach the crayon holder to the pad holder with glue and four countersunk round head wood screws as shown in the Side View.

### 5 CUTTING THE LEGS AND ASSEMBLING THE EASEL

Cut the four legs to size and round all edges. Cut a 1-inch end rabbet in the top of each leg to accommodate the hinges. Sand the legs and finish them in the same manner as the blackboard and drawing pad holder. When dry, attach two of the legs to the blackboard and two to the drawing pad holder. Use twelve 1 1/4-inch countersunk round head wood screws, driving them from the backs of the legs into the blackboard frame and drawing pad holder at top, center, and bottom.

### 6 MAKING THE STOP LATCH AND FINAL ASSEMBLY

Screw a 1-inch butt hinge to the inside edge at the top of each pair of legs. Use a saber saw to cut the stop latch from 1/2-inch stock and shape as shown in the detail drawing. Drill a 1/4-inch hole in the center of the rounded end and attach the stop latch to one of the legs with a 1 1/4-inch round head wood screw as shown in the Side View. Drive in another 1 1/4-inch round head wood screw on the directly opposite leg (check exact location by marking with the stop latch in position). This screw must protrude slightly more than 1/2 inch so the stop latch will hold on it. Fasten a small brass safety chain with 1/2-inch screws about 3 inches below the stop latch to prevent the easel from falling down should the stop latch accidentally get knocked open.

### MAKING THE DRAWING PAD HOLDER

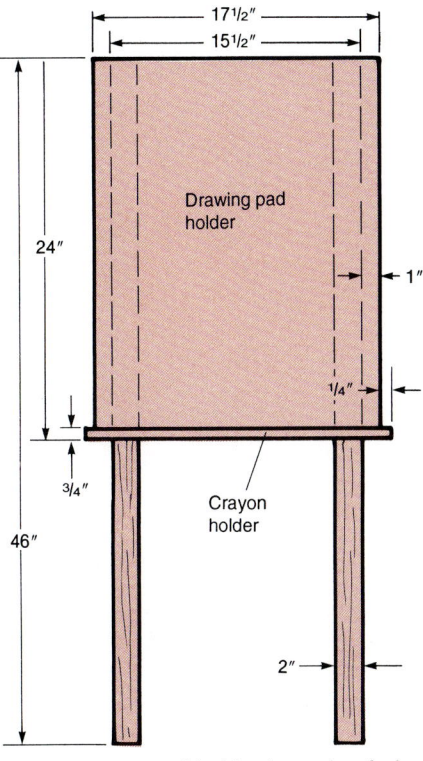

The drawing pad holder is made of plywood.

### MAKING THE STOP LATCH AND FINAL ASSEMBLY

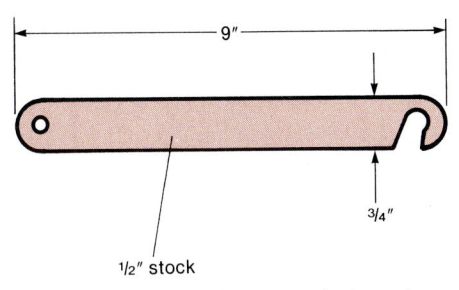

The stop latch must be cut and shaped precisely for it to do its job.

103

*projects for quiet time*

# GAME TABLE AND STOOLS

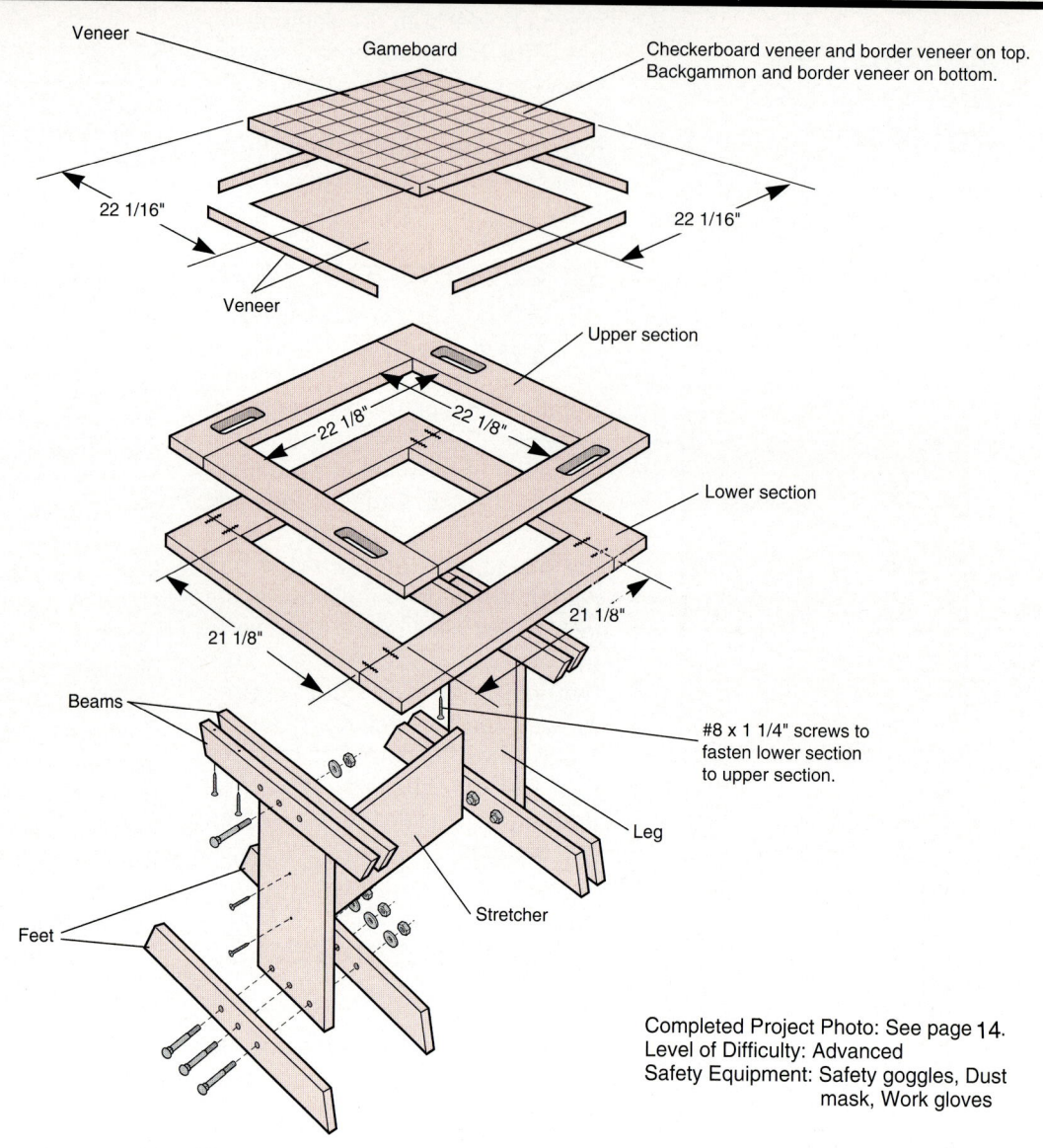

Veneer
Gameboard
Checkerboard veneer and border veneer on top.
Backgammon and border veneer on bottom.
22 1/16"
22 1/16"
Veneer

Upper section
22 1/8"
22 1/8"
Lower section
21 1/8"
21 1/8"
Beams
#8 x 1 1/4" screws to fasten lower section to upper section.
Leg
Stretcher
Feet

Completed Project Photo: See page 14.
Level of Difficulty: Advanced
Safety Equipment: Safety goggles, Dust mask, Work gloves

### MATERIALS, PARTS, AND CUTTING LIST—GAME TABLE

| Material/Part Name | Qty. | Size |
|---|---|---|
| Clear heart redwood | 1 | 5/4 x 12" x 10' |
|     Beams | 4 | 11/16" x 2 11/16" x 24" |
|     Feet | 4 | 11/16" x 2 11/16" x 32" |
|     Legs | 2 | 11/16" x 8 1/2" x 19" |
|     Stretcher | 1 | 11/16" x 5 1/2" x 23 13/16" |
| Clear heart redwood | 1 | 1 x 12 x 10' |
|     Upper section pieces | 4 | 3/4" x 5" x 27 1/8" |
|     Lower section pieces | 4 | 3/4" x 5 1/2" x 26 5/8" |
| Particleboard | 1 | 3/4 x 22" x 22" |
|     Game board | 1 | 3/4" x 22" x 22" |
| Checkerboard assembled veneer | 1 | 18" x 18" |
| Backgammon assembled veneer | 1 | 20" x 20" |
| Veneer cement | 1 | pint |
| Carriage bolts/nuts/washers | 12 | 5/16" x 3 1/2" |
| Stainless steel flat head and Phillips head wood screws | 16 | #10 x 3" |
| Stainless steel flat head and Phillips head wood screws | 60 | #8 x 1 1/4" |
| Stainless steel corrugated fasteners | 8 | 1/2" x 5" |

### MATERIALS, PARTS, AND CUTTING LIST—STOOLS

| Material/Part Name | Qty. | Size |
|---|---|---|
| Clear heart redwood | 3 | 1 x 2 x 4' |
|     Front aprons | 2 | 3/4" x 2" x 10 1/2" |
|     Back aprons | 2 | 3/4" x 2" x 10 1/2" |
|     Side aprons | 4 | 3/4" x 2" x 12" |
|     Leg braces | 8 | 3/4" x 1 1/2" x 6" |
| Clear heart redwood | 1 | 1 x 3 x 6' |
|     Seat slats | 5 | 3/4" x 2 1/2" x 13" |
| Clear heart redwood | 2 | 2 x 2 x 6' |
|     Legs | 8 | 1 1/2" x 1 1/2" x 11 3/4" |
| Brass round head wood screws | 40 | #8 x 1 1/2" |
| Waterproof urea resin or resorcinol glue | 1 | can or bottle |

# projects for quiet time

Children will enjoy this all-wood gaming table and accompanying stools. They're ideal for backyard or patio use. The table stands 20-1/2 inches high and the stool seats are 12 1/2 inches off the ground, making this project a perfect fit for youngsters. The gameboard table insert can be flipped over for instant conversion from backgammon to checkers. For smaller tykes who aren't playing board games, the table and stools can be used for open-air arts and crafts.

The tabletop is equipped with four chip pockets. These make it appropriate for most board games, as well as card games. For smaller children, the chip pockets make ideal pencil and crayon holders.

The basic building material is redwood, which is used for the table feet, legs, and supporting structure. The stools are made entirely of redwood; note that the Materials, Parts, and Cutting List is intended for building two stools.

The game board is made from particleboard that is veneered on all surfaces. The veneers on the top and bottom are checkerboard and backgammon marquetry arrays with a mitered mahogany border and a matching edge. The entire game board has several coats of protective urethane varnish.

With the "use zone" figured in, the game table and stools require an area at least 8 feet long and 7 feet wide for optimum safety.

## MAKING THE TABLE

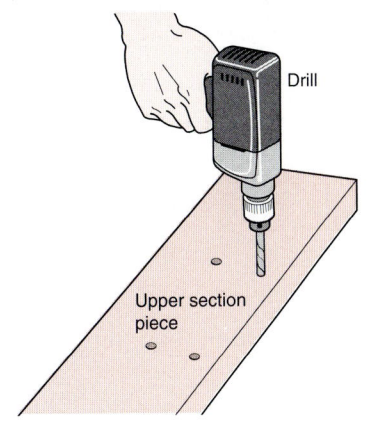

Drill starting holes for the jigsaw in all four corners of the chip pocket layout on the four upper section pieces.

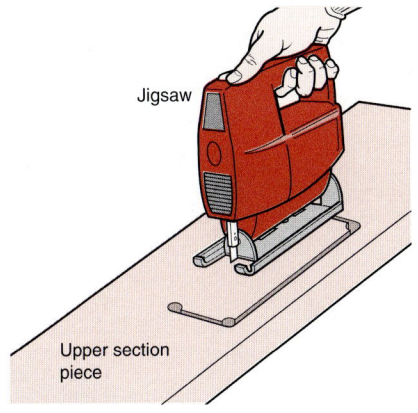

Place the workpiece good-side down, insert the jigsaw blade into a hole, and cut out the pocket.

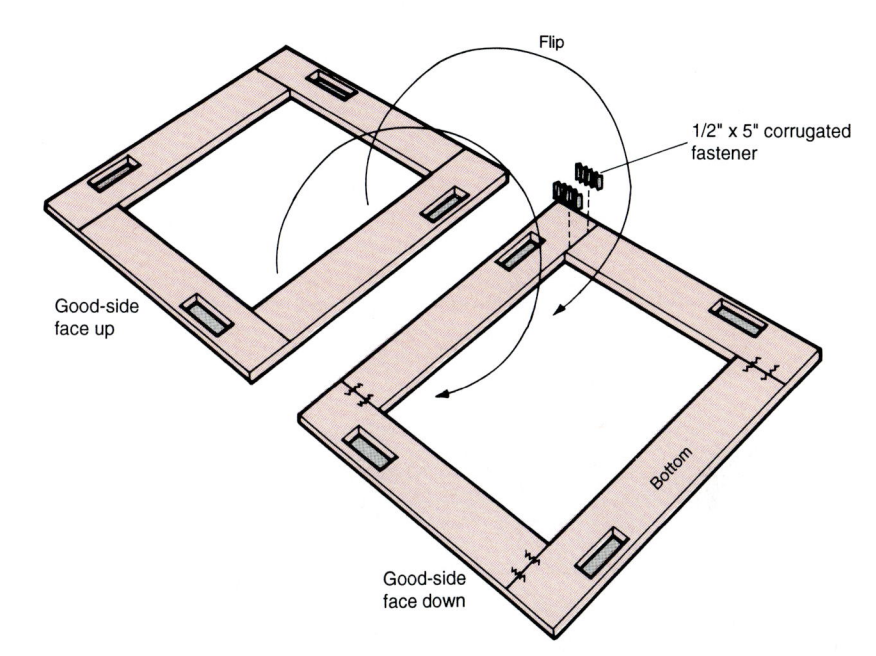

Set the upper section pieces in position, good-side face down, and drive in four pairs of corrugated fasteners for temporary assembly. Repeat the procedure for the lower section pieces.

## 1 MAKING THE GAME BOARD

It will probably take you as long to make the game board as it will to make the rest of the table. First, saw the particleboard to size. If the veneer is somewhat lumpy, follow the supplier's instructions for flattening it out before use.

Mark the outline for the checkerboard marquetry array on one side of the board, and for the backgammon array on the other.

Then tape the border pieces in position, with each one overlaying its neighbor. Double cut the 45° corner miters, as you would when making wall-covering matches. Make sure to identify each piece and its matching board location.

The veneer supplier should furnish a work sheet that explains the whole procedure, as well as special veneer cement and saws. Following are a few tips that you may find useful.

Apply the cement to both the particleboard and the back of the veneer. The cement must be allowed to dry until a brown paper bag can be slid across the surface without grabbing. The veneer sticks immediately, so get it right the first time. You can prevent mistakes by slipping a waxed paper separator between the core and the veneer as you move them into position.

Note that the game arrays are held together by thin paper and

105

*projects for quiet time*

## MAKING THE TABLE (CONTINUED)

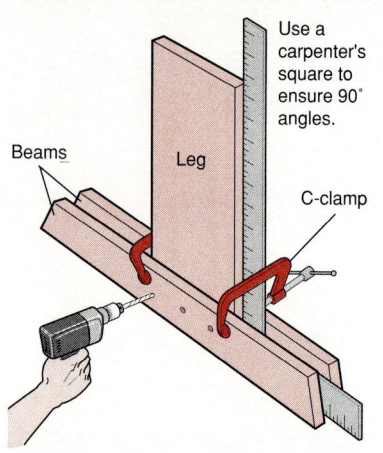

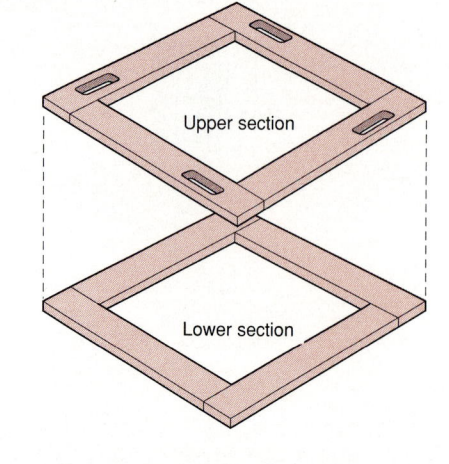

Square and clamp the legs into sandwiches with both the beams and feet; this will ensure accuracy when drilling the bolt holes.

The upper and lower sections are permanently fastened together with screws.

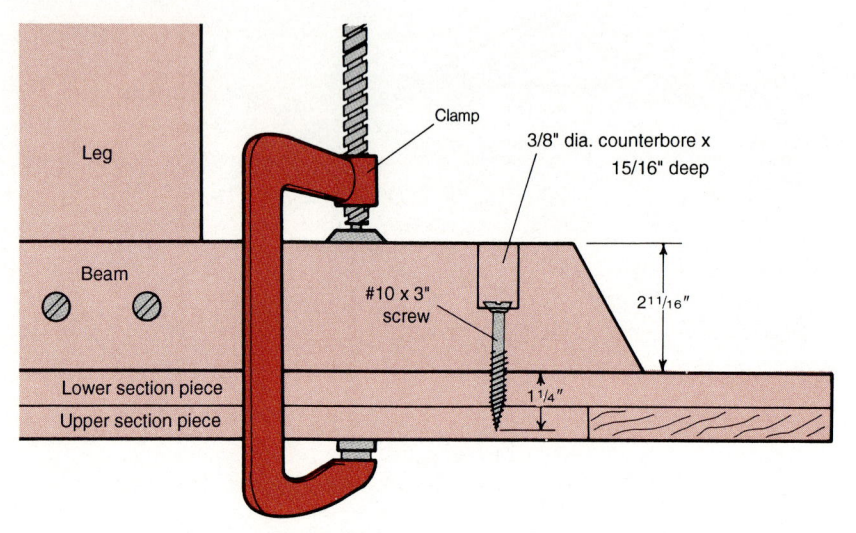

The legs are secured to the tabletop with #10 x 3" flat head wood screws.

four-sided ledge that supports the game board.

Both the upper and lower sections are temporarily assembled with corrugated fasteners. This keeps the parts together until the two sections can be permanently screw-assembled with the overlapping joints.

When you are ready to drill through and bolt up the sandwich formed by the beams and legs at the top, and the feet and legs at the bottom, clamp all the parts together to freeze them in proper position. Use a carpenter's square to ensure a right angle at these assembly points.

Be careful when drilling and screwing through the beams into the laminated tabletop. Avoid the chip pockets and use the depth control on your drill to avoid piercing the laminate.

With the assembly complete, do any final sanding. Stain or finish the table as desired.

### 3 MAKING THE STOOLS

Cut the apron pieces to the given dimensions and sand them. Make a frame as shown in the exploded view on the next page, and assemble using glue and two #8 x 1 1/2-inch brass round head wood screws at each corner. Use a carpenter's square to make sure that the apron frame is square.

Secure the seat slats to the apron, using four #8 x 1 1/2-inch brass round head wood screws in each slat. After cutting the legs to the given dimensions, notch two adjacent corners in the top of each leg. The notches should be 3/8 deep and 2 inches long so that the apron will sit over them for extra strength, as shown in the corner detail on the next page.

Cut the corner braces to the given dimensions. Hold one of the legs in position against the apron, measure the braces against the

glue; the cement is applied to the other side. After the arrays have been cemented to the particleboard and the cement has fully dried, the paper attached to the finish side must be removed carefully by applying a mist of water, followed by scraping. Additional watering and scraping may be necessary.

Veneer the edge first, the game array second, and the border last. After the veneer pieces are laid down, they must be set by striking a small, flat wooden block randomly over the surface. Trim the edges carefully with a razor blade or sharp utility knife. When all of the veneer has been set, wipe down the area with a tack cloth and apply a coat of varnish.

### 2 MAKING THE TABLE

The tabletop is a laminate consisting of an upper and lower section. The upper section pieces have chip pocket cutouts, which are made with a drill and jigsaw. The lower section provides the base for these pockets and includes a small

106

## projects for quiet time

### MAKING THE STOOLS

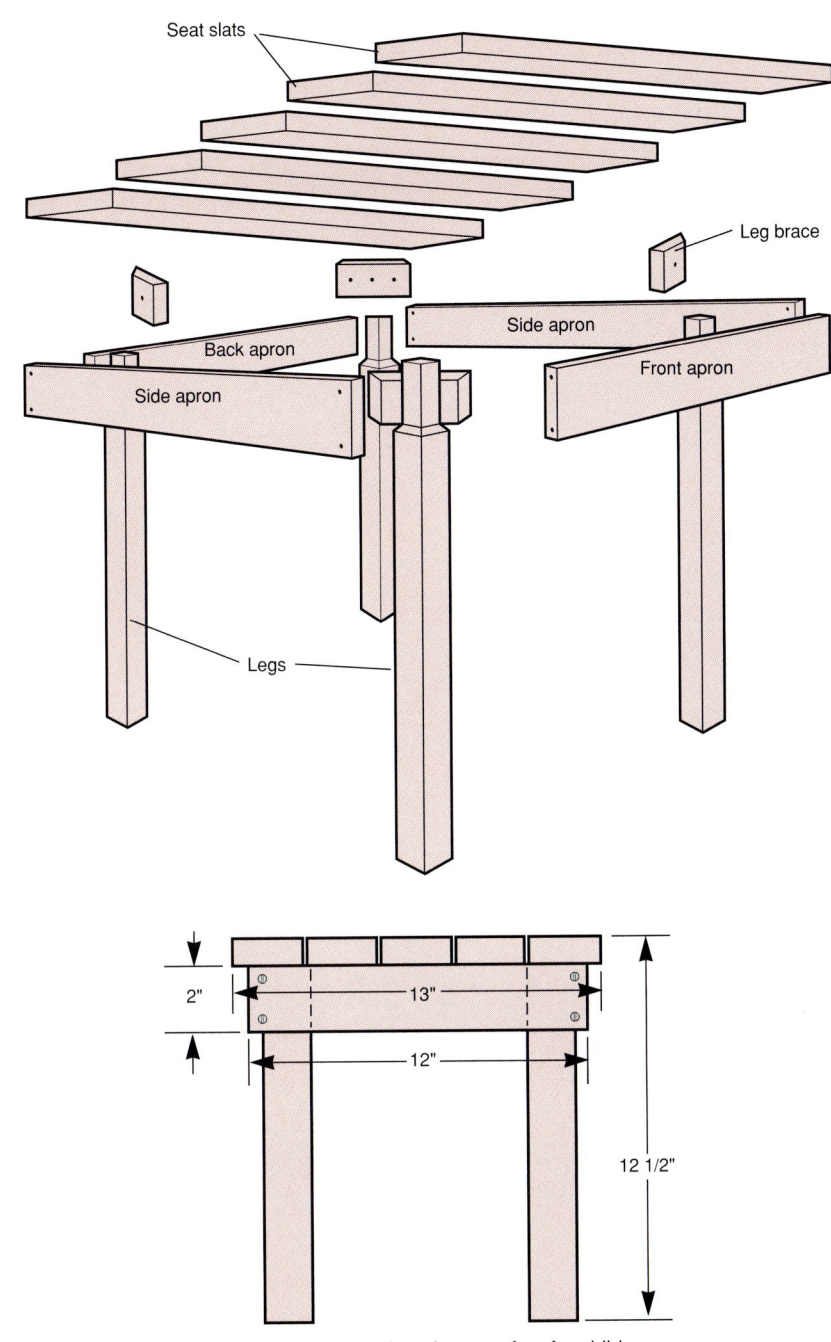

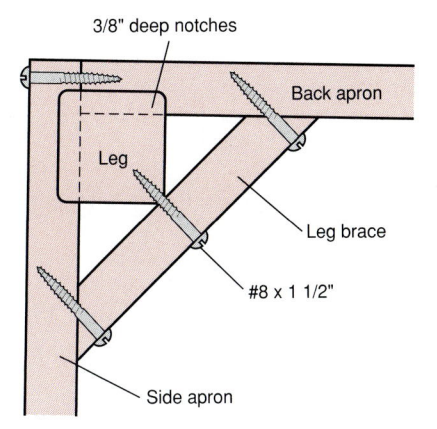

Use three screws at each corner to install the braces and legs.

corners of the apron (up against the leg), and cut 45° miters at either end so that they will hold the legs against the apron. Install the braces and legs, as shown in the illustration, with #8 x 1 1/2-inch brass round head wood screws.

Sand the stools thoroughly, then stain or finish to match the game table.

The 12 1/2-inch height of the benches makes them perfect for children.

107

*projects for quiet time*

# ADIRONDACK CHAIR

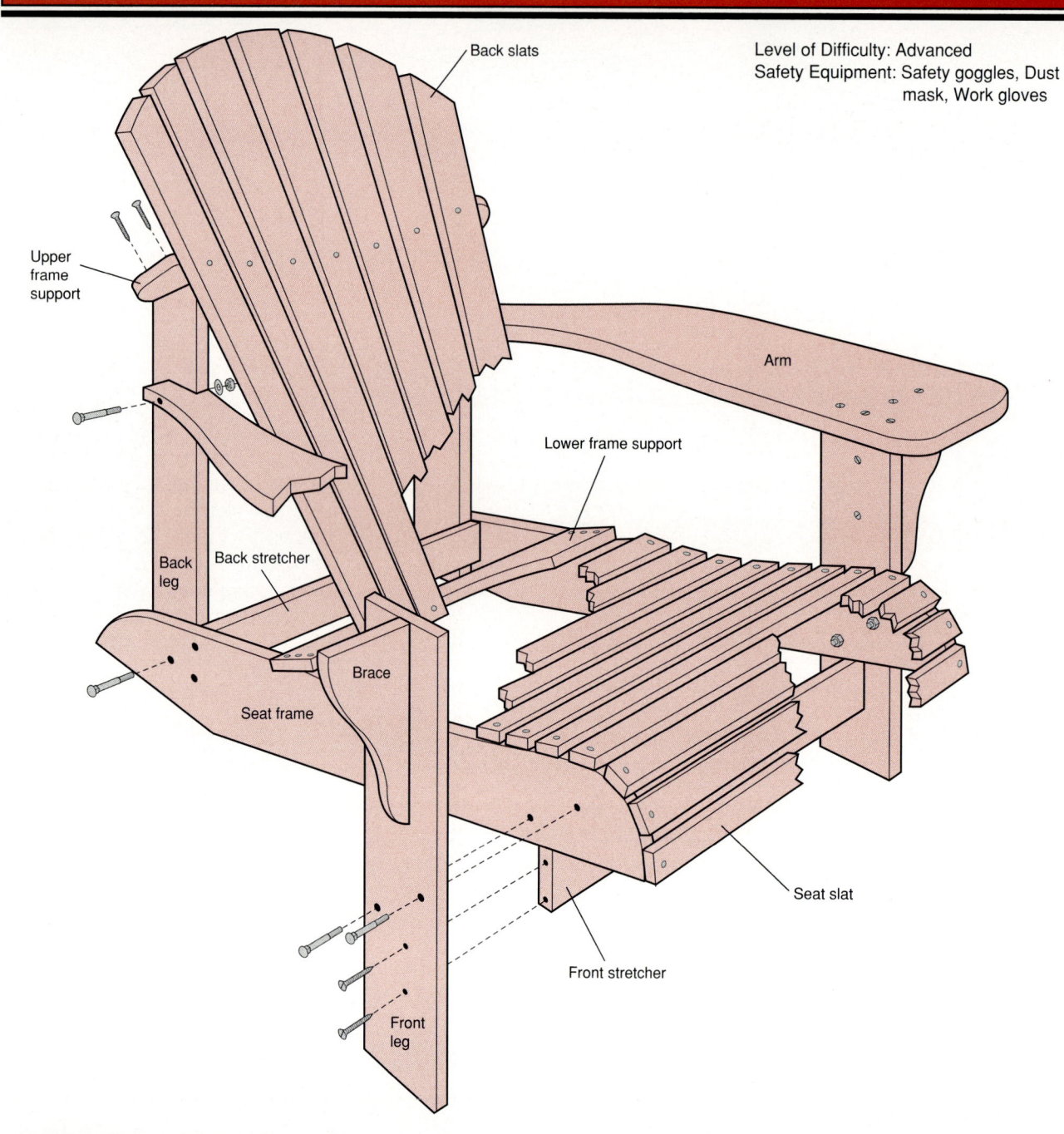

Back slats

Level of Difficulty: Advanced
Safety Equipment: Safety goggles, Dust mask, Work gloves

Upper frame support

Arm

Lower frame support

Back leg

Back stretcher

Brace

Seat frame

Seat slat

Front stretcher

Front leg

## MATERIALS, PARTS, AND CUTTING LIST

| Material/Part Name | Qty. | Size |
|---|---|---|
| Pressure-treated select #3 pine | 4 | 1 x 2 x 5' |
| Seat slats | 11 | 3/4" x 1 3/16" x 20" |
| Pressure-treated select #3 pine | 7 | 1 x 4 x 3' |
| Back slats | 7 | 3/4" x 2 3/4" x 32" |
| Pressure-treated select #3 pine | 2 | 1 x 4 x 5' |
| Back legs | 2 | 3/4" x 3 1/2" x 21 1/2" |
| Back stretcher | 1 | 3/4" x 3 1/2" x 18 1/2" |
| Front stretcher | 1 | 3/4" x 3 1/2" x 20" |
| Lower frame support | 1 | 3/4" x 3 1/2" x 20" |
| Braces | 2 | 3/4" x 3 1/2" x 6" |
| Pressure-treated select #3 pine | 1 | 1 x 5 x 2' |
| Upper frame support | 1 | 3/4" x 4 1/2" x 22" |

| Material/Part Name | Qty. | Size |
|---|---|---|
| Pressure-treated select #3 pine | 3 | 1 x 6 x 3' |
| Seat frames | 2 | 3/4" x 5 1/2" x 32 1/2" |
| Front legs | 2 | 3/4" x 5 1/2" x 16" |
| Pressure-treated select #3 pine | 1 | 1 x 8 x 4' |
| Arms | 2 | 3/4" x 5 3/4" x 24" |
| Galvanized deck screws | 54 | #8 x 2" |
| Galvanized carriage bolts | 6 | 1/4" x 2" |
| Galvanzied carriage bolts | 2 | 1/4" x 3 1/2" |
| Waterproof urea resin or resorcinol glue | 1 | can or bottle |

108

## projects for quiet time

With its steeply angled back and long curved seat both slatted, it would be understandable to doubt just how comfortable this Adirondack chair could be. But rest assured, it will quickly become a favorite of your children for reading, playing, and (rare as this may be for youngsters) just plain relaxing. While this version is scaled to child-size, it is nevertheless very durable and designed to withstand its share of abuse. With the exception of the back slats, all of the parts are made from 3/4-inch common pine boards that require no ripping.

With the "use zone" figured in, the Adirondack chair requires an area at least 6 feet long and 7 feet wide for optimum safety.

### CUTTING THE ARMS AND BRACES

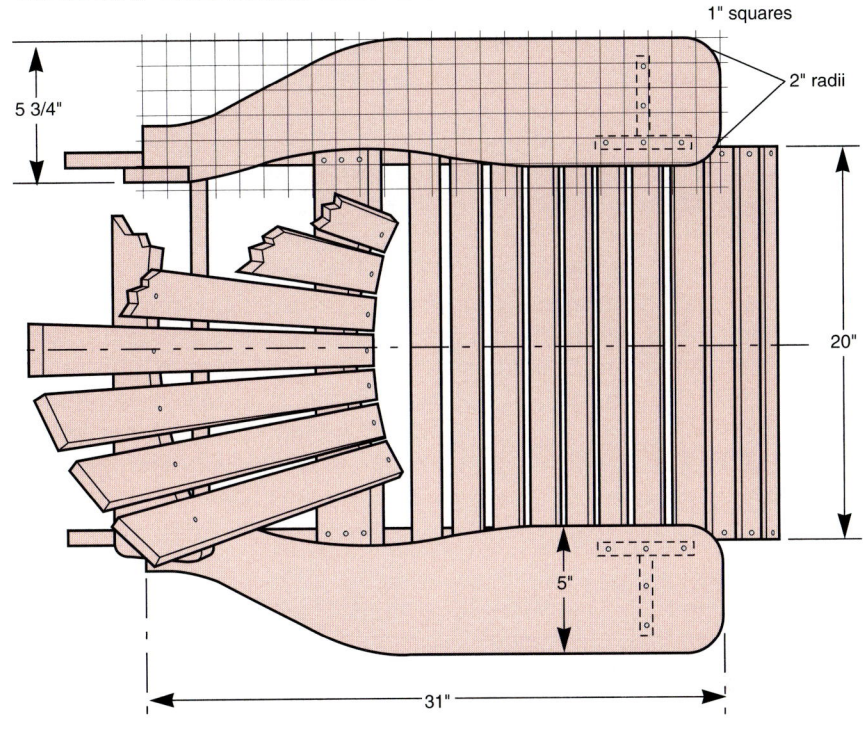

This Top View also includes a graph drawing to aid in cutting the arms.

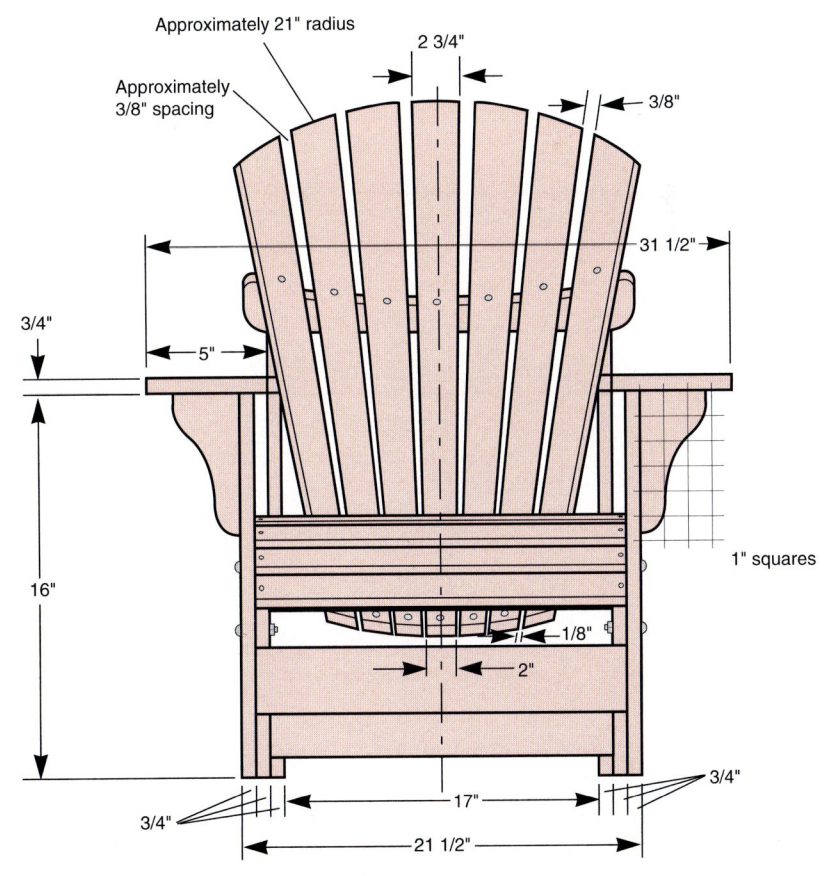

### PREPARING THE SEAT FRAME

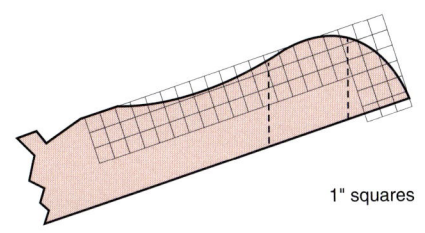

Use the graph drawing to make a pattern for the curved front portion of the seat frame pieces.

### CUTTING THE LEGS, STRETCHERS, AND SLATS

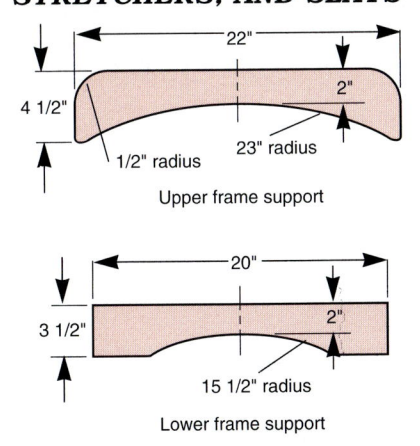

Upper frame support

Lower frame support

The radii of the frame supports can be marked using a pencil tied to a string and anchored by a nail.

This Front View also includes a graph drawing to aid in cutting the braces.

109

*projects for quiet time*

## 1 PREPARING THE SEAT FRAME

Start with the two seat frame members. After cutting an 18° taper on the bottom of the back of each piece, enlarge the graph drawing for the front. Make a full-size pattern, transfer it to the stock, and cut the seat curves. Cut a notch in the top of each seat frame member to accommodate the lower frame support, then radius the back corners as shown in the Side View.

## 2 CUTTING THE LEGS, STRETCHERS, AND SLATS

Cut the front and back legs to length. The top of the back legs must be mitered to 57° as shown in the Side View. Next, cut the two stretchers and eleven seat slats to length. The trick to cutting the radii on the two frame supports is to use a pencil tied to a string and anchored by a nail. For the lower frame support, the length of the string between the pencil and nail should be 15 1/2 inches, while 23 inches is required for the upper frame support.

The seven back slats are initially cut to the same dimension, as given in the Materials, Parts, and Cutting List. The 2 3/4-inch top width tapers to 2 inches at the bottom of the slats. After the tapers are cut, line up the back slats side-by-side, clamp securely, and scribe a 21-inch radius to make the curved top.

## 3 CUTTING THE ARMS AND BRACES

Enlarge the graph drawing for the two arms and make a full-size pattern. Transfer the pattern to the stock, and cut out the arms. Do the same for the two braces. Notch each arm as shown to accept the back legs. You are now ready to put the chair together.

## 4 ASSEMBLING THE CHAIR

The chair is assembled using waterproof glue, round head screws, and carriage bolts, as shown in the exploded view and the assembly drawing below. When laying out the back slats, note that their spacing is about 3/8 inch at the top and then tapers to less than 1/8 inch at the bottom. Be sure to chamfer any sharp edges, and sand the corners and edges as needed to prevent splintering. Finish the chair with a durable exterior finish.

**ASSEMBLING THE CHAIR**

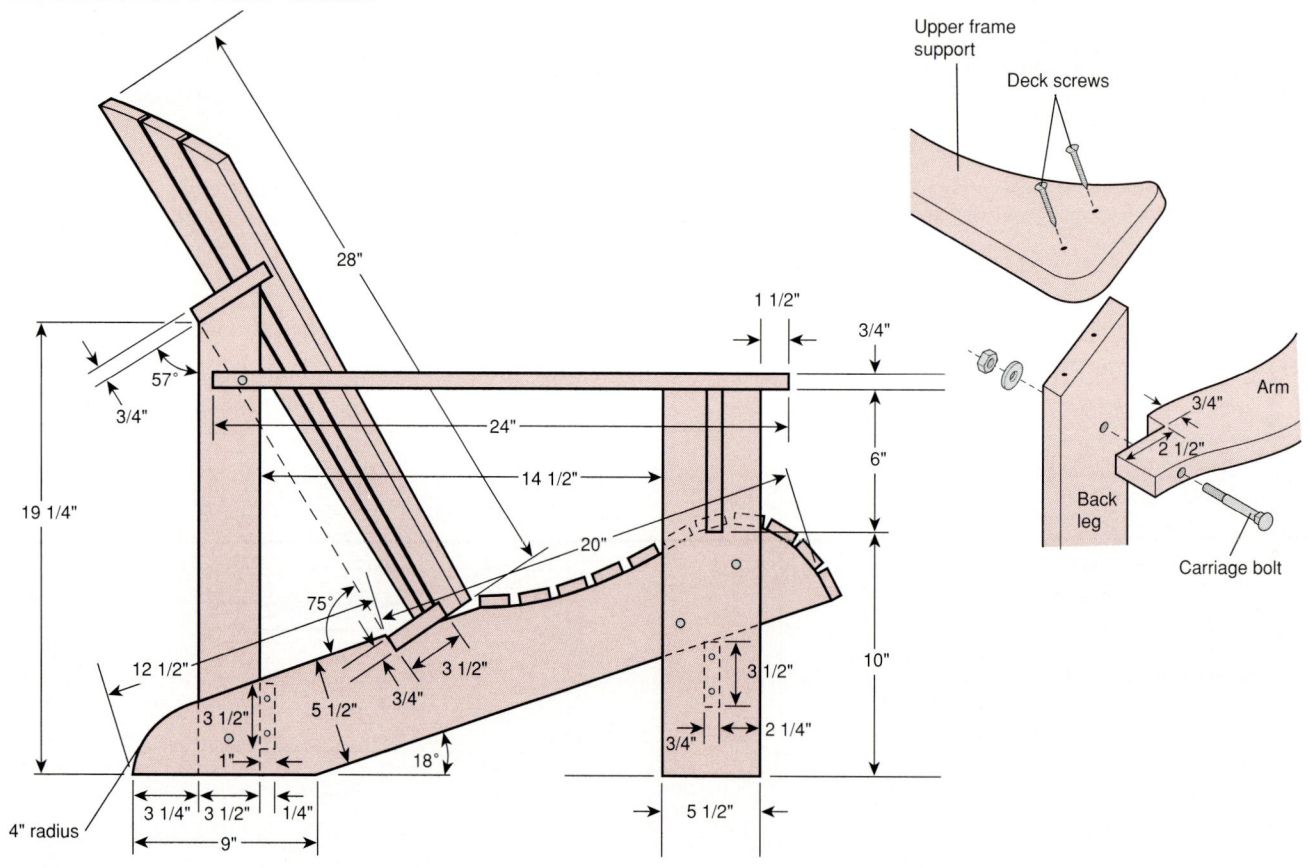

The Adirondack chair is assembled with carriage bolts and deck screws, as shown in this Side View and arm assembly drawing.

*projects for gardening*

# Six-Sided Garden Plot

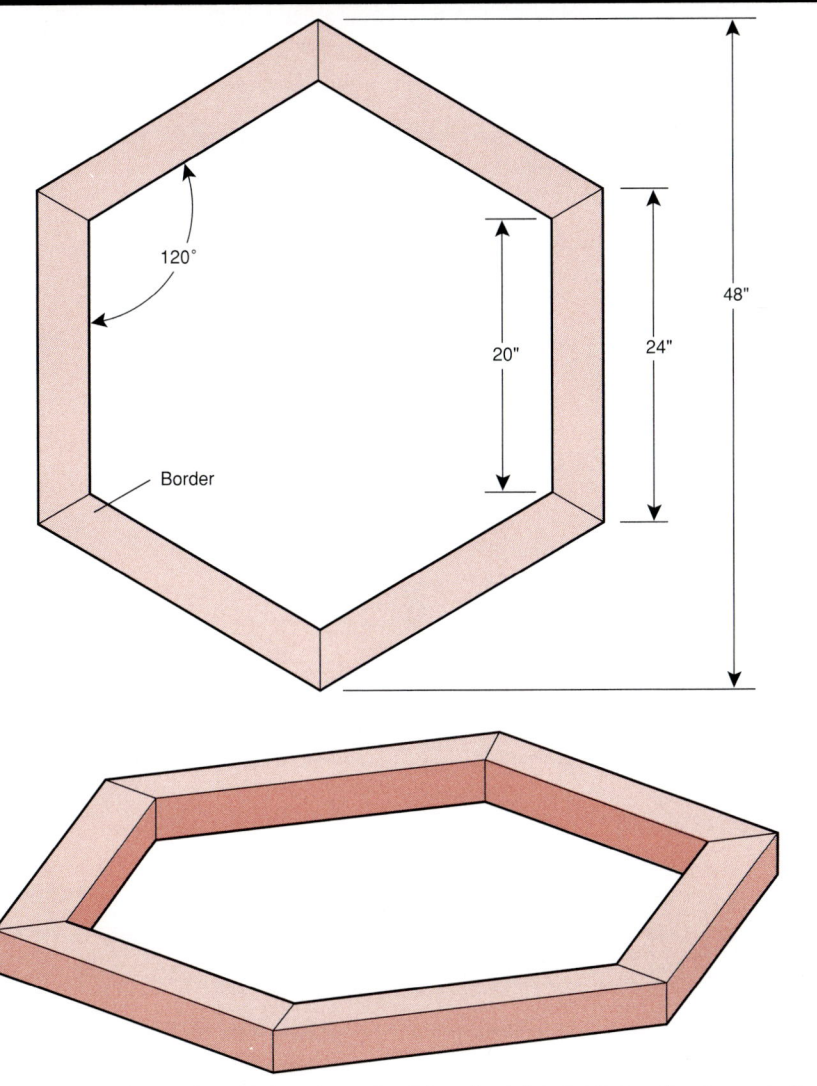

Completed Project Photo: See page 15.
Level of Difficulty: Basic
Safety Equipment: Safety goggles, Work gloves

### SIZING THE TIMBERS

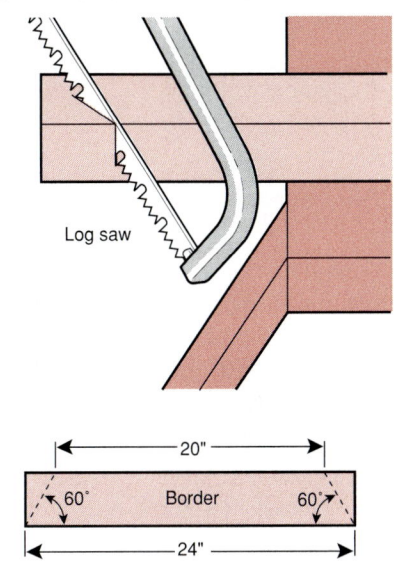

Make the miter cuts on the timber ends with a handsaw or log saw.

When laying out the garden plot, butt the ends of the miter joints tightly together to create the hexagonal shape.

**MATERIALS, PARTS, AND CUTTING LIST**

| Material/Part Name | Qty. | Size |
|---|---|---|
| Landscape timbers | 6 | 2 x 6 x 2' |
| Borders | 6 | 1 1/2" x 5 1/2" x 2' |
| Galvanized nail spikes | 12 | 30d |
| Topsoil | 2 | 50-lb. bag |
| Sand | 5-6 | Handfuls |

Any child will enjoy his or her own personal garden. This hexagonal plot bordered with landscape timbers is the perfect size for a young farmer or botanist to learn the skills needed to grow prize-winning vegetables or blooms.

With the "use zone" figured in, the six-sided garden plot requires an area at least 7 feet long and 8 feet wide for optimum safety.

## 1 SIZING THE TIMBERS

The majority of work involved in this project will be done when cutting the mitered ends on the 2-foot landscape timbers. The timbers are too large to be angle-cut using a standard 7 1/4-inch or 8 1/4-inch circular saw, so be prepared for some substantial cutting using a good sharp handsaw or log saw. Mark out the 60° cut lines on the ends of each timber, using a combination set. Make sure the cut on one end of the timber is the mirror image of the cut on the other end. Work slowly and follow the cut line carefully.

## 2 PREPARING THE BASE

Lay out the timbers at the garden site, butting the ends of the miter joints tightly together to create the hexagon shape. Mark the inside border of the plot by cutting into the soil with a square mouth shovel or pickax. You can also sprinkle

111

## projects for gardening

### PREPARING THE BASE

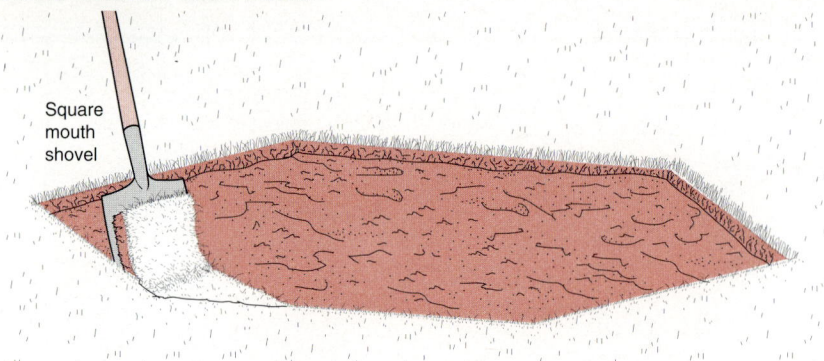

Square mouth shovel

Remove all sod from the inside of the plot.

### INSTALLING THE TIMBERS

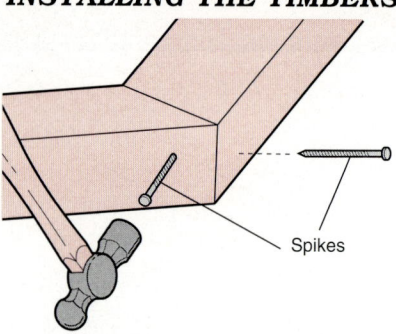

Spikes

Drive the spikes at the miter joints deep into the wood.

a small amount of sand along the inside edges of the timbers to mark off the plot. Now remove the timbers and cut away the sod using the shovel or pickax.

### 3 INSTALLING THE TIMBERS

Once all sod has been removed, reposition the timbers around the perimeter of the plot. Tie the timbers together at the mitered joints by driving two 30d spikes through the joint ends. This will give the border the stability it needs when a young gardener decides to use it as a balance beam or seat.

### 4 FINAL PREPARATION

Dump in fresh topsoil and level. You are now ready to sow seeds or transplant seedlings.

### FINAL PREPARATION

Add fresh topsoil to the garden plot, and you're ready to plant.

112

*projects for gardening*

# WHEELBARROW

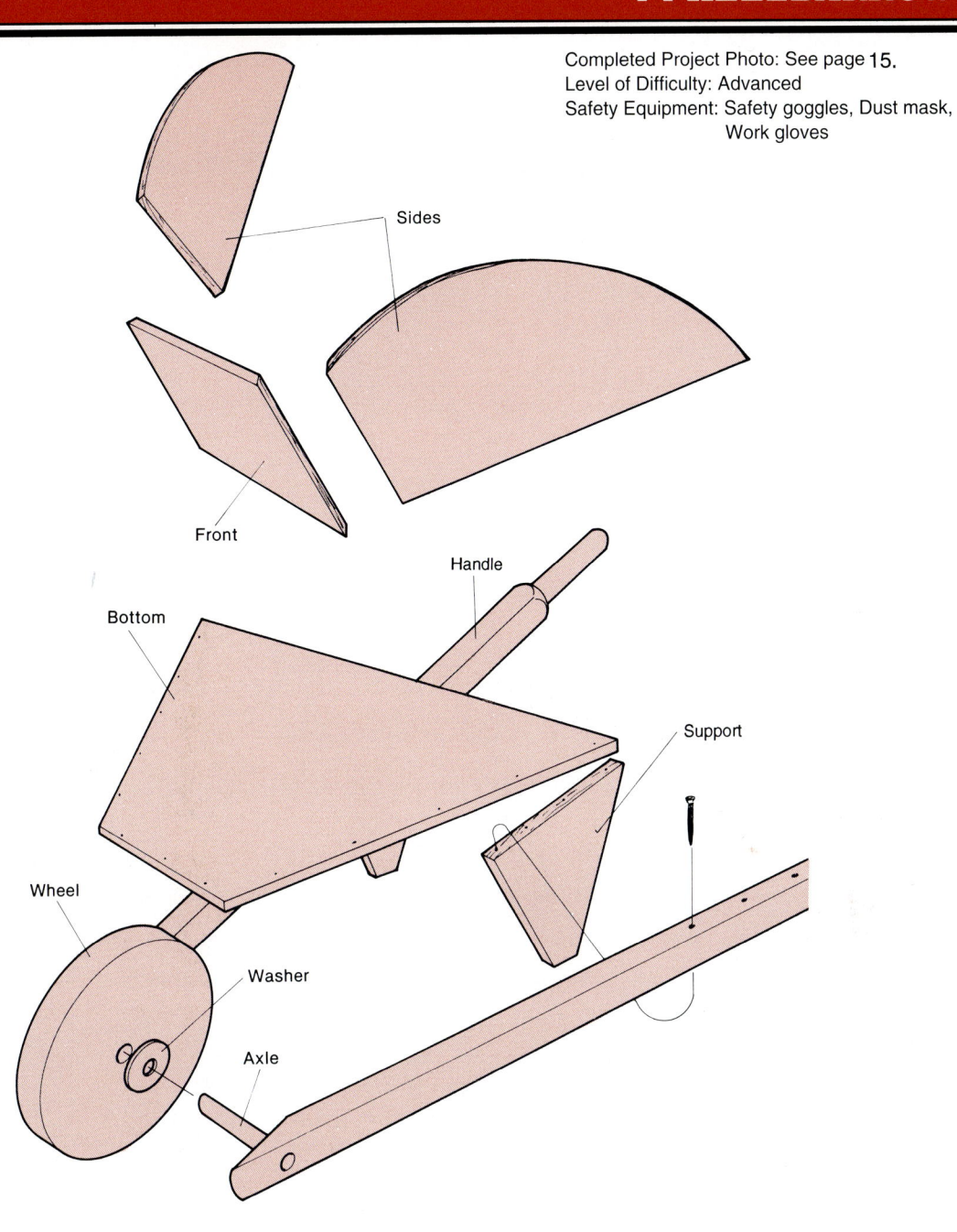

Completed Project Photo: See page 15.
Level of Difficulty: Advanced
Safety Equipment: Safety goggles, Dust mask, Work gloves

Sides
Front
Handle
Bottom
Support
Wheel
Washer
Axle

## MATERIALS, PARTS, AND CUTTING LIST

| Material/Part Name | Qty. | Size |
|---|---|---|
| Pressure-treated #2 select white pine | 1 | 1 x 10 x 4' |
| Sides | 2 | 3/4" x 8 1/2" x 19" |
| Front | 1 | 3/4" x 8 3/4" x 9" |
| Pressure-treated #2 select white pine | 1 | 2 x 3 x 5' |
| Handles | 2 | 1 1/4" x 1 3/4" x 25" |
| Pressure-treated #2 select white pine | 1 | 2 x 6 x 1' |
| Supports | 2 | 1 1/4" x 5" x 5 1/2" |
| Pressure-treated #2 select white pine | 1 | 2 x 8 x 1' |
| Wheel | 1 | 1 1/4" x 6 1/2" x 6 1/2" |

| Material/Part Name | Qty. | Size |
|---|---|---|
| Exterior grade plywood | 1 | 3/4" x 4' x 8' |
| Bottom | 1 | 3/4" x 14 3/4" x 15" |
| Hardwood dowel | 1 | 1/2"-dia. x 4" |
| Axle | 1 | 1/2"-dia. x 4" |
| Galvanized flat head wood screws | 8 | #8 x 2" |
| Galvanized flat head wood screws | 42 | #8 x 1 1/4" |

113

## projects for gardening

A sturdy toy wheelbarrow is an item that all youngsters seem to enjoy. Not only is it the perfect accessory for the budding gardener, but children can use it to carry loads of toys—and for that reason it must be constructed to withstand hard knocks. The one shown here is made of white pine, with 3/4-inch stock for the sides, front, and bottom, and 1 1/4-inch stock for the handles, wheel, and supports. The 1 1/4-inch stock is available at many lumberyards, but you may have to order it. You can also use 1 1/2-inch stock—such as a 2 x 6 for the supports—and run it down with a portable belt sander to the required thickness. The supports and wheel can be made of 3/4-inch stock, if necessary, but this thickness will not be as sturdy.

The only difficult parts of this project are cutting the beveled edges on the barrow front and the curved edge of the sides. A saber saw does a good job on the curved edge of the sides, and a portable circular saw is fine for cutting the beveled edges.

### 1 CUTTING THE PIECES

Enlarge the graph drawing for the sides and transfer the pattern to 3/4-inch stock. Cut out the sides with a saber saw. Bevel the edges of the front to the dimensions and angles shown in Detail A. Cut the bottom to the dimensions given, as shown in Detail B. Sand all the pieces; the edges on the bottom, the upper edge of the front piece, and the top and curved edge of the side pieces must be smooth.

### 2 ASSEMBLING THE BARROW

Fasten the front piece between the sides with glue and countersunk #8 x 1 1/4-inch flat head wood screws.

### CUTTING THE PIECES

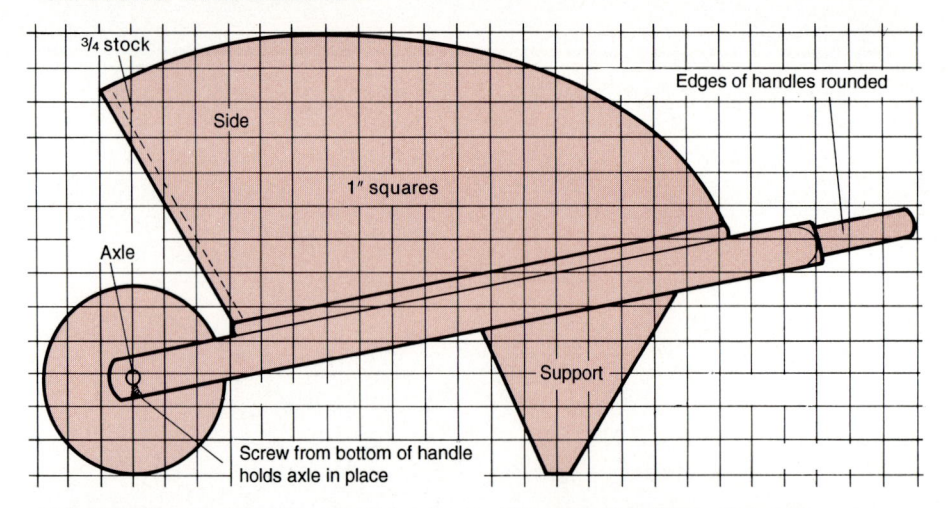

This Side View also includes a graph drawing to aid in cutting the sides and supports.

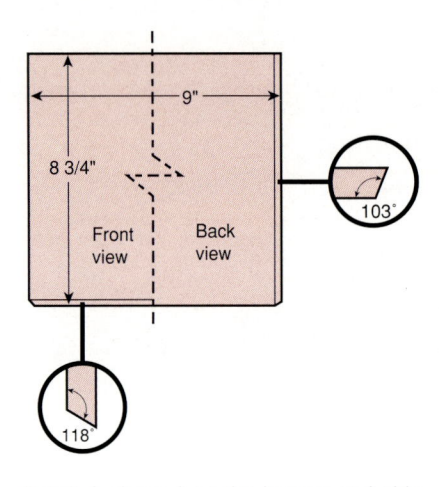

Detail A shows how the bottom and side edges of the barrow front are beveled.

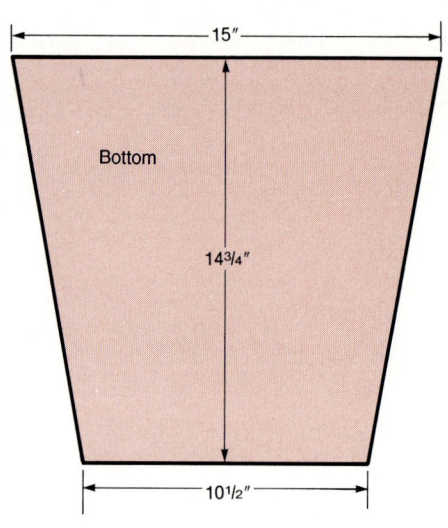

Then fasten this assembly to the bottom as shown in Detail C, using glue and countersunk #8 x 1 1/4-inch flat head wood screws. Cover the countersunk screws with wood plugs and sand them down. Sand the entire barrow and set it aside.

### 3 CUTTING THE HANDLES

Cut the handles to the given dimensions; then mark for the angled ends, as shown in Detail D, and make the cuts. Position each handle as shown in Detail E, and

Cut the bottom to the exact shape shown in Detail B.

bore a 1/2-inch hole straight through the center, 1 inch from the end. Round the front ends of the handles with a saber saw, as shown on the graph drawing. Cut a 4-inch rounded portion for the gripping end of the handles.

### 4 CUTTING THE WHEEL AND SUPPORTS

Use a compass to mark a 5 3/4-inch circle on 1 1/4-inch stock and cut it out with a saber saw. Smooth

## projects for gardening

### ASSEMBLING THE BARROW

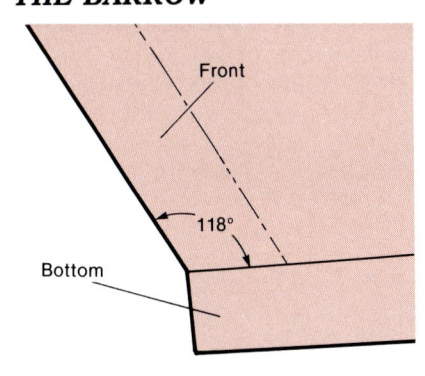

The front attaches to the bottom at a 118° angle, as seen in Detail C.

### CUTTING THE HANDLES

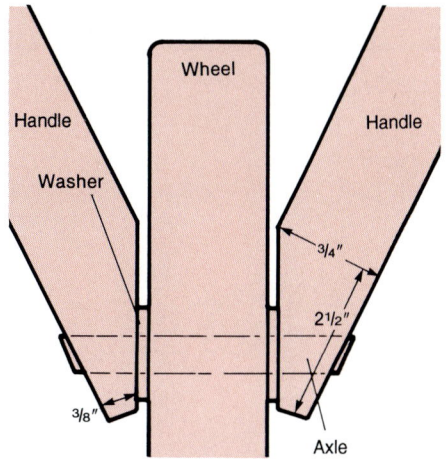

Detail D illustrates the axle assembly. A 1/2-inch-diameter hardwood dowel acts as the axle.

Detail E: Drill at a right angle to the flat surface of the handles to accommodate the axle.

the saw cuts with a disc sander so that the wheel is perfectly round and rolls smoothly. Then use a wood rasp and sandpaper, and round the edges of the wheel. Enlarge the graph drawing for the supports, transfer the pattern to 1 1/4-inch stock, cut out the supports, and sand them smooth.

### 5 ASSEMBLING THE HANDLES, WHEEL, AXLE, AND SUPPORTS

Fasten the supports to the handles, as shown on the graph drawing, with glue and #8 x 2-inch flat head wood screws. The screws should be countersunk and driven down through the top edge of the handles. Bore a 1/2-inch hole exactly in the center of the wheel and sand it out with sandpaper wrapped around a piece of scrap wood until a 1/2-inch dowel will turn easily in the hole. Cut a 4-inch length of 1/2-inch dowel for the axle. Put the wheel between the angled handle ends and drive the axle through one handle, the wheel with a washer on either side, and the other handle. Turn the assembly on its back and drive a #8 x 1 1/4-inch flat head wood screw through one of the handle ends into the axle to secure it in place. Work the handles apart or together so that there is room enough for the washers to turn easily. Then cut the ends of the axle flush with the edges of the handles.

Sand the assembly thoroughly. If you plan to paint the barrow, handles, and wheel in contrasting colors, do it now. If you plan to paint the entire project in one color or use a single finish over the whole piece, proceed with final assembly first.

### 6 FINAL ASSEMBLY

Lay the handle assembly on a flat, smooth surface and fit the barrow in place for marking positions. The outside edge of the back of the barrow should be flush with the outside edges of the handles when the front of the barrow is 1 inch away from the back edge of the wheel and is centered over the front of the handle assembly. After marking the location of the handles on the underside of the barrow, use glue and countersunk #8 x 1 1/4-inch flat head wood screws to fasten on the handles, driving the screws down through the barrow. Cover the screws with wood plugs and sand them smooth.

115

*projects for gardening*

# Window Box Planter and Stand

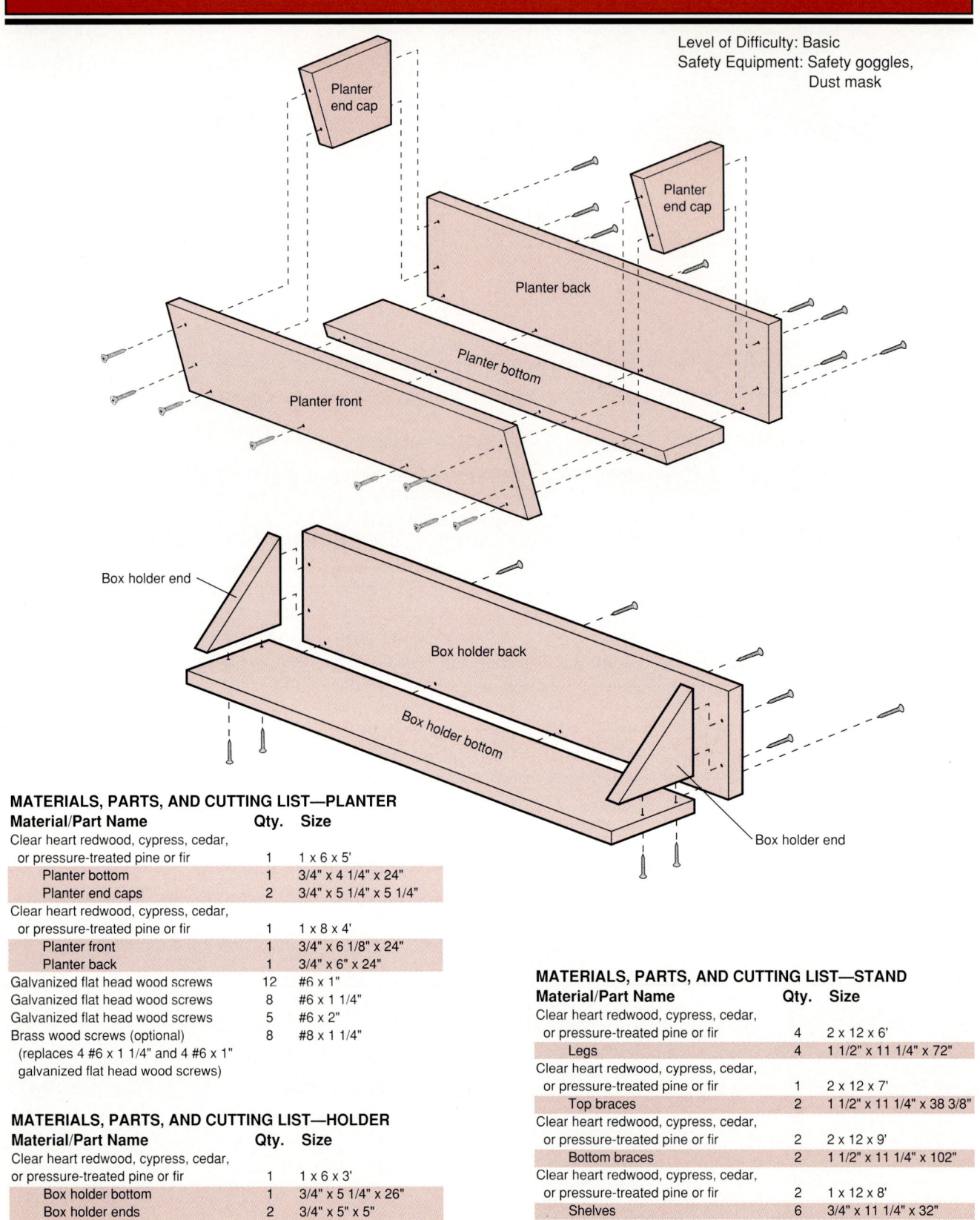

Level of Difficulty: Basic
Safety Equipment: Safety goggles, Dust mask

### MATERIALS, PARTS, AND CUTTING LIST—PLANTER

| Material/Part Name | Qty. | Size |
|---|---|---|
| Clear heart redwood, cypress, cedar, or pressure-treated pine or fir | 1 | 1 x 6 x 5' |
| Planter bottom | 1 | 3/4" x 4 1/4" x 24" |
| Planter end caps | 2 | 3/4" x 5 1/4" x 5 1/4" |
| Clear heart redwood, cypress, cedar, or pressure-treated pine or fir | 1 | 1 x 8 x 4' |
| Planter front | 1 | 3/4" x 6 1/8" x 24" |
| Planter back | 1 | 3/4" x 6" x 24" |
| Galvanized flat head wood screws | 12 | #6 x 1" |
| Galvanized flat head wood screws | 8 | #6 x 1 1/4" |
| Galvanized flat head wood screws | 5 | #6 x 2" |
| Brass wood screws (optional) (replaces 4 #6 x 1 1/4" and 4 #6 x 1" galvanized flat head wood screws) | 8 | #8 x 1 1/4" |

### MATERIALS, PARTS, AND CUTTING LIST—HOLDER

| Material/Part Name | Qty. | Size |
|---|---|---|
| Clear heart redwood, cypress, cedar, or pressure-treated pine or fir | 1 | 1 x 6 x 3' |
| Box holder bottom | 1 | 3/4" x 5 1/4" x 26" |
| Box holder ends | 2 | 3/4" x 5" x 5" |
| Box holder back | 1 | 3/4" x 6" x 26" |
| Galvanized flat head wood screws | 4 | #6 x 1" |
| Galvanized flat head wood screws | 4 | #6 x 1 1/4" |

### MATERIALS, PARTS, AND CUTTING LIST—STAND

| Material/Part Name | Qty. | Size |
|---|---|---|
| Clear heart redwood, cypress, cedar, or pressure-treated pine or fir | 4 | 2 x 12 x 6' |
| Legs | 4 | 1 1/2" x 11 1/4" x 72" |
| Clear heart redwood, cypress, cedar, or pressure-treated pine or fir | 1 | 2 x 12 x 7' |
| Top braces | 2 | 1 1/2" x 11 1/4" x 38 3/8" |
| Clear heart redwood, cypress, cedar, or pressure-treated pine or fir | 2 | 2 x 12 x 9' |
| Bottom braces | 2 | 1 1/2" x 11 1/4" x 102" |
| Clear heart redwood, cypress, cedar, or pressure-treated pine or fir | 2 | 1 x 12 x 8' |
| Shelves | 6 | 3/4" x 11 1/4" x 32" |
| Galvanized carriage bolts | 16 | 3/8" x 1 1/2" |
| Galvanized flat head wood screws | 48 | #6 x 1" |
| Galvanized "L" braces | 24 | |

*projects for gardening*

Your child doesn't even need a window to enjoy this window box planter. It offers an optional holder that can be screwed to the mounting area of your choice; or you can build the stand, which accommodates up to six planters. The planter shown is built of clear heart redwood, which is naturally resistant to ground rot. Cypress and cedar are two other naturally rot resistant woods, but you can also use pressure-treated pine or fir.

Dimensions are based on lumber that measures 3/4 inch in thickness. If the thickness of the stock you use varies slightly from 3/4 inch (7/8 inch, for example), you will have to alter the cutting dimensions of the side pieces slightly.

The planter measures 2 feet long, 6 inches high, 5 3/4 inches wide at the base, and 6 3/4 inches wide at the top. Inside widths are 4 1/4 inches at the base and 5 1/4 inches at the top.

The stand is made from 1 x 6 lumber; it is actually two A-frame assemblies tied together by shelves. The tiered shelf design ensures that all of the planters receive their fair share of sun and rain.

With the "use zone" figured in, the window box planter and stand require an area at least 6 feet long and 6 feet wide for optimum safety.

### ASSEMBLING THE PLANTER

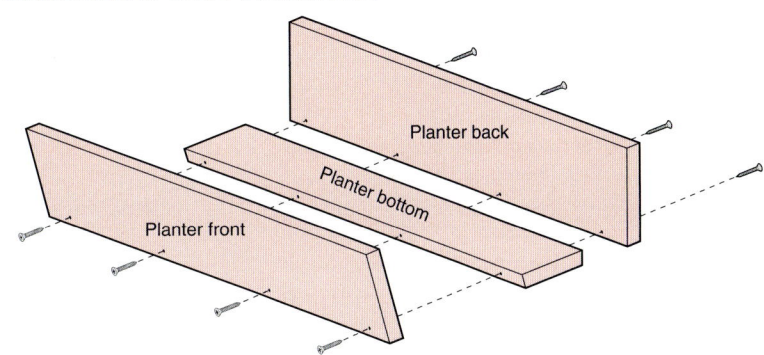

Join the bottom and back pieces first, then add the angled front.

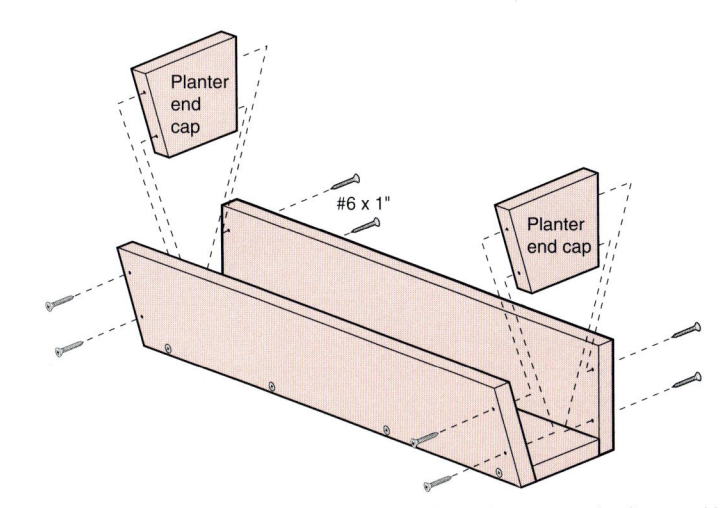

Secure the end caps using two #6 x 1-inch flat head wood screws at the front and back.

## 1 CUTTING PLANTER AND HOLDER LUMBER TO SIZE

Cut all planter and holder stock to size, following the cutting diagram.

Both the planter front and bottom pieces require 10° bevel rip-cutting. The table saw is the most accurate tool for this task, but a portable circular saw can also be used. Make a test-cut in scrap

### CUTTING PLANTER AND HOLDER LUMBER TO SIZE

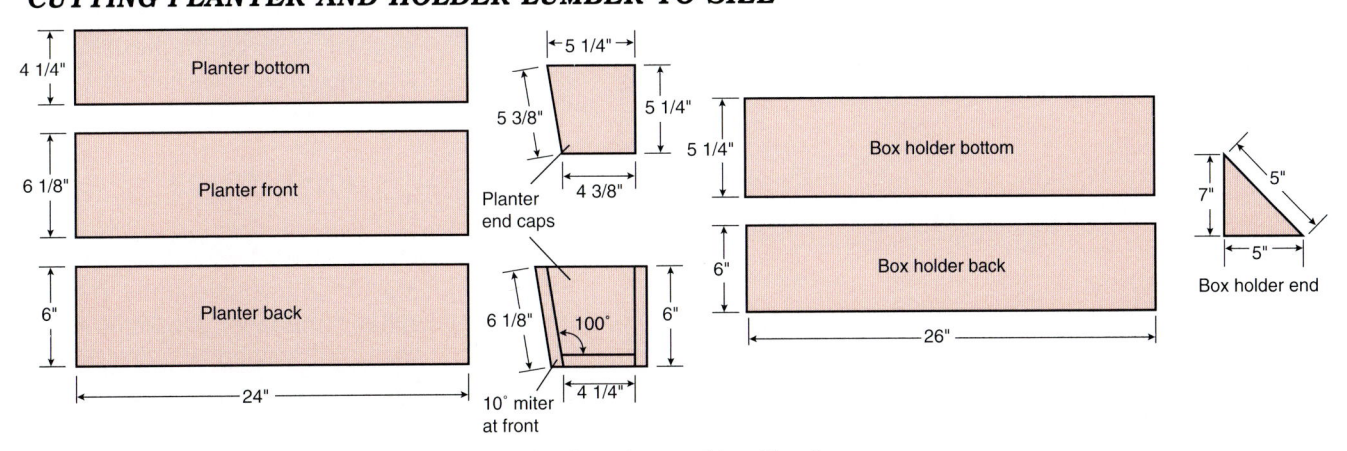

Cut the lumber for the planter and holder according to the dimensions on this cutting diagram.

117

# projects for gardening

material to check the bevel setting and results before cutting the actual pieces.

Each planter end cap requires a 10° miter at its front, as illustrated. The holder ends are cut from a single 5 x 5 piece of stock that is cut diagonally from corner to corner.

## 2 ASSEMBLING THE PLANTER

The planter is constructed by assembling the bottom and back pieces to provide a base on which to position the angled front piece. Position the bottom against the back and drill four equally spaced 1/8-inch-diameter pilot holes through the back piece. Install four #6 x 1 1/4-inch flat head wood screws to fasten the back to the bottom.

Install the front piece to the bottom piece using four #6 x 1 1/4-inch flat head wood screws or #8 x 1 1/4-inch decorative brass screws.

## ASSEMBLING THE HOLDER

The holder assembles easily; follow these construction details.

### MOUNTING THE HOLDER

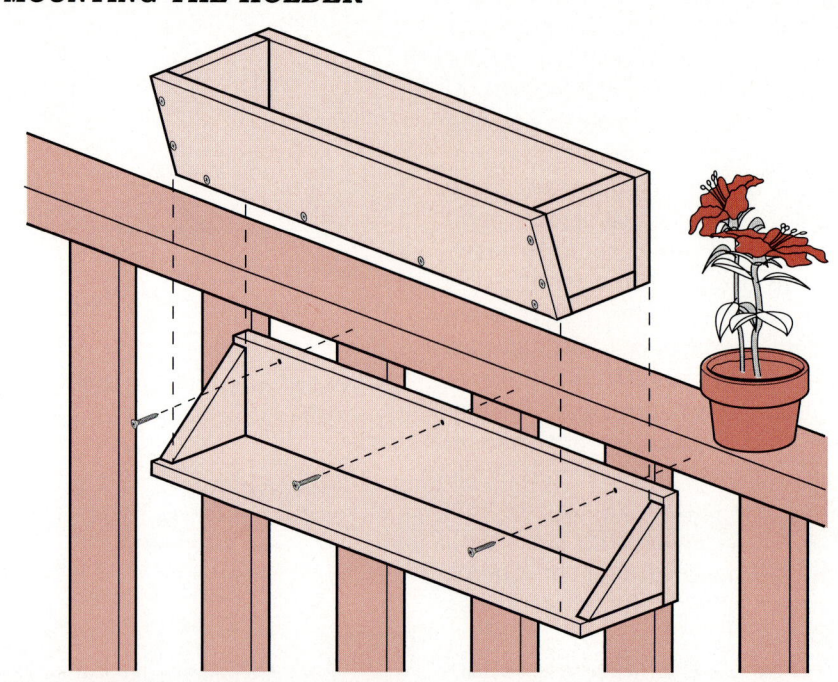

Mounting the holder requires hardware to match your particular mounting situation.

Install the end caps inside the front/back/bottom assembly using two #6 x 1-inch flat head wood screws at both the front and back as shown. Drill 1/8-inch pilot holes for all screws. Angle the pilot holes in the front pieces slightly so the screw head will rest flush against the angled front. Decorative brass screws can be used if desired.

## 3 ASSEMBLING THE HOLDER

The holder assembles quickly using four #6 x 1 1/4-inch flat head wood screws to fasten the back to the bottom and four #6 x 1-inch flat head wood screws to fasten the triangular ends to the bottom/back assembly. Drill 1/8-inch pilot holes for all screws.

## 4 FINISHING

Sand down all sharp edges on the planter and holder using medium grade sandpaper. Redwood is normally not stained or painted, but a

## projects for gardening

**CUTTING THE STAND LUMBER TO SIZE**

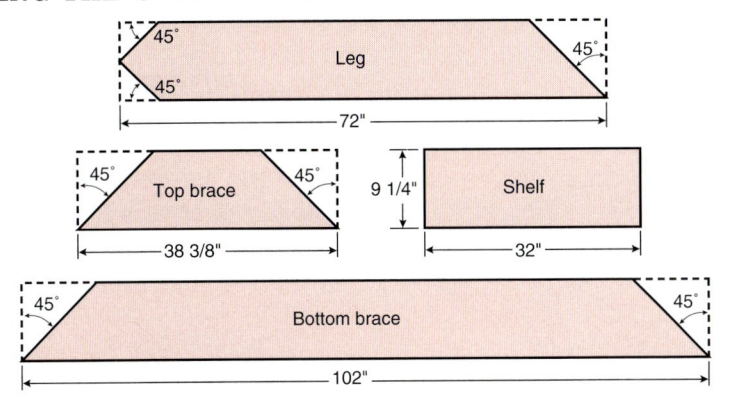

*(Leg: 72", 45° miters at both ends)*

*(Top brace: 38 3/8", 45° miters; Shelf: 9 1/4" × 32")*

*(Bottom brace: 102", 45° miters at both ends)*

**ASSEMBLING THE STAND**

*3/8" x 1 1/2" carriage bolts*

coat of clear polyurethane or sealer will prevent it from turning grey as it weathers. Pressure-treated lumber can be painted or stained to match surrounding decor.

## 5 MOUNTING THE HOLDER

The holder can mount directly to the windowsill or other surface using #6 x 2-inch flat head wood screws or expansion anchors (for masonry). Mounting hardware such as brackets or "L" braces may be required for special mountings.

## 6 CUTTING THE STAND LUMBER TO SIZE

Cut the legs, braces, and shelves to size according to the dimensions given. Miter the ends of the legs at 45° angles as shown so they fit together at the top and rest flat on the ground at the bottom. Miter the top and bottom braces at 45°

**ASSEMBLING THE STAND (CONTINUED)**

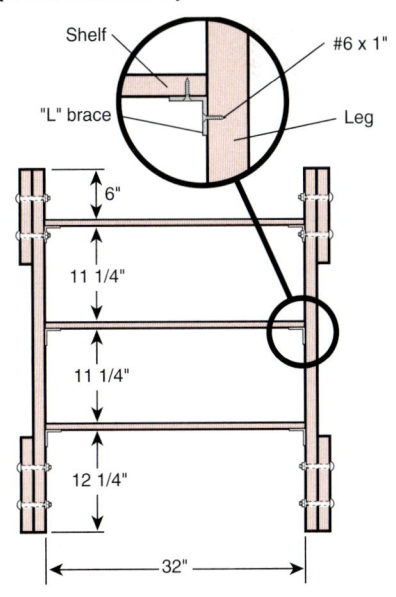

*(Dimensions: 6", 11 1/4", 11 1/4", 12 1/4"; width 32"; hardware #6 x 1")*

Metal "L" braces provide the necessary support for the shelves.

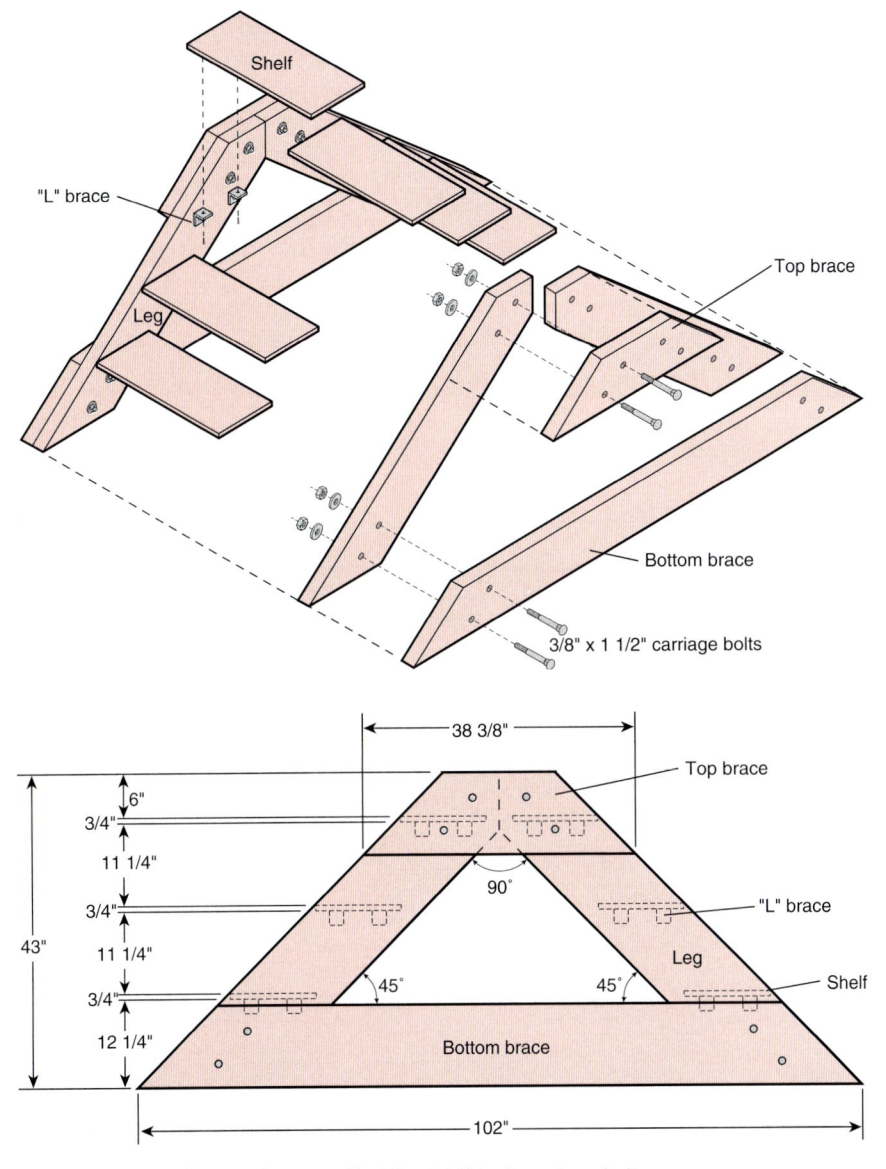

Attach the top and bottom braces with 3/8 x 1 1/2-inch carriage bolts.

*(Front view dimensions: 38 3/8" top brace width, 102" bottom brace width, 43" overall height; 6", 3/4", 11 1/4", 3/4", 11 1/4", 3/4", 12 1/4"; 90° at top, 45° angles at base)*

119

## projects for gardening

**ASSEMBLING THE STAND (CONTINUED)**

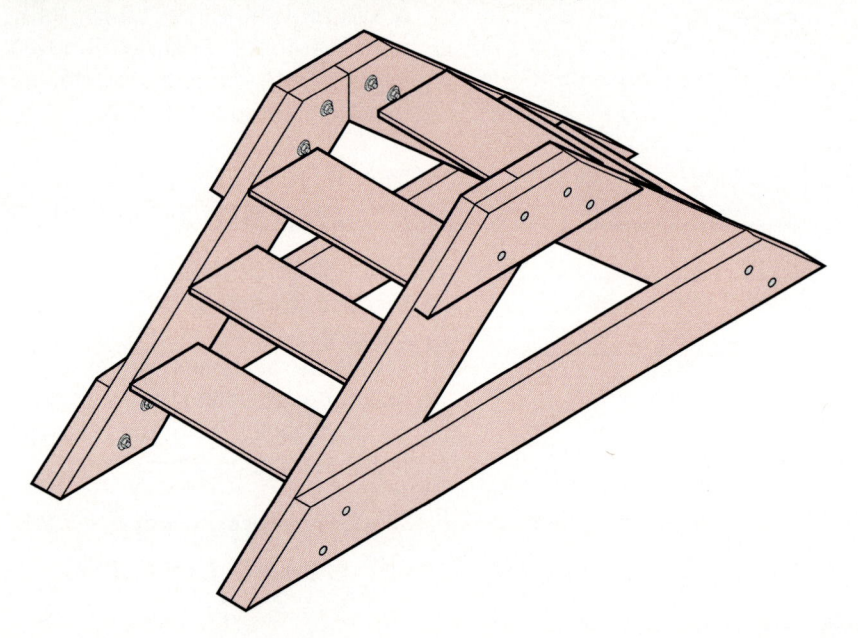

The completed stand can hold six window box planters.

angles so they match the contour of the legs.

### 7 ASSEMBLING THE STAND

Drill two 1/2-inch-diameter holes at each end of each brace. Make 1/2-inch-deep counterbores on the back of the legs, and bolt the braces to the legs using 3/8 x 1 1/2-inch carriage bolts.

Stand the leg assemblies upright. Assemble the stand by attaching the six shelves between the legs using "L" braces (four per shelf) and countersunk 1-inch flat head wood screws. Mark out the screw locations on the shelves and drill 3/4-inch deep pilot holes for the screws. The top shelves are mounted 6 inches from the top of the stand, and the bottom shelves are mounted 12 1/8 inches from the bottom of the stand. The middle shelves are equidistant from the top and bottom shelves.

Finish the stand to match the window box planter.

## projects for toys and games

# STICK PONY

Completed Project Photo: See page 16.
Level of Difficulty: Basic
Safety Equipment: Safety goggles, Dust mask, Work gloves

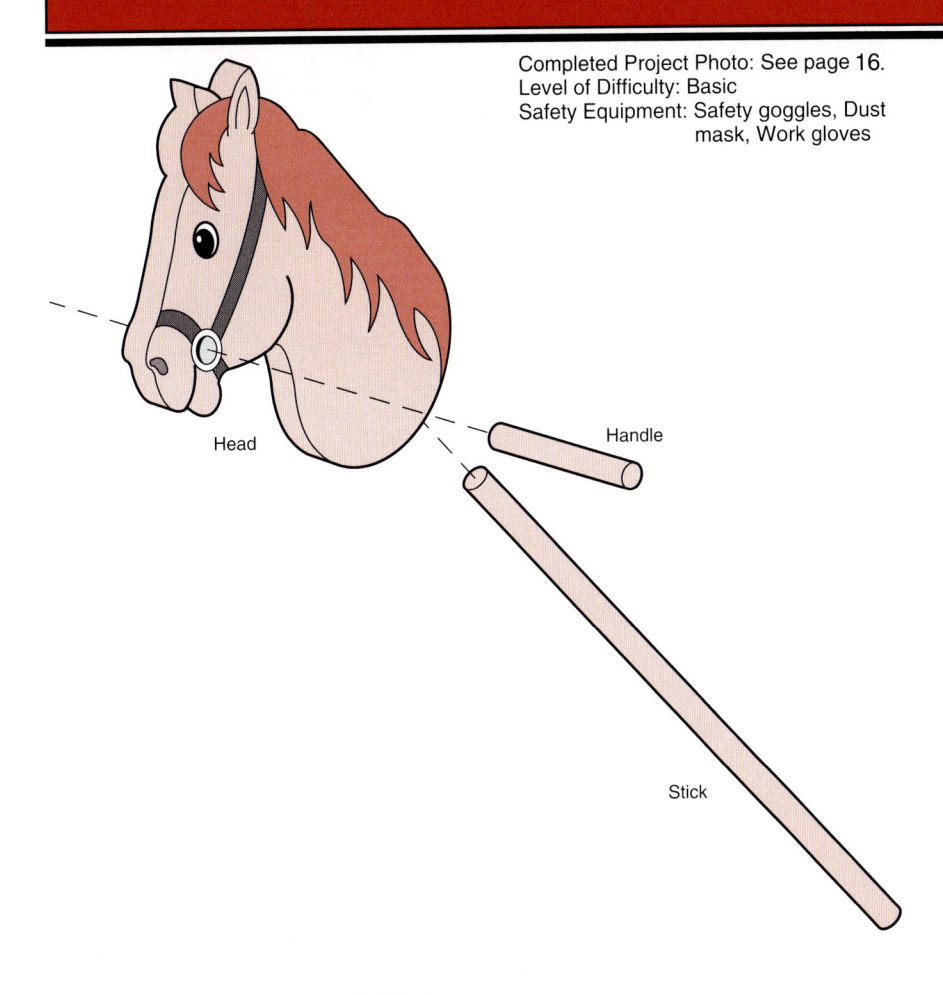

## CUTTING OUT THE HEAD

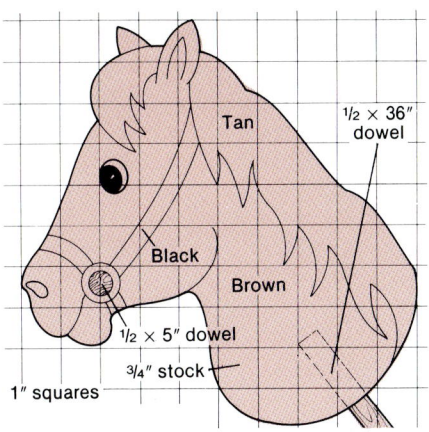

Use the graph drawing for cutting the horse head profile. Note that two holes must be drilled: one for the stick and one for the handle.

## 1 CUTTING OUT THE HEAD

Enlarge the graph drawing and transfer the pattern to the stock. Cut out the pattern with a saber saw or coping saw. Sand the edges of the head thoroughly, taking care that they are smooth.

## 2 FITTING THE HANDLE AND STICK

Place the head in a vise and drill a 1/2-inch-diameter x 2-inch deep hole in the bottom edge to accommodate the stick, as indicated on the drawing. Then bore a 1/2-inch-diameter hole through the head at the bridle to accommodate the handle. Sand away any rough spots caused by the drill. Cut the stick and handle to length and glue them in place. Allow the glue to set overnight; then paint as indicated on the drawing or to your own taste.

### MATERIALS, PARTS, AND CUTTING LIST

| Material/Part Name | Qty. | Size |
|---|---|---|
| Pressure-treated white pine or A-C exterior grade plywood | 1 | 3/4" x 10" x 10" |
|    Head | 1 | 3/4" x 10" x 10" |
| Hardwood dowel | 1 | 1/2"-dia. x 42" |
|    Stick | 1 | 1/2"-dia. x 36" |
|    Handle | 1 | 1/2"-dia. x 5" |
| Waterproof urea resin or resorcinol glue | 1 | can or bottle |

Stick ponies and their variations are among the oldest toys known, and they happen to be just about the simplest to make. As any youngster can tell you, even a broom turned upside down with the brush for the pony's head will do fine. For fancier riding, the stick pony is a good example of what an hour's work can produce. You can vary the basic pattern or the painting scheme to suit your imagination or the specifications of the rider.

The pony's head can be cut from almost any 3/4-inch scrap, such as plywood left over from a larger project or a piece of white pine; for the best balance, the lighter the wood, the better.

121

*projects for toys and games*

# Bad-Guy Bean Bag Game

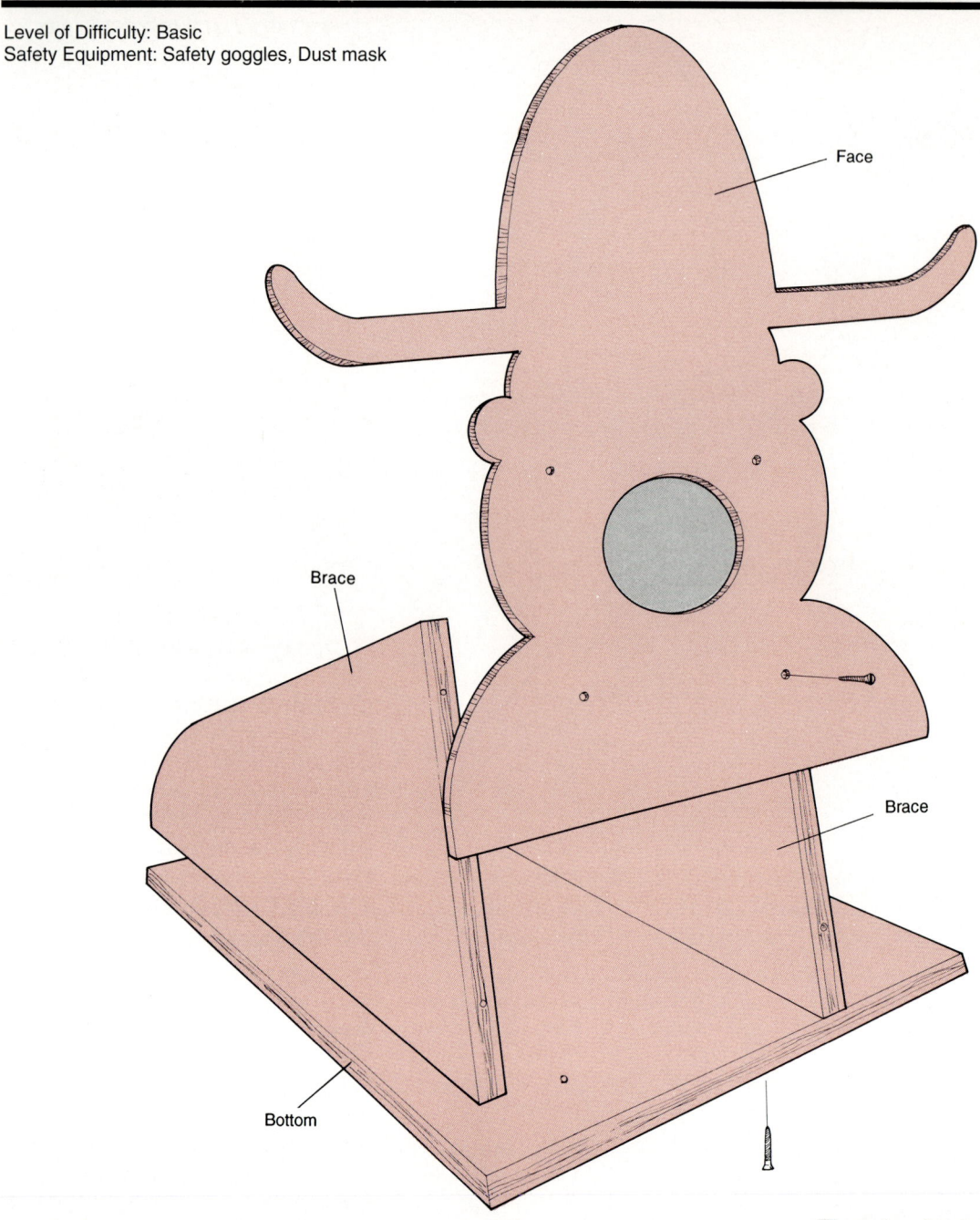

Level of Difficulty: Basic
Safety Equipment: Safety goggles, Dust mask

*Labels on diagram:* Face, Brace, Brace, Bottom

### MATERIALS, PARTS, AND CUTTING LIST

| Material/Part Name | Qty. | Size |
|---|---|---|
| A-C exterior grade plywood | 1 | 1/4" x 4' x 8' |
|     Face | 1 | 1/4" x 24" x 30" |
| A-C exterior grade plywood | 1 | 3/4" x 4' x 8' |
|     Braces | 2 | 3/4" x 16" x 16" |
|     Bottom | 1 | 3/4" x 16" x 24" |
| Galvanized flat head wood screws | 8 | #8 x 1 1/4" |
| Galvanized flat head wood screws | 8 | #8 x 1 1/2" |
| Cloth squares | 6-10 | 4" x 4" |
| Thread | | |
| Dried beans | | |

Throwing bean bags at a target is a game that never loses its appeal—grownups can't resist a toss any more than a four-year-old can. This bean bag game is extra fun for youngsters because a good throw makes the Bad-Guy swallow the beans. Plan to make several bean bags; children want lots of ammunition.

122

## projects for toys and games

### CUTTING OUT THE HEAD

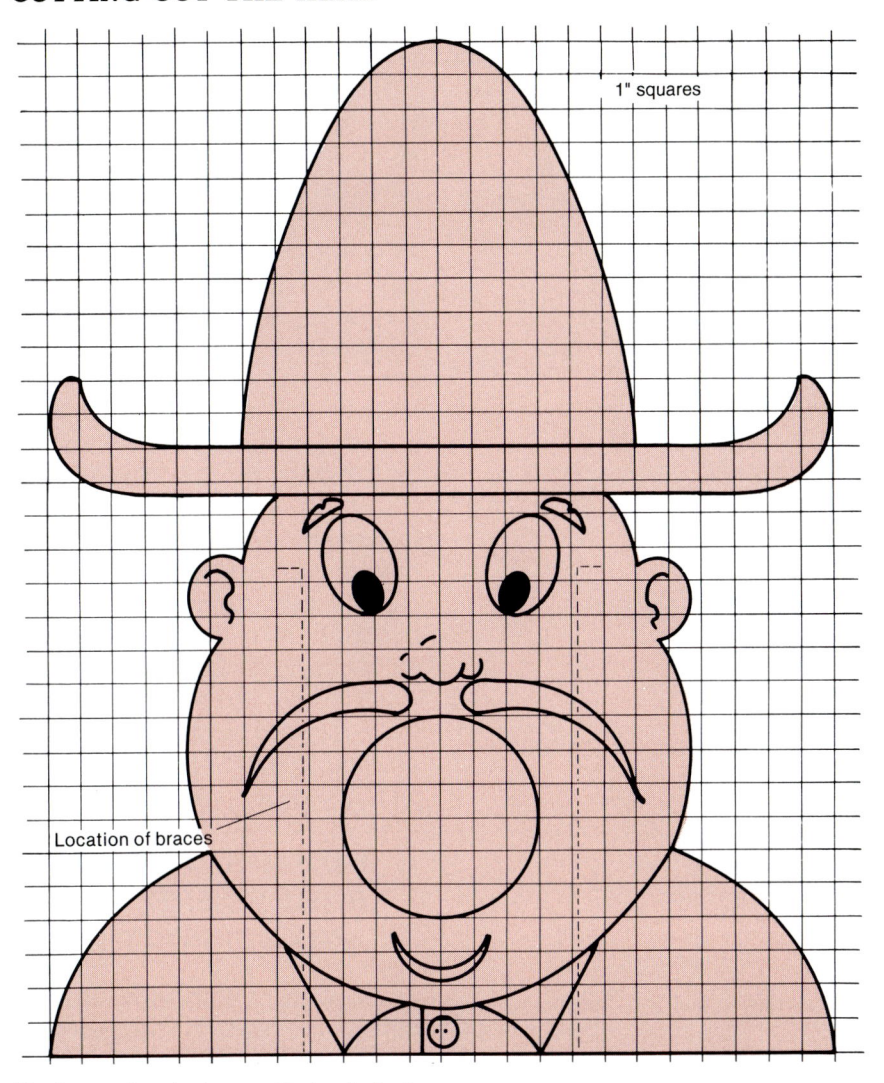

*The face pattern is also used to locate the braces.*

### ASSEMBLING THE TARGET

*Make the bags from 4" x 4" squares of cloth sewn together. Fill with dried beans.*

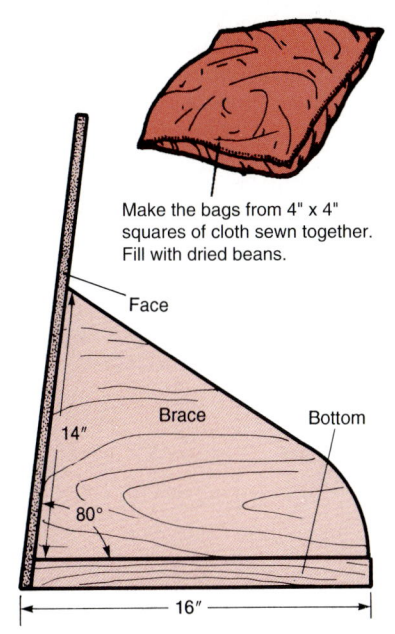

When the bean bag game is assembled correctly, the face is at an angle, as shown in this Side View.

With the "use zone" figured in, the bad-guy bean bag game requires an area at least 6 feet long and 15 feet wide for optimum safety.

## 1 CUTTING OUT THE HEAD

Enlarge the graph drawing and transfer the face pattern to a sheet of 1/4-inch plywood. Cut it out with a saber saw or coping saw. Draw the outline of the mouth, drill a starting hole inside it, and cut out this opening.

## 2 CUTTING THE BRACES AND BOTTOM

Make a pattern for the braces following the measurements given in the Side View. The curved back edges do not have to look exactly as shown, but they should be rounded off to eliminate sharp corners where the braces meet the bottom. Be sure to mark off the correct angle or the face won't tilt back correctly. Cut the braces and bottom to size from plywood. For the bottom, cut the front edge to the same angle as the braces, as shown in the Side View, and round the corners on the back edge.

## 3 ASSEMBLING THE TARGET

Sand all the pieces; check the fit, and make any necessary adjustments. Attach the face to the bottom with four #8 x 1 1/2-inch flat head wood screws, countersunk to avoid rough edges. Attach the face to the braces in the same way. Finally, secure the braces to the bottom by driving countersunk #8 x 1 1/4-inch screws up through the bottom. Follow the design on the graph drawing to paint the face or use your own imagination.

## 4 MAKING THE BEAN BAGS

Make the bags by stitching together 4-inch squares of sturdy cloth, leaving an opening on one side. Fill the bags with dried beans, but don't overfill; the bags should be limp. Stitch the bags closed.

*projects for toys and games*

# BASKETBALL BACKBOARD

Level of Difficulty: Basic
Safety Equipment: Safety goggles, Dust mask, Work gloves

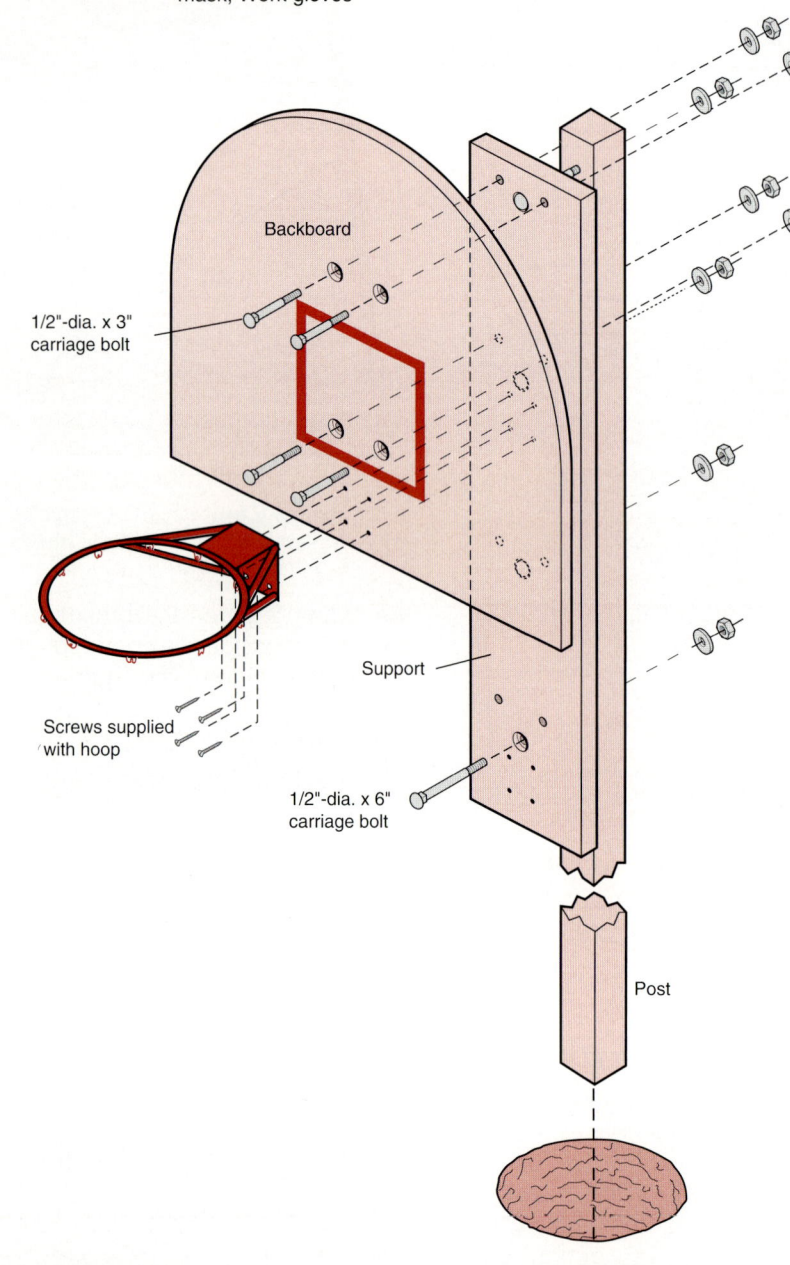

"Shooting hoops" has appeal for both the young and the young-at-heart, so you're sure to get a lot of mileage out of this project. The plans that follow include directions for mounting the backboard on a post and installing the post in the ground. As an added feature, the backboard is adjustable, so it can grow as your children do. If desired, you also have the option of simply mounting the backboard on a garage or other outbuilding. Naturally, where you place the backboard should be a departure from the grass surface desired for most of the projects in this book; concrete or macadam is needed for bouncing the basketball.

With the "use zone" figured in, the basketball backboard requires an area at least 10 feet long and 15 feet wide for optimum safety.

## 1 CUTTING THE BACKBOARD AND SUPPORT

Enlarge the graph drawing and transfer the pattern to the plywood. The backboard can be easily cut out using a portable circular saw. Cut the support to the given dimensions out of 2 x 12 stock. For

### CUTTING THE BACKBOARD AND SUPPORT

30" at highest point
36"
1" squares

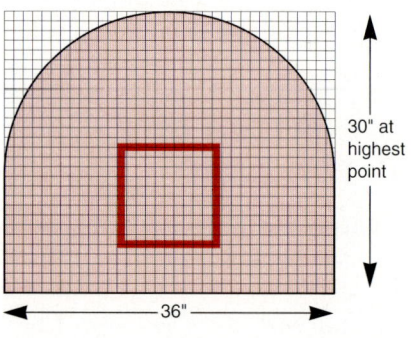

The "shooting square" can be painted on or made using red tape.

### MATERIALS, PARTS, AND CUTTING LIST

| Material/Part Name | Qty. | Size |
|---|---|---|
| A-C exterior grade plywood | 1 | 3/4" x 4' x 8' |
|     Backboard | 1 | 3/4" x 30" x 36" |
| Pressure-treated common Douglas fir | 1 | 2 x 12 x 4' |
|     Support | 1 | 1 1/2" x 11 1/4" x 20" |
| Pressure-treated common Douglas fir | 1 | 4 x 4 x 16' |
|     Post | 1 | 3 1/2" x 3 1/2" x 16' |
| Galvanized carriage bolts | 4 | 1/2"-dia. x 6" long |
| Galvanized carriage bolts | 4 | 1/2"-dia. x 3" long |
| Premixed concrete | 1 | 50-lb. bag |

124

# projects for toys and games

optimum strength, the pole should be a 4 x 4 approximately 14 to 16 feet in length; this allows for at least a full 2 feet below ground.

With red tape or paint, put a 10-inch x 10-inch square on the backboard directly above where the hoop will be. Attach the hoop to the backboard using the hardware provided with the hoop.

## 2 ATTACHING THE SUPPORT TO THE POST

Use four 1/2-inch-diameter x 6-inch long countersunk carriage bolts to secure the support to the post. The addition of the support will lend much needed stability to the backboard.

## 3 SETTING THE POST

Because structural support is so important to the success of this project, be sure to bury the post at least a full 2 feet in the ground. If a 16-foot post is used, you can bury it 3 feet deep. The diameter of the

### ATTACHING THE SUPPORT TO THE POST

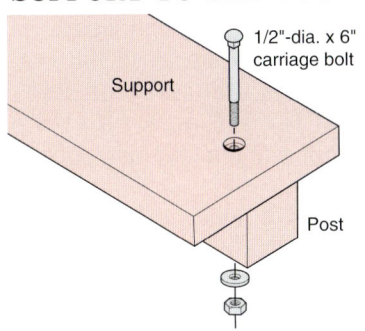

By attaching the support to the post with carriage bolts, the backboard will be less prone to sway.

### SETTING THE POST

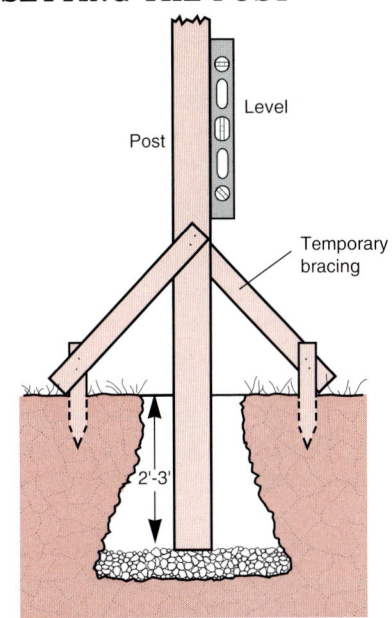

It is important to undercut the base of the posthole for added structural support.

### MOUNTING THE BACKBOARD

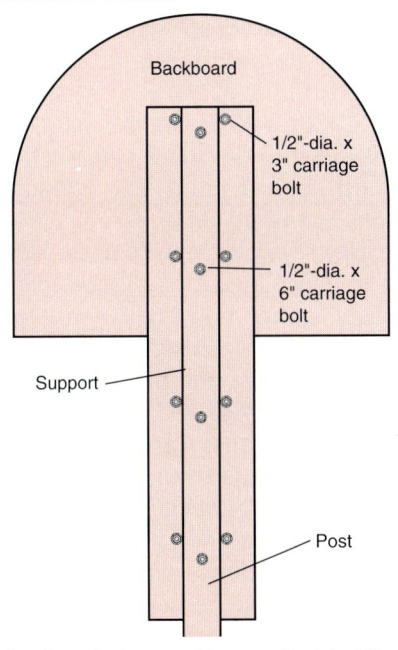

Carriage bolts provide excellent holding power when mounting the backboard.

posthole should be two to three times the width of the post; in this case, make the hole at least 12 inches in diameter. Undercut the base of the hole by making it wider at the bottom as shown to provide increased support strength. Place a 6-inch layer of crushed stone or gravel in the hole to aid in drainage.

With the aid of a helper, insert the post in the hole and check to make sure it is level and plumb. After mixing and pouring the concrete, tamp it firmly to compact the surface. Slope the concrete away from the post so rainwater will not collect around the base. Recheck for plumb and add any temporary bracing as needed. Allow the concrete a full 24 hours to cure before attempting to attach the backboard.

## 4 MOUNTING THE BACKBOARD

To mount the backboard, you will need a ladder and some assistance. Use four 1/2-inch-diameter x 3-inch-long countersunk carriage bolts to secure the backboard to the post-and-support assembly. For smaller children, use the four lower mounting holes; for taller children, use the four upper mounting holes. Drive the bolts through the front of the backboard and into the support, with one bolt in each corner. By countersinking the bolts, they will be seen from the front of the backboard, but they will not project out and interfere with the flight of the basketball.

If you wish to turn your driveway into a mini-basketball court, special paint is available for concrete to make a free-throw line and boundaries.

# play yards, play things

# GLOSSARY

**Abrasive** Any material used to wear away, smooth, or polish a surface, such as sandpaper used to smooth wood.

**Backsaw** Short saw having a reinforced back; ideal for cutting molding and fine woodworking.

**Bevel** The inclination that one line or surface makes with another when not at right angles.

**Bevel joint** Miter joint in which two pieces meet at other than a right angle.

**Blindhole** A hole that does not go all the way through a piece of material, commonly used with dowels; also called a stopped hole.

**Block plane** An adjustable plane used to trim end grain and other fine work.

**Braces** Structural supports that add strength to a wood assembly.

**Brads** Slender nails having either a small, deep head or a projection to one side of the head end; commonly 1 1/2 inches or less in length.

**Butt joint** Joint formed by two pieces of wood united end to end without overlapping.

**Carriage bolt** A flat head bolt that is threaded only part of the way up the shaft; its design makes this bolt impossible to be turned from the head.

**Chamfer** A flat surface made by cutting the corners or edges of the end of a piece of stock.

**Circular saw** Power saw consisting of a circular disk, usually with a toothed edge; used to make straight and angle cuts.

**Clear finish** Any of a number of wood finishes that allow the wood grain to be seen.

**Cleats** Structural members that serve to hold other parts in place.

**Combination set** A layout tool with a built-in protractor head used to mark off or measure angles.

**Common nails** Nails having a flat head and a grooved shank; ideal for nailing framing lumber and other applications where gripping power is more important than appearance.

**Compass** Instrument for drawing or describing circles or measuring distances, consisting generally of two movable, rigid legs hinged to each other at one end.

**Coping saw** Saw consisting of a light, ribbonlike blade held in a three-sided, U-shaped frame with a handle; used for cutting small curves.

**Counterbore** The use of a counterbore drill bit to bore a hole at the end of a pilot hole in order to accommodate a wood plug or other covering to hide a screw head.

**Countersink** The use of a countersink drill bit to bore a beveled hole at the end of a pilot hole in order to accommodate the head of a flat head screw so that it sits slightly below the surface when driven in.

**Crosscut saw** Handsaw used for cutting across the grain of the wood, with a point size ranging from 8 to 12 points.

**Dowel** A wood pin frequently used to join two pieces of wood. The dowel fits into holes drilled in each piece; this creates a dowel joint. In longer lengths, and different diameters, the dowel has varied uses.

**Dressing** Planing down of rough wood to various sizes.

**Drill guide** An accessory used to guide drill bits and to align matching holes for dowel joints.

**Dust mask** A device to cover the nose and mouth and prevent inhalation of sanding dust, chemicals in paints and stains, and other materials in the air.

**Edge-nailing** Fastening method in which nails are driven into the edge of one of the pieces of wood.

**End grain** The end of a board showing the grain of the wood in cross section.

**Face-nailing** Preferred fastening method in which nails are driven into the broad face of both pieces of wood.

**Fasteners** Nails, screws, brads, and other items that are used to join two pieces of wood or to secure hardware.

**Finishing nails** Nails having a small globular head, more slender than common nails of the same length; used for finish work, they are driven slightly beneath the surface and covered with putty or wood filler.

**Framing square** An "L"-shaped steel square used to mark work for squaring and to verify the accuracy of angles.

**Gauge** A number assigned to screws and other fasteners to show relative differences in diameters.

**Grain** The growth pattern in the tree. The grain will look different in different woods and as a result of different sawing techniques.

**Hardwood** Wood that is cut from deciduous (leaf-bearing) trees. Although designated as hardwood, some types are actually physically soft and easy to dent.

**Kerf** The space created by a saw blade as it cuts through wood. All cuts should be made on the outside, or waste side, of lines marked for cutting so that the inside edge of the kerf just touches the mark.

**Line level** A level with a hook at either end for hanging on a taut line to ensure that the line is perfectly horizontal.

**Log saw** Saw consisting of a combination of pegged teeth and gullets to provide cutting action in both directions; used to cut landscape timbers and logs to length.

**Miter** To cut a beveled edge on a piece of lumber for the purpose of making a miter joint. A miter joint is usually the mating of two 45° angled ends to make a 90° corner.

# glossary

**Miter box** A jig with slots designed to guide the blade of a saw to cut 45° miters and squared ends.

**Molding** Various types of wood used for decorative or practical trim. Molding styles range from flat lath to ornately grooved, carved, or stamped picture frame moldings. Molding is usually applied to cover joints of dissimilar surfaces.

**Nail set** Short rod of steel used to drive a nail below or flush with the surface.

**Nominal dimension** The size of lumber before it is planed down, as opposed to the actual size.

**On center** A phrase designating the distance between the centers of regularly-shaped holes.

**Particleboard** Inexpensive sheet material composed of wood chips, or particles, and adhesives pressed into sheets. Fairly brittle and not as easy to nail through as wood.

**Pattern** The outline, usually on a scaled grid, of a piece composed of curves and angles that cannot be given as dimensions. Some patterns are full-sized and can be used as templates; others must be enlarged.

**Pilot holes** Holes drilled in stock to make it easier to drive a screw through the stock. Pilot holes are slightly narrower than the diameter of the screw to be used.

**Plywood** Manufactured wood made up of piles, or layers, for strength and uniformity.

**Point size** Number of teeth per inch on a saw blade. Lower point sizes cut faster, higher point sizes cut finer and smoother.

**Pressure-treated wood** Wood treated with special preservatives, making it highly resistant to moisture and decay.

**Rabbet** A steplike corner cut into the edge of a board so that another board can be seated in the cut to make a rabbet joint.

**Resorcinol** Two-part glue that is extremely waterproof; ideal for use with wood.

**Ripsaw** Handsaw used for cutting with the grain of the wood, with a point size of 5 1/2 or 6 points.

**Router** Power tool used for hollowing out and for cutting grooves, rabbets, and dadoes; also used for rounding off edges of stock.

**Saber saw** Portable electric jigsaw with varied blades capable of making intricate cuts.

**Sanding block** A padded wood block around which a piece of sandpaper is wrapped for hand sanding of a surface.

**Sandpaper** A coated abrasive—usually flint, garnet, or aluminum oxide—glued to a paper, cloth, or plastic backing. It is used for smoothing or polishing woods.

**Scroll saw** Power saw used to cut even, tight curves; also known as a bench jigsaw.

**Setscrew** Screw passing through a threaded hole in a part to tighten the contact of that part with another.

**Softwood** Wood that comes from logs of cone-bearing (coniferous) trees.

**Solid stock** Milled lumber, as opposed to composition woods like plywood or particle board.

**Stain** Any of various forms of water, latex, or oil-based transparent or opaque coloring agents designed to penetrate the surface of the wood to color (stain) the material.

**Starter holes** Holes drilled inside the outline of a shape to be cut out of a larger shape for the purpose of inserting the blade of a coping saw or saber saw to start the cut.

**Straightedge** Strip of wood or metal for use in drawing or testing straight lines, plane surfaces, etc.

**Tack cloth** A piece of cheesecloth or other lint-free fabric treated with turpentine and a small amount of varnish to create a sticky or tacky quality so the rag will pick up and hold all dirt, dust, and lint that it touches.

**T-bevel** A layout tool with a parallel sided steel blade for marking off and checking angles on the work.

**Texture 1-11 plywood** Plywood manufactured with ship-lapped edges and parallel grooves for simplified construction.

**Toe-nailing** Fastening method in which nails are driven into the workpiece at an angle for greater holding power.

**Tongue and groove** Milling treatment of the edges of a board resulting in a protruding tongue on one side and a groove the same size on the other; used to join several boards.

**Try square** Device for testing the squareness of carpentry work, consisting of a pair of straightedges fixed at right angles to one another.

**Use zone** Any activities or movements which can be expected on and around a piece of play yard equipment. The use zone should always be considered so as to allow sufficient space between equipment.

**Warp** A distortion of lumber from its milled shape caused by uneven shrinkage. Warped boards should be avoided when purchasing lumber, and precautions should be taken to prevent stored lumber from warping.

**Wood filler** Liquid, paste, putty, or plaster material designed to fill in holes or grain lines so that final finishes may be applied to a smooth surface.

**Wood rasp** A hand tool used for rough shaping of edges or curves.

# Metric Conversion Charts
## LUMBER

**Sizes:** Metric cross-sections are so close to their nearest Imperial sizes, as noted below, that for most purposes they may be considered equivalents.

**Lengths:** Metric lengths are based on a 300mm module which is slightly shorter in length than an Imperial foot. It will therefore be important to check your requirements accurately to the nearest inch and consult the table below to find the metric length required.

**Areas:** The metric area is a square meter. Use the following conversion factors when converting from Imperial data: 100 sq. feet = 9.290 sq. meters.

### METRIC SIZES SHOWN BESIDE NEAREST IMPERIAL EQUIVALENT

| mm | Inches | mm | Inches |
|---|---|---|---|
| 16 x 75 | 5/8 x 3 | 44 x 150 | 1 3/4 x 6 |
| 16 x 100 | 5/8 x 4 | 44 x 175 | 1 3/4 x 7 |
| 16 x 125 | 5/8 x 5 | 44 x 200 | 1 3/4 x 8 |
| 16 x 150 | 5/8 x 6 | 44 x 225 | 1 3/4 x 9 |
| 19 x 75 | 3/4 x 3 | 44 x 250 | 1 3/4 x 10 |
| 19 x 100 | 3/4 x 4 | 44 x 300 | 1 3/4 x 12 |
| 19 x 125 | 3/4 x 5 | 50 x 75 | 2 x 3 |
| 19 x 150 | 3/4 x 6 | 50 x 100 | 2 x 4 |
| 22 x 75 | 7/8 x 3 | 50 x 125 | 2 x 5 |
| 22 x 100 | 7/8 x 4 | 50 x 150 | 2 x 6 |
| 22 x 125 | 7/8 x 5 | 50 x 175 | 2 x 7 |
| 22 x 150 | 7/8 x 6 | 50 x 200 | 2 x 8 |
| 25 x 75 | 1 x 3 | 50 x 225 | 2 x 9 |
| 25 x 100 | 1 x 4 | 50 x 250 | 2 x 10 |
| 25 x 125 | 1 x 5 | 50 x 300 | 2 x 12 |
| 25 x 150 | 1 x 6 | 63 x 100 | 2 1/2 x 4 |
| 25 x 175 | 1 x 7 | 63 x 125 | 2 1/2 x 5 |
| 25 x 200 | 1 x 8 | 63 x 150 | 2 1/2 x 6 |
| 25 x 225 | 1 x 9 | 63 x 175 | 2 1/2 x 7 |
| 25 x 250 | 1 x 10 | 63 x 200 | 2 1/2 x 8 |
| 25 x 300 | 1 x 12 | 63 x 225 | 2 1/2 x 9 |
| 32 x 75 | 1 1/4 x 3 | 75 x 100 | 3 x 4 |
| 32 x 100 | 1 1/4 x 4 | 75 x 125 | 3 x 5 |
| 32 x 125 | 1 1/4 x 5 | 75 x 150 | 3 x 6 |
| 32 x 150 | 1 1/4 x 6 | 75 x 175 | 3 x 7 |
| 32 x 175 | 1 1/4 x 7 | 75 x 200 | 3 x 8 |
| 32 x 200 | 1 1/4 x 8 | 75 x 225 | 3 x 9 |
| 32 x 225 | 1 1/4 x 9 | 75 x 250 | 3 x 10 |
| 32 x 250 | 1 1/4 x 10 | 75 x 300 | 3 x 12 |
| 32 x 300 | 1 1/4 x 12 | 100 x 100 | 4 x 4 |
| 38 x 75 | 1 1/2 x 3 | 100 x 150 | 4 x 6 |
| 38 x 100 | 1 1/2 x 4 | 100 x 200 | 4 x 8 |
| 38 x 125 | 1 1/2 x 5 | 100 x 250 | 4 x 10 |
| 38 x 150 | 1 1/2 x 6 | 100 x 300 | 4 x 12 |
| 38 x 175 | 1 1/2 x 7 | 150 x 150 | 6 x 6 |
| 38 x 200 | 1 1/2 x 8 | 150 x 200 | 6 x 8 |
| 38 x 225 | 1 1/4 x 9 | 150 x 300 | 6 x 12 |
| 44 x 75 | 1 3/4 x 3 | 200 x 200 | 8 x 8 |
| 44 x 100 | 1 3/4 x 4 | 250 x 250 | 10 x 10 |
| 44 x 125 | 1 3/4 x 5 | 300 x 300 | 12 x 12 |

### NAILS — NUMBER PER POUND OR KILO

| Size | Weight Unit | Common | Casing | Box | Finishing |
|---|---|---|---|---|---|
| 2d | Pound | 876 | 1010 | 1010 | 1351 |
|    | Kilo | 1927 | 2222 | 2222 | 2972 |
| 3d | Pound | 586 | 635 | 635 | 807 |
|    | Kilo | 1289 | 1397 | 1397 | 1775 |
| 4d | Pound | 316 | 473 | 473 | 548 |
|    | Kilo | 695 | 1041 | 1041 | 1206 |
| 5d | Pound | 271 | 406 | 406 | 500 |
|    | Kilo | 596 | 893 | 893 | 1100 |
| 6d | Pound | 181 | 236 | 236 | 309 |
|    | Kilo | 398 | 591 | 591 | 680 |
| 7d | Pound | 161 | 210 | 210 | 238 |
|    | Kilo | 354 | 462 | 462 | 524 |
| 8d | Pound | 106 | 145 | 145 | 189 |
|    | Kilo | 233 | 319 | 319 | 416 |
| 9d | Pound | 96 | 132 | 132 | 172 |
|    | Kilo | 211 | 290 | 290 | 398 |
| 10d | Pound | 69 | 94 | 94 | 121 |
|     | Kilo | 152 | 207 | 207 | 266 |
| 12d | Pound | 64 | 88 | 88 | 113 |
|     | Kilo | 141 | 194 | 194 | 249 |
| 16d | Pound | 49 | 71 | 71 | 90 |
|     | Kilo | 108 | 156 | 156 | 198 |
| 20d | Pound | 31 | 52 | 52 | 62 |
|     | Kilo | 68 | 114 | 114 | 136 |
| 30d | Pound | 24 | 46 | 46 | |
|     | Kilo | 53 | 101 | 101 | |
| 40d | Pound | 18 | 35 | 35 | |
|     | Kilo | 37 | 77 | 77 | |
| 50d | Pound | 14 | | | |
|     | Kilo | 31 | | | |
| 60d | Pound | 11 | | | |
|     | Kilo | 24 | | | |

### METRIC LENGTHS

| Lengths Meters | Equivalent Ft. & Inches | Lengths Meters | Equivalent Ft. & Inches |
|---|---|---|---|
| 1.8m | 5' 10 7/8" | 5.1m | 16' 8 3/4" |
| 2.1m | 6' 10 5/8" | 5.4m | 17' 8 5/8" |
| 2.4m | 7' 10 1/2" | 5.7m | 18' 8 3/8" |
| 2.7m | 8' 10 1/4" | 6.0m | 19' 8 1/4" |
| 3.0m | 9' 10 1/8" | 6.3m | 20' 8" |
| 3.3m | 10' 9 7/8" | 6.6m | 21' 7 7/8" |
| 3.6m | 11' 9 3/4" | 6.9m | 22' 7 5/8" |
| 3.9m | 12' 9 1/2" | 7.2m | 23' 7 1/2" |
| 4.2m | 13' 9 3/8" | 7.5m | 24' 7 1/4" |
| 4.5m | 14' 9 1/3" | 7.8m | 25' 7 1/8" |
| 4.8m | 15' 9" | | |

NOTE: All the dimensions are based on 1 inch = 25 mm.

### LENGTH AND DIAMETER IN INCHES AND CENTIMETERS

| Size | Length Inches | Length Centimeters | Diameter Inches | Diameter Centimeters |
|---|---|---|---|---|
| 2d | 1 | 2.5 | 68 | 17 |
| 3d | 1.2 | 3.2 | 102 | 26 |
| 4d | 1.4 | 3.8 | 102 | 26 |
| 5d | 1.6 | 4.4 | 102 | 26 |
| 6d | 2 | 5.1 | 115 | 29 |
| 7d | 2.2 | 5.7 | 115 | 29 |
| 8d | 2.4 | 6.4 | 131 | 33 |
| 9d | 2.6 | 7.0 | 131 | 33 |
| 10d | 3 | 7.6 | 148 | 38 |
| 12d | 3.2 | 8.3 | 148 | 38 |
| 16d | 3.4 | 8.9 | 148 | 38 |
| 20d | 4 | 10.2 | 203 | 51 |
| 30d | 4.4 | 11.4 | 220 | 58 |
| 40d | 5 | 12.7 | 238 | 60 |
| 50d | 5.4 | 14.0 | 257 | 66 |
| 60d | 6 | 15.2 | 277 | 70 |